CU01023056

SUMMER ON THE ITALIAN LAKES

LUCY COLEMAN lives in the Forest of Dean
in the UK with her lovely husband
and Bengal cat, Ziggy. Her novels have been
short-listed in the UK's Festival of Romance
and the eFestival of Words Book Awards. Lucy
won the 2013 UK Festi-
val of Romance: Innovation in Romantic
Fiction award.

ALSO BY LUCY COLEMAN

The French Adventure
Snowflakes Over Holly Cove
Summer on the Italian Lakes

SUMMER ON THE ITALIAN LAKES

Lucy Coleman

First published in the United Kingdom in 2019 by Aria, an imprint of
Head of Zeus Ltd

9 7 5 3 1 2 4 6 8

A CIP catalogue record for this book is available from the British Library.

ISBN 9781035903559

Aria
an imprint of Head of Zeus
First Floor East
5–8 Hardwick Street
London EC1R 4RG

To Lawrence – for one glorious summer in Italy, in a villa set high up in the hills.

Love you forever!

Prologue

Sniff. Sniff. Sniff.

My hand gropes around in the semi-darkness for yet another tissue; the flow of tears is now almost completely obliterating my vision. When all that my fingers succeed in finding is a gaping cardboard hole, it is with great reluctance that I drag my watery gaze away from those adoring eyes in front of me.

Empty? How can the box be empty?

I scowl in disgust, scanning the sofa and taking in the profusion of crumpled whiteness caught in the flickering glow from the TV screen. I'm surrounded on one side by what looks like a surreal stack of miniature snowballs and, despite my tears, I begin laughing. With a defeated shrug, I drag the sleeve of my PJ top across each cheek in a quick swiping action. Then I return my gaze to its original position staring, mesmerised, into Jude Law's eyes.

He's looking directly at me as if it's just the two of us here and I take in every little detail of that half-smile he's trying so hard to disguise. Okay, so it's aimed at Cameron Diaz and not at me because I'm watching *The Holiday* and it's just a film; but on pause Cameron isn't even in the frame. Jude is all mine to savour for as long as I want.

To my horror, suddenly the screen goes black as the TV switches into standby mode and the room is consumed in an eerily bleak darkness. With a thudding heart, I frantically scrabble around, desperately trying to locate the remote control and in the process upending the remains of a bowl of crisps.

'Damn it! Now is not the time to be eco-friendly!' I cry out angrily, at my so-called intelligent TV system.

My fingers continue to rake across the surface of the sofa, each passing second making me feel increasingly desperate. Home alone. And in the dark I'm feeling scared. A creak behind me sets me on edge, my heart beginning to race and increasing the urgency of my search. I discover the half eaten bar of chocolate and push it carefully to one side, then move on to discover the almost empty bag of popcorn. Swallowing hard to disperse a lump that has risen in my throat, I'm painfully aware that binge eating isn't the answer to anything. But you know how it is, one handful turns into two… then three.

As my eyes finally begin to adjust to the gloom, I see a dark shape poking out from beneath the discarded scatter cushion. I snatch it up, stabbing my index finger on the power button. Two clicks and Jude is back, bathing us both in a comforting glow of light. Warmly wrapped up in his navy blue, wool overcoat and sporting that festive red scarf, the ground around him is dusted with snow. I settle back, feeling happy once more.

'I missed you,' I whisper, softly. My voice wavers a little. I wish he could talk back. To me. And not to Cameron.

That gorgeously cheeky little glint in his eye threatens to melt my now calm heart, as I surrender to his powerfully romantic gaze. Stuffing a generously sized square of chocolate into my mouth, I rather reluctantly press play and the film continues. The camera pans around to catch the utterly gorgeous Cameron fluttering her eyelashes at Jude, and in that instant she snatches him back. Once more the tears start to fall. Sometimes life can be so cruel.

Why can't I find my own Jude Law?

Sniff.

Swipe.

Sniff.

I

Word Count: Zero

It's 6 a.m. and I should be online stoking the flames of my social media train and littering the internet with my sexy book covers. After all, who doesn't want to look at a gorgeous, half-naked man with an eight-pack at this time of the morning? Well, the truth is me, for one. Unless it's the real thing, of course.

Instead, I hop out of bed and slink downstairs to make a strong cup of coffee and grab a packet of biscuits, before I head back to write. Which is ironic, because I haven't written a word now for over a month. Well, not one that still exists on the blank page beneath a rather lonely looking title, as they've all been consigned to the electronic bin.

I have no idea why I can't seem to break this cycle which feels as if I'm going around in a never ending circle. Write, delete; write, delete. And I'm even hiding myself away from everyone – except the enigmatic Jude Law, of course, but I don't think that counts. It's been weeks since I ventured outside. Apart from brief exchanges with the postman and the online supermarket delivery guy, I'm turning into a virtual recluse. I haven't looked at my inbox for days now and I can't remember the last time I wore anything other than PJs or a tracksuit.

I'm supposed to be working towards a deadline, but the line is well and truly dead, with a zero word count so far. I mean, this inability to settle down and make a real start can't last forever, can it?

With a dozen plus novels under my belt, over half of which are international bestsellers, the expectations of me are high. I'm a professional and if I can't fill the screen with meaningful words then it's over and the bills won't get paid. I don't have a back-up plan if the day job goes awry and I don't think I'm capable of doing anything else. It's the only job I've ever had and therein lies the problem, I suspect. Do all writers eventually run out of things to say, the spring of inspiration reduced to a dribble? Or in my case, drivel.

Come on, Brie, pull yourself together. Have a shower, brush your teeth and your hair and instead of lying in bed battling with a string of words that aren't inspiring you at all, sit down in front of that very expensive desk of yours.

Maybe I need to feel the part again, rather than glancing in the mirror and wondering why it doesn't shatter when I see that Medusa head staring back at me.

Make this the day when things start to pick up, lady. The little voice inside my head is adamant. There is a story in there somewhere, but it isn't the one my agent, or publisher, is expecting. I groan out loud. The price you pay for not being true to yourself is that it's rather like wearing a mask. At some point it could slide off and that's precisely why I'm in this mess now.

When your birthday just happens to fall on the fourteenth of February you are pretty much marked for life. It was my fourth birthday and the memories are still vivid in my mind. After I'd opened a stack of presents, my dad gave my mum a large bouquet of flowers and a box of chocolates tied up with a big red bow. I'd never even heard of Valentine's Day, until a friend broke the news later that day. Well, she was more of an acquaintance really: the playground is a tough place and kids can be crushingly mean.

'You aren't special at all,' Carol Ann had taunted. 'They aren't happy just because you're another year older. No one really cares about that. Everyone has a birthday!' And in a split second the party was over.

But as time passed the significance became an ever increasing thrill. So many people expressing their love at the same time: sending a wave of good karma rippling outwards to warm the hearts of even the least romantic folk amongst us. I also came to believe that I had been doubly blessed; I hadn't just been born a true romantic at heart, but also an eternal optimist. I awaited each birthday with eager anticipation because it was a day when a lot of people were very happy. To be surrounded by couples pledging their love and giving each other thoughtful gifts, flowers, and even engagement rings, was special. And that made me feel extra special too, as if the promise of finding a perfect love had been bestowed upon me. I simply had to bide my time until our paths crossed. And, of course, I would instantly know he was the one I was destined to be with forever.

My first crush was a brief and painful experience; he broke my heart by not reciprocating my overwhelming feelings. I was distraught for a while, but my heart eventually healed. My second crush, Lucas, happened when I was nine years old and he broke my heart, too. The pattern was set and as the years rolled on, so the *former* boyfriend count continued to mount.

The problem with being a dreamer and a wistful romantic is that it's hard to find a man to live up to your dreams. At the tender age of fifteen I began writing and creating my own heroes. Four years later I finally had a manuscript worthy of getting some attention and after an editor knocked off the edges and corrected my erratic punctuation, it was good to go. My first publisher believed in the sort of stories I wanted to write, but three novels later the sales figures weren't exactly setting the charts alight. And I was still living at home with my parents. Then I met my agent, the awe inspiring, Carrie Preston. She is the definition of a bubbly personality and an uber confident person. So much so, that she has become the role model for my feisty heroines. Our first meeting was brutal. She didn't hold back.

'The truth is, Brie, that sex sells books. Do you want to earn some money, or languish in the charts and scrape by?'

I remember recoiling in horror. Sex? As it turned out, what I lacked in experience I made up for in imagination. Well, aided by a copy of the *Kama Sutra*, which turned out to be a tax deductible item – according to my accountant. I let my imagination run riot. It was bestseller time and I enjoyed basking in the glory.

Living with my parents had allowed me to save a satisfying large nest egg. I only needed a small mortgage to buy a quirky, thatched, five bedroom cottage in the Forest of Dean and finally I had my independence. This was my investment for the future and enough of a project that there would be a handsome profit at the end of it. With the messy building work out of the way, yes, I do rattle around in it, but one day I hope to share it with someone special. And a couple of kids… if I'm lucky. Or sell it and have the sort of financial freedom only a big chunk of cash in the bank can give you.

Then, a little over a year ago, I met the gorgeous Paul Turner, bass guitarist with Haphazard. He swept me off my feet, literally, and I was admittedly flattered. As a writer my life is governed by deadlines, interspersed with prolonged periods spent in the company of people I've made up. Add in a few book signings, a handful of literary dinners and the odd awards ceremony, and it's not a glamorous lifestyle by any means. On balance, most of the time it's a rather solitary existence. The truth is that I bumped into him at a point when I was beginning to feel that something was missing from my life.

When another batch of those glossy magazines had arrived with the shopping and I found myself flicking through them, I began to feel a tad lacklustre. My life was whizzing by – what exactly was I waiting for to kick start it? Would I wake up one day to find that my best years had passed me by while I was otherwise occupied? Doing more of the same, which is *working*, because it is an amazingly satisfying substitute and I will admit that, quite freely.

My sedentary lifestyle has meant that over the last couple of years I've piled on a few extra pounds. I don't have a problem with that, as I was never designed to be straight up and down, but… there's always a but, isn't there? It had become increasingly apparent that my eating was getting just a little out of control. Doctor Carter, who guided me through my difficult teen years, hasn't been happy with me for a while. After my last MOT, he didn't mince his words.

'Your blood sugar levels indicate you have a pre-diabetic condition, Brie. It's your body giving you a warning signal loud and clear. If you don't lose at least a stone and a half by reviewing your diet and getting active, you are storing up problems for the future. The solution is in your hands, my dear.'

I remember walking home from the surgery that day knowing that something had to change, but it's easy to think that and hard to make it happen. Then I met Paul.

The first time I saw the face I knew so well from MTV up close, my jaw dropped. I was rooted to the spot, so much so that he nearly knocked me over as he swept through the lobby at The Protocol with his entourage that night. It was a smart new restaurant in Bristol that Mel had convinced me was a must, and she kept on and on about it until I gave in.

We were waiting in the queue when this mass of people suddenly descended and it was like a whirlwind had touched down. Two beefy security guards made their presence very obvious and there was an exciting buzz in the air. As one of the guys backed into me and I started to fall, Mel shrieked. Suddenly, Paul span around and within an instant he was there and I found myself in his arms. It was a moment from one of my novels, re-enacted, I swear. After apologising profusely, he asked me – well, *us* – to join him for dinner.

I remember so clearly, gazing into his eyes and saying *yes*. Later in the evening he asked me out on a real date. Could I be the life and soul of the party, dancing until dawn, I wondered? Well, I wasn't convinced, but I wanted to find out. And the way Paul looked at me that night fooled me, for a while, into thinking I could be that person. I was excited and exhilarated by the thought of what was to come. Being with him changed me in ways that felt good at the time. I was caught up in the permanent high that existed around him. I felt alive, really alive, for the first time in ages.

Mel was delighted for me, of course. She genuinely felt she had achieved something by prising me, after a few moans and groans, out of my cosy little cottage that night to socialise. And when date one's intimate little dinner for two turned out to be a resounding success, she was ecstatic. I looked at myself in the mirror and decided it was time. I cleared out the shameful piles of high sugar, high fat comfort foods that had become my daily snacks. Then, I pulled out my running gear and started jogging each morning.

My skin started to glow again and my hair was shinier. I had more energy and I was sleeping so much better. Mel was relieved, as she had tried to intervene when she saw I was becoming a hermit and always seemed to have a packet of biscuits within easy reach.

'It's fate,' she'd said to me, with a huge grin. 'You needed something to motivate you and I'm so happy for you, Brie. You look like you're enjoying life again.' And I was.

Just being around Paul was intoxicating at first because he was so attentive and it made me feel special. Until the paparazzi started snapping less than flattering photos, which seemed to prove I didn't have one single good angle on me. Or a way of getting out of a car elegantly, even though by then I was a whole stone lighter. Slowly it began to erode my confidence whenever I was out and about with him.

Then, to my shame, the press started comparing me to Paul's former girlfriends. They even congratulated him on the fact that the size of a woman's thighs clearly didn't bother him. I mean, how dare they? *Amply proportioned* was one of the terms used and that was only the start of the fat-shaming. But I wasn't fat. I was a size twelve for goodness' sake, and I'm never going to be stick thin. Nor do I want to be. But freedom of speech is a dangerous thing and it was impossible to stem the flow, or even correct the lies.

Worse was to come and that's when I began reaching for the family size chocolate bars. For the first time in my life I regretted not writing under a pen name. As soon as Paul introduced me to someone and they heard the name Brianna Middleton, I swear their eyes would open wide in surprise.

'Not the author?' They'd query. Or, 'Really?' with that little lift in their voice implying I wasn't what they were expecting at all.

If I thought that was bad, what happened next was a disaster. The name calling and trolling on Twitter sent me into panic mode. The whole world could see these very personal attacks and virtually all of them were about my appearance.

'Have you seen the latest?' I'd screeched down the phone at Mel one morning in a traumatised state.

'No. But it's only jealousy, Brie, anyway. They're the ones who look pathetic and you shouldn't take it to heart.' Her empathy had been real, but her grasp of the situation was tenuous.

'Okay – and I quote: "Seriously??? She needs a stylist… Poor Paul." Then someone named CutieSue: "Another clinger-on. Book sales must be down lol!" Even the guys, MDR53 says: "Dude, what's happening – is this a joke? Sizeable ass going on there." And this! Pussykins1982: "Who do you think you are, lady? One burger too many in that dress." There are whole threads, laughing and joking over the footage of me getting my coat caught in that revolving door! Someone has even posted a video clip of it on a continual loop set to music.' I'd gasped, as my lungs ran out of air and I began to hyperventilate.

The clip made it look like I was simply too wide to get through the doorway because of the angle. The reality was that the hem of my coat jammed between the inner and outer revolving walls and the mechanism ground to a halt. With five paparazzi snapping away the other side of the glass, and my face getting redder by the moment as I tugged and tugged, it wasn't a pretty sight.

Mel had been speechless and all she could do was to try and calm me down, saying eventually the haters would tire and I'd become old news.

I got it. Paul was a heartthrob; meltingly gorgeous and he only had to roll out of bed in the morning, grab a wrinkled T-shirt off the floor and he looked amazing. Even better when he forgot to shave, which he often did because he knew it made women's jaws drop. It's too easy for men, isn't it?

Me? Well, I kept up my daily exercise regime to convince myself I was on the right track. But, once more, my cupboard was brimming over with the very things I knew I shouldn't be eating.

I was also back and forth to the beauty salon waxing bits of me I hadn't glanced at in a long while and wearing the weirdest nail combos going. Blingy bits aren't really me and it was an utter nightmare typing, letting alone pulling up my leggings. But I felt the need to make myself better in some way to justify Paul's attention. The irony was that he didn't seem aware of the agonies I was going through. He seemed to like me the way I was, but I didn't like me the way I was and neither did the haters, or the press.

I felt a little like Cinderella. The excitement of being a part of Paul's life was rather like going to a big party you've been looking forward to for ages. As the night draws to a close, though, you simply want to crawl under the duvet and sleep for hours and hours. I ran out of steam. The negativity overwhelmed me and I stopped trying. In fact, I did the reverse. It wasn't one slice of cake, it was the whole cake and it showed. Quickly I gained back the stone in weight that I'd lost and added another eight pounds to that. My daily jog was now a slow walk.

Paul grew concerned about the backlash and the changes he could see in me. Then his manager became involved. He tried talking me out of going to one of Paul's promotional events because, clearly, I wasn't feeling very happy with myself. I was devastated. I ended up having a mini meltdown when I decided to go anyway, but later found I could no longer get into the dress I'd bought expressly for the event. And that was even yanking on an industrial set of Spanx. I'd gone from a size twelve to a size sixteen virtually overnight. Or so it seemed.

I was growing tired of trying to prove I was… what, suitable girlfriend material? That I could look glamorous enough to justify being in his life? My thoughts went beyond shallow. Beyond any level-headed person's thought processes. And, yes, I am ashamed to admit that I fell into that pit for a while. The negativity coming at me from all sides, though, began to brainwash me.

When we eventually split up, his actual words chilled my heart like an icy blast from the arctic.

'It's no longer fun, Brie, and my agent says this isn't doing me any favours. Image is everything these days. It goes with the job, as they say and you either live up to that, or you walk away. You're a serious little thing, aren't you? You really buy into this love stuff you write, but from what I've seen that's a rather naïve way of handling relationships. I'm building a brand and the woman in my life is just another piece of that.'

I spent my thirty-first birthday drowning my sorrows in Prosecco and eating the contents of a box of Thornton's chocolates.

Unfortunately, the press didn't instantly let up. Oh no! Because then people wanted to know why our relationship had gone south and the speculation fuelled the trolls once more; that ardent legion of angry female fans who never thought I was good enough for him in the first place. And yes, I was well aware of some of the glamorous women he'd been linked to in the past, although I didn't believe he'd actually dated all of them.

But for a while there, he made me feel special enough not to worry about the hype going on around us. I did let my hair down and I did have a good time. But the next day I knew there'd be a snap of me with one eye half-shut as if I was drunk, when I wasn't, or with my skirt having ridden up far enough to show my – and I quote – *generously* proportioned thighs. I even came off Twitter after the name calling and sheer vindictiveness shocked me to the core. I'd constantly dissolve into tears and Mel would sit there, trying to reassure me that decent people would be horrified, too.

'Why do you keep reading them, Brie? Pass it over. I'll block and report every single one of them. Look, some are already disappearing, so other people are complaining on your behalf.'

One of the most vociferous was @PaulTILoveUBabe.

What a joke! This is a PR stunt... never heard of her before. Paul marry me! At least I look in the mirror before I leave the house.

One morning I opened the door to the postman, who asked me if I knew my car had been trashed. A fan had decided to scratch Paul's name in twelve inch high letters, alongside a broken heart, on the bonnet with a key. Just in case I needed a permanent reminder that he was never truly in love with me, I suppose. Although, admittedly, I was too busy worrying about not letting him down and looking the part to listen to what my own heart was telling me at the time.

Since then my morale has taken a gradual downwards slide, despite the ironic fact that my book sales are rapidly climbing. But suddenly everything seems to be gathering speed. I'm a passenger on a train that is out of control. It's only a matter of time before my entire world comes crashing down around me because I can no longer function.

I was made to look foolish to the world at large. And now my fear is that real, heart-stopping romance only truly exists on the big screen, or in the haunting lyrics of a love song. Absolutely nothing in my life so far has prepared me for that. Even Valentine's Day is no longer the little thrill it was after what I witnessed this year. I was queuing for some flowers for Mum – she spent one of those precious occasions in labour with me, so it's something I do every year. The guy in front of me was picking up a dozen red roses. When he handed over his credit card and saw the amount appear on the screen, he gasped.

'Are you sure I'm only paying for a dozen?' His voice was full of disbelief.

'Yes, sir. One dozen red roses.'

'I don't know who invented this Valentine's Day lark, but I bet it was someone who was going to be raking in the cash. It wouldn't be so bad, but when you take in the cost of an expensive meal out and the taxi there and back, it's ludicrous. I hope she bloody well appreciates it. Last year's girlfriend didn't seem overly impressed. Her previous boyfriend, she took delight in telling me, took her away for a spa weekend!'

His eyes had flickered over me at that point and instantly dismissed me, as if I was invisible. He was shaking his head as he slid the card back into his wallet, leaving the sales girl unmoved. I realised then that she had probably heard it what must feel like a million times over. Even before he was an arm's length away she was greeting me with a smiley face, eager to ring up another sale. No doubt she was counting down the hours until it was time to shut up shop for the day. Florist's shops aren't heated and it was bitingly cold. It had been a grim day all round.

Dringggg. Dringgg. Dringgg.

The shrill ring of the doorbell makes my heart almost leap out of my chest. It must be a parcel because ringing three times is unnecessarily insistent. Delivery drivers these days need to zip around and I always feel guilty if

I can't instantly fling open the front door, because every second counts. A glance at the bedside clock tells me it's only just after eight. But I do have a dozen sentences on the page in front of me that I haven't yet deleted, so I haven't totally wasted the last two hours.

Reluctantly, I push back the duvet cover and rush downstairs, feeling guilty that I'm still in bed and so far away from the door. It doesn't help that I seem to have developed this unstoppable urge to buy things online. I'm waiting for a tempered glass screen protector for my iPad at the moment. It's shatterproof and resistant to fingerprints. And it was on sale at the bargain price of two pounds and ninety-nine pence! How could I resist?

I pop on the chain and open the door a full six inches, peeking out and with my hand ready to grab the parcel. Three familiar faces stare back at me with looks ranging from mildly uncomfortable to horror-struck. To my utter dismay, standing on the doorstep is not only my mother, Wendy, but my best friend, Mel, and the fearsome Carrie herself.

'Darling, can we come in?' Mum's voice is soft and full of compassion. A fourth person suddenly appears.

'Morning, lovely.' It's Dad and he's trying to sound upbeat. It comes out staccato fashion and even his lop-sided smile smacks of discomfort.

'Can you take the chain off, Brie? I'm gasping for a cup of tea.' Mel, too, sounds decidedly awkward.

I snap the door shut and stand, half leaning against the wall for a few moments while I try to collect my thoughts. I'm in no fit state to receive company and neither is the cottage. I wonder what the hell they want at this time of the morning?

I leave the chain on and ease the door open to peer around the edge once more.

'Um… it's a bit early, guys, and I'm not up yet. Can you come back later?'

Carrie suddenly strides forward blocking out my view of the others.

'Open the door, Brie, this is an intervention. We aren't going anywhere, so you might as well let us in now.'

One look at her face and I quiver, my hand reluctantly sliding back the chain. As I step aside it feels like a crowd is filtering into the hallway of my sanctuary.

'Right,' Dad says, looking decidedly embarrassed as he tries not to stare at me. And I can't blame him. Even I don't recognise me sometimes when I catch sight of myself unexpectedly in the mirror. 'I'll, um, put the kettle on then.'

I watch as he heads off to the kitchen and when I turn back, everyone is staring at me.

'What on earth have you done to your hair?' Mel asks, looking appalled.

Glancing in the mirror on the wall behind her, I groan inwardly. With my hair pulled up into a scrunchy, it looks like a furry animal is sitting on top of my head. It's debatable whether it's dead or alive.

'It needs washing,' I offer, lamely.

'Come on,' she replies. 'We should sit down and have a bit of a chat. We're all very worried about you, Brie, and you can't go on like this ignoring all contact. Don't you ever answer your phone or your emails, these days?'

I hang my head, bringing up the rear like some wayward child as everyone files into the sitting room. It looks like there has been an explosion and most of it is snack related.

After indicating for everyone to follow my lead and clear a little space, I take the seat next to Mum on one of the sofas. She leans across to place a hand over mine, giving it an encouraging squeeze before drawing back.

Carrie sits opposite us and Mel draws back the curtains before lowering herself down, rather strategically, next to her. The eye contact is awkward; no one seems to know quite where to look. I'm conscious that the place isn't looking quite as pristine as usual but then I have been spending a lot of time in bed waiting for inspiration to come. And every night I'm peering at the other sort of screen. To my shame, instead of clearing up my clutter I've been working my way from room to room. Having four TVs is actually quite handy, I've discovered.

'It's been weeks since any of us have heard from you, Brie. Shutting yourself away isn't doing you any good at all. We all have problems at times and that's what family and friends are for – to be here for you when you need us.' Mel speaks softly as if I'm some sort of invalid.

Dad appears with a pot of tea and five mugs on a tray. I only ever drink tea if I'm unwell or I've had a bit of a shock. Like the day I signed my first publishing contract and it wouldn't sink in. Every other author probably cracks open a bottle of champagne and makes a lot of noise. I said a little 'Woo-hoo!' and had a brew to calm me down, then went straight back to work.

'I'm fine, really. My head has been full of the story I'm writing at the moment, and you know how I work. I like to withdraw from the world and pop up again when it's done.' Well, it seems I could have a second career as an actress because that had a positive ring to it.

Carrie raises one eyebrow. 'The work in progress is going well?'

It's obvious to everyone she doesn't believe me. I have two choices here. I can lie and hopefully they won't stay very long, or I can come clean.

'Very well, indeed.'

'So, you could send me a few sample chapters to read through today?'

It doesn't help that all eyes are still on me and Dad has made no attempt to pour out the tea, which would at least be a distraction.

'Well, I could but I had an epiphany and decided to change the plot a little. That's why I've been so quiet. I'm having to go back through the whole thing. It's annoying but it happens.'

Oh, that was a little too bright and breezy.

'You haven't written a single word, have you?'

I don't think I've ever seen such a deep frown on Carrie's face before. She'll probably need Botox now, because of me.

'Okay, so I've scrapped most of it. There's another story in my head but it isn't the one you're expecting. Until it's written I can't seem to move on.' It's the truth; I'm tired of writing about sex. If I don't pander to my romantic core soon, then I'll probably combust! I've never felt so desolate before; it's like I'm in imminent danger of giving up on love, and myself, completely. That's why I'm indulging my unhealthy addiction to Jude. Of course, I know that's not normal, but he's keeping me sane.

Mum, Dad and Mel begin to look a little relieved, but Carrie's face doesn't alter.

'If I negotiate a revised deadline, can you work on both at the same time? We can take a look at this… other story, but I need a reassurance from you. You can't let your publisher and your readers down, Brie. If you don't publish a new book every six months your sales will lose momentum. That's the game you're in and this is so unlike you.'

I nod guiltily, casting around for something to say to deflect the attention.

'Um, any chance you can pour out that tea, Dad?'

It's judgement day and if I don't pull myself together then I'll be admitting I have a problem and I'm not in control. But that isn't strictly true as I'm not depressed or having a breakdown, it's simply that my heart is feeling forlorn. Traditionally when that happens, I turn to food.

If I can just write a love story with no bedroom action in it at all, ending with one simple kiss, something that will make the reader's heart squish, then I'll know that my romantic soul hasn't given up. And then everything will be fine. The only teeny-weeny problem I can foresee is, how on earth am I going to find any inspiration for that?

2

Getting Rid of the Cobwebs

Mel stays behind after I manage to get Mum, Dad and Carrie out of the door. When it swings shut, my entire body sags as I lean against it and Mel stares at me in abject horror.

'You're really struggling, aren't you?'

I nod.

'I'm out of control. I love what I do, but I'm not loving what I'm doing because I feel like recent events have undermined my credibility. I can't let anyone see the mess I've gotten myself into.' I indicate my new, even curvier self. 'I'm eating for the sake of eating and hating myself with every bite I take. And I feel rubbish, inside and out.'

'Oh, Brie. That's awful.'

I survey Mel's slim physique and realise how difficult this must be for her to understand.

'When you're stressed, your natural coping mechanism is to get to the gym and I envy that discipline, Mel,' I admit. 'You work out your anxiety and come back floating on a cloud of good endorphins. What hurts is that I know all this stuff, because one of my heroines used food as a coping mechanism after the death of her soul mate. I've spent time researching the subject inside and out. The solutions aren't rocket science, but they require me to get my act together and at the moment I'm doing the denial thing. But knowing that doesn't help exactly.'

Mel's frown grows even deeper.

'Do you need professional help? I know it's hard to reach out, but if we hadn't come here today how much longer would you have put off doing something about it?'

I shrug and sigh. 'Every day I wake up I tell myself today is the day I start making those changes and stop doing this to myself. But that's been going on for a month now. It's not so much the physical changes, but it's what it's doing to me in here.' I tap my head with a finger. 'Can you understand how this extreme need to grab whatever comfort I can affects me when I'm working? I don't write from personal experience obviously, but my confidence levels are at an all-time low and even my thought processes are going slowly. So I grab something to eat, hoping the feel good factor will kick in. But it's transient and I feel even worse afterwards.'

'Well, a good start would be to stop monitoring your social media accounts. All you are doing is torturing yourself needlessly because it will fizzle out at some point. I know that sounds harsh, but it's the only way.'

I know she's right.

'Have you seen some of the trolls' book reviews popping up everywhere? They are looking for other ways to make my life a misery. I doubt some of them can even read given the awful spelling mistakes and poor grammar of their one-liner rants. They're cruel and downright merciless in their attacks. Because I'm not strikingly beautiful and thin, they have turned me into a target.'

'I know this is easy for me to say, Brie, but you can't let a bunch of sad, attention seeking, green eyed individuals drive you into the ground. Their problem is that they need to get a life. You have a very productive life, but it's out of balance and your reaction to the pressures reflects that. I know it's not fair but you have to shake it off and rise to the challenge.'

I can see by the look on her face that she understands, today is the day to draw the line.

'Not everyone is on Twitter, Facebook or Instagram, Brie. And decent folk will ignore what they see in print because everyone knows most of it is made up. It hasn't harmed your career. If it had, then they wouldn't be pressing you to finish that next book. Not all bad press is necessarily bad publicity, is what I'm trying to say.'

I sigh, not even sure that makes sense. Either way it's publicity I don't want.

'The truth is that my heart feels starved of love and now I'm not even loving myself. I've lost hope that there are other true romantics still out there, so what's the point in what I do? Every book I sell seems to endorse the fact that it's all about physical love, but the most intense part should come from in here.' I thump my chest.

Mel chews on her lip, looking at me sorrowfully.

'Oh, Brie! You are your own worst enemy, you know. I love your books and so do a whole army of loyal readers. You add the spice we need to perk up our lives a bit when things feel rather mundane. I've spent many a lonely night imagining I'm wrapped up in the arms of one of your testosterone filled heroes. Your stories have gotten me through some of my difficult moments, which is a wonderful thing. Don't let anything erode that kudos, because escapism is like taking a break to get away from the negativity. Goodness knows there's enough of that in everyone's lives these days.

'Paul Turner looked the part and he seemed genuine enough, but he's a marketable commodity and he knows that. Falling in love is a luxury he can't afford, even if he wanted to. He has to make money while he can and that means as much red carpet, tabloid and TV exposure as he can get. Everyone he dates is scrutinised and I should have warned you what you were getting yourself into. He's so charming, though, and I don't for one minute think his attraction to you was fake. But his business head dictates his decisions, because no one knows how long fame and public favour lasts. You mustn't confuse that type of existence with real life. It's about putting on a show.'

I look at her, shame-faced; she's trying so hard to make me feel better.

'He thought I was… boring, Mel. That bit was real. And I am. Look at me – I'm thirty-one years old and I live in my PJs most of the time. I seldom go out these days and I've lost touch with the world out there. All the posh frocks, facials and professionally applied make-up couldn't disguise the *me* underneath it all.'

'Look, Paul was one smooth guy in public, but in private even he was using drink and a few choice recreational drugs to cope with the pressure. That alone would have been tough to handle in a relationship, but the personal attacks you suffered were beyond belief. Now, well, you're just going through a bit of a rough patch in the aftermath of it all.'

'And some. Every time I look at myself, I fear the trolls have won. I don't go out any more because none of my clothes fit me and I don't feel like *me*. I've let myself down by allowing the trolls to erode my confidence and that's a horrible feeling. They've stolen my sense of… worth. The truth is that I've done this to myself and now I feel like I'm a prisoner in someone else's body.' Mel sidles up to give me a hug as the tears begin to roll down my cheeks.

'Hey, it's not that bad. We can fix this. You're one strong lady, Brie, and now you've come to your senses you will turn this around. You wouldn't be human if you didn't occasionally get a bit lost. Personally, I think we learn more from our mistakes than we do from our successes, but it's a painful process. First of all, we have to sort out that hair. I mean, it looks like you're wearing a stuffed cat.'

I look at her and laugh. 'It's a bit matted, I'm afraid.'

She looks around the room.

'How about we do a makeover of the house and you at the same time? I'll get on the phone and call in the cleaners to spruce this beautiful cottage up a bit. You and I can then head off to a spa at the weekend to kick start your programme. What do you think?'

That gives me two days to get my act together, ready to face the world outside my door. My brain might have stopped functioning but at least I still have a sense of pride.

'I think you're a life saver, Mel. You're the one person who really understands me. So yes, let's do it.'

'Your problem is, Brie, that you spend too much time talking to your characters rather than talking to the people who love you. And that includes Carrie. She isn't just your agent, she's a good friend and she's concerned about you. This was her idea, actually.'

I smile. 'That doesn't mean she still doesn't scare me at times. She's ballsy and I wish I had a fraction of her energy and bubbly personality. When she enters a room, everyone is well aware of her presence whereas I slink in and hide in the corner.'

Mel stands back, giving me a stern look.

'Don't you ever apologise for being you! We wouldn't be friends if you were some over the top, conceited author who was constantly seeking the spotlight. That's why I should have realised Paul was wrong for you, from the start. You aren't an attention seeker, Brie. But you wear your heart on your sleeve and maybe you need to toughen up a little. Let's get the old, confident Brie back. The one who was content and optimistic about finding her Mr Right one day soon.'

I sigh. 'I guess I was a little dazzled by Paul's charm and it was a bit like stepping into one of my own storylines. Do you think my hair is fixable?'

'Well, I think a short style might be the only answer.'

My heroines always have long hair; but they're not all body perfect and don't wear their clothes like models. I put my hands around my waist, gently squeezing the wobbly tyre that fills my hands as it sits upon my hips.

'I've gained nearly two stone in weight. When I'm standing, I can't see my feet any more,' I moan, dejectedly.

'Pack your trainers and we can also hit the gym. Dieting isn't the answer to this, Brie. It's time for a lifestyle change that will turn your mental approach to stress around. In future, everything in moderation. That includes easing back a little on work to give yourself time to take care of you.'

Mel has come to rescue me as the loyal and caring friend she is, so the least I can do is not let her down.

'Have you been ill?'

The hairdresser, whose name is Zena, stares at my reflection in the mirror and I glance nervously at Mel. She's standing behind my chair with a look of optimism reflected on her face.

'Yes, Brie had a bad case of the 'flu and couldn't do much with her hair. She's thinking of a complete change. What do you think would work?'

Given that this young woman is probably about nineteen years old and is sporting a bright pink Mohican style cut, I'm wondering if this is going to be a little too radical for me.

'What are we aiming for?' She tilts her head to one side, gazing at my now lop-sided up-do.

'Something vibrant, a bit of a statement, isn't that right Brie?'

I take a hard swallow. 'Yes. But not too short. Or too bright.'

She turns, grabbing a hair magazine from the shelf and flicking through it, before stopping and holding it out for us both to see.

'How about this? A tapered bob cut longer at the front and allowing some of that wave to give it some bounciness? I'm thinking I just lighten the brown a little to lift it and then maybe do a few red highlights to make it pop.'

I let out a weary sigh and then realise they are both staring at me.

'Yes, that sounds perfect, thank you.'

Mel gives me a reassuring look and saunters off in the direction of the coffee machine.

Zena begins using a detangling brush on my hair.

'You're better now, then? The new style is going to really perk you up. There's a lot of that 'flu going around, and some people have had it quite badly. How long were you off work?'

Oh, here we go. I hate telling little white lies.

'I work from home, so it doesn't really affect me too much if I take a little time off. I often work long hours which might mean starting very early or working through the night if I'm on a roll.'

'What do you do?'

'I'm a writer.'

'Ooh, anything I might have read?'

Warning bells sound in my head. Duck and dive, Brie, duck and dive.

'Probably not. It's very busy in here today, isn't it?'

'It always is on a Saturday. Wednesday is our quietest day but even then, we have at least three stylists on shift. The spa offers mid-week discount breaks so you could grab yourself a bargain next time around. Brie, that's an unusual name.'

I can almost hear her brain ticking over.

'Yes, although it's growing in popularity.'

Suddenly she stands upright and peers at me.

'All I can think of is that Brianna Middleton. Wow, that lady knows how to write a sex scene. Just thinking about the gorgeous guys she features in her books is enough to get me in the mood to jump into someone's arms!' She laughs and for one moment a look of horror passes over my face.

Oh, dear! Am I unwittingly killing the art of romantic love by concentrating on the intense passion and the hot sex? Isn't that a modern day disease, anyway? We want everything instantly and it seems that people forget that some things are worth waiting for. Wasn't it more exciting when couples didn't jump into bed before they'd had a chance to get to know each other? And then when they did get to that point it held more meaning. How many people wake up the next morning regretting the night before, I wonder?

'Guess we're all looking for a hero.' I smile up at her in the mirror, doing my best to push aside my concerns.

'Tell me about it! I can't remember the last time a guy held a door open for me. Or picked up the tab for a meal out without expecting to go Dutch.'

I nod, glancing in the mirror and relieved to see that my face isn't giving anything away.

Zena excuses herself to go and mix up the colour for the first step in the transformation. She returns wheeling a cart with two black bowls both containing a creamy white mixture. I'm keeping my fingers crossed the colours aren't too loud.

'Can you turn up the music, please?' She addresses the receptionist who is manning the desk. 'I love this one.'

Relief washes over me. It's not a record I know but at least it curtails the conversation. I'm not being moody but the less said the better.

Closing my eyes for a moment to rest them, I'm horrified when a sudden jolt rouses me. There's a buzzer on the shelf in front of me and it's jumping around. I can't believe I fell asleep.

Zena returns, and I follow her over to the basin. I'd forgotten how good it feels to be pampered and the head massage alone is a tonic. I didn't realise I was quite so stressed out and now I'm longing for that full body polish and massage Mel and I have booked for later this morning.

After wrapping a towel around my head, Zena and I walk back to her styling station. She begins by twisting the majority of my hair up on top my head, securing it with a clip. Scissors in hand, she turns her attention to the first layer at the back and begins cutting.

With my head tilted forward slightly, I look at the growing pile of debris on the floor. The colour looks okay but then it's still wet and it's hard to tell how it will look once dry. It's been a long time since I wore my hair this short, that's for sure. I glance across at Mel but she's engrossed, listening to her iPod. Usually I love thinking time, but my head is in such a mess that what I need now is a distraction. So instead I grab a magazine from the shelf in front of me and read about the latest red carpet event in Hollywood. I can identify with the sadness behind some of those fake smiles.

The cutting seems to go on forever and I lose interest. I decide it's time to stop looking in the mirror and wait for the reveal. Eventually the scissors disappear back into the neat little pouch strapped around Zena's slender hips. She uses a generous squirt of mousse to scrunch up the longer hair at the front, with her hands, then the blow drying starts in earnest. My head is feeling curiously lighter and it's a fight to avoid glancing in that mirror.

'I think we're done.' Zena takes a step backwards, sounding pleased with herself. The girl from the reception desk walks by on her way to the coffee machine.

'On fleek, Zena. A hot new look there, Ms Middleton, it's time for a new author photo! I rang my mum and she just popped in with one of your books, so I wondered if you'd sign it for me? I have them all! I couldn't bear to miss one of your hot, sexy heroes.'

I feel the heat rising up around my ears as my cheeks begin to burn; Zena's jaw has dropped. Fortunately, Mel steps in, making a big fuss over my new hairdo and then whisks me off to the reception desk. I do my usual writerly scrawl just inside the front cover of the book lying on the counter, while raising a smile and trying to look composed.

It isn't until we're out through the doors and walking down the corridor to find the nail technician that I feel I can finally breathe. I stop to catch my reflection in a glass panel and swish my hair from side to side.

'You look gorgeous, Brie. On fleek, even!'

She looks at me with a big smile on her face.

'I don't feel like me. I look my age; I look like I'm ready to party.'

'Well, after some new nails and a relaxing massage you will be. Tomorrow we hit the gym and I've booked us a session with a personal trainer. Tonight, we are dining in the spa's acclaimed Nature's Best restaurant. Nude food is the theme, as nature intended. They've stripped everything away and it's all about the quality of the produce and keeping it simple.'

'You have to let me pay for this, Mel. It's way too much. Just the fact that you've organised all this is more than I deserve. I've been a very bad friend, lately.'

I lean in to give her a hug.

'Hey, it's me. Remember? The one you bailed out when I couldn't make the mortgage repayments on my flat and you wouldn't let me repay you. It was a tough time but now I'm through it and things are looking up.'

It's no wonder that every single one of my heroines has at least one staunch friend who is always there for her. Mel is, unwittingly, the role model.

3

The Butterfly Emerges

With gorgeous new gel nails, eyebrows shaped to perfection and all the knots in my shoulders nicely pummelled away, I'm feeling renewed. In fact, even better than the old me.

'You really do look the part now, Brie. You're a kick-ass author whose heroines give the guys a run for their money. It's like the cover now matches the contents. Just don't mention the L-word and no one would be any the wiser.'

I'm really enjoying the plate of mostly raw food in front of me, with delicately poached chicken on the side as if it were an afterthought.

'So, Mel, what's new with you? And don't try to fob me off, as I can tell there's something on your mind.' As soon as I finish speaking Mel gives me a decidedly shifty look.

'I've joined a dating website. I haven't been on an actual date yet, but I do have a shortlist of potential candidates. I've narrowed it down to three and am thinking I might make contact and see how it goes. I'd want to chat a little first before I meet up with anyone.'

My eyebrows shoot up.

'That's good to hear and it's about time, Mel,' I enthuse.

After a very long engagement, Mel's world was turned upside down when out of the blue Justin broke the news that he'd had a one-night stand – and it wasn't his first, apparently. It was simply the first time he'd been caught out, after a mutual friend had spotted him. She gave him an ultimatum – come clean or she'd do it for him. Mel was off work, virtually inconsolable, for two whole weeks. I stayed over at her flat for the best part of that first week and after that I called in on her every day until I could see she was going to be okay. So this is a big step and I'm proud of her.

'If it works out then maybe you could join, too.' She toys with the food on her plate, while casually trying to assess my reaction.

The waiter comes across to replace our glasses with two more very healthy, non-alcoholic cocktails. He smiles down at me and his eyes linger for a second or two. I look away nervously and see that Mel is fidgeting in her seat.

As soon as he's out of earshot she leans forward and whispers excitedly, 'Did you see that? He was so checking you out, Brie. Honestly, this new look suits you, lady. Even your body language has changed. And you must get a new author photo taken. The old one is cute but now you're in another league. It's time to acknowledge your achievements, I think, and become that inspiring woman who grabs what she wants in life. Just like the stories you write. You haven't really given up on finding love, have you?'

I chew on my raw carrot stick, wondering the exact same thing.

'First I have to nail the start of my next story and reassure myself that what I've been through is merely a temporary blip. Then I need to write this other story that keeps fogging up my brain, even though I have no real sense of direction with it. But at least if I get the words out of my head and onto that screen then maybe it will be content to sit there untouched for a while.'

Mel looks at me expectantly. 'And then you'll consider giving online dating a go?'

'Definitely maybe.'

'Even I know that's bad grammar and it doesn't make sense. I'm not letting you slip backwards again, Brie. If I can find a decent guy, then perhaps he'll have a friend who is also looking for love. I can't believe all the solid, hard working and reliable guys are taken. That's just too depressing to even consider.'

I roll my eyes. Mel is right, of course, and there are probably a lot of great, available guys out there, but I hate first dates. They're such a lot of effort and then there's the awkwardness when you know within the first few minutes it's going to be a complete waste of time.

'Okay. Let's wait and see what happens. In the meantime, I'll continue to live in hope. I promise. Maybe I'm destined to meet the guy of my dreams when I'm waiting in line at the supermarket. You never know.' I can see by her expression she's not impressed, and now she's on my case she won't give up easily.

But my thoughts are already trying to write the opening paragraph for my love story. A second, lingering glance at our meltingly broody waiter is enough to convince me that he's going to be my inspiration for the character whose name is Ethan. Ethan Turner. I close my eyes for a moment and I can feel that connection. I don't need a dating website because I'm going to enjoy spending my days with Ethan. In between discovering the sexual exploits of the larger than life, Jed Jackman, to keep Carrie happy. A feeling of writerly excitement begins to surge through me. Once I have my hero the story practically writes itself and it seems I now have two voices in my head, which means I can do this! I'm back in business.

I end up throwing a sleeveless, baggy cotton top over my Lycra gym wear to disguise that barrel like middle section. It feels like I'm wearing a padded jacket all the time that constricts my movement. When I catch sight of fitness guru, Rob, I'm grateful for that foresight. He's hero worthy, that's for sure, and all credit to him because you don't get a body like that unless you work very hard indeed. He's also charming and although I'm feeling rather self-conscious to begin with, as the hour slips by I stop worrying about how I look and focus on the exercises. Mel is doing a circuit and looking good. This is a natural environment for her and I can see a few male heads turning to check her out as she struts her stuff.

'I'll print out the full programme for you, Brie. As I explained, once you've shed that excess weight, if you start to pile on the pounds again it's down to two things. One, you aren't doing enough exercise, which also means you are probably losing muscle density. Two, you're eating the wrong foods. Everything in moderation when it comes to treats, so no comfort eating. Instead, try exercising rather than reaching for the chocolate as that's a natural high, not a sugar induced one.'

I nod; knowing something is one thing, adhering to it is the bit I now have to put into practice. Rob has one cute smile though, and when he folds his arms across his chest like that who can keep their eyes off those guns of his? I bet he could lift me up as if I was a feather and not two stone overweight.

'Thank you, Rob. It's been a wake up call and I'm on it now.'

He grins back at me and I find myself involuntarily moving my head a little so that my hair flicks around the side of my face. In my mind I see it in slow motion and then our eyes engage. But when I focus I can see that he's actually looking over the top of my head and he raises a hand to wave to one of the guys working out behind me. I hear a loud grunt and a bang as weights hit the floor merely feet away, almost lifting me off the ground.

I don't like attending gyms where the weights area isn't in a separate room. There's something about all that testosterone flying around in the air that's a little too Neanderthal for my liking. I mean, I love the results, obviously. Most women drool over a muscular physique but watching a man train puts me off a little. Unless it's The Rock, of course.

'I'm sure you'll stick with it, Brie, and you'll love the results. You sound like one committed lady. Pop in sometime so I can see for myself how you're getting on; we could grab a coffee.'

I don't know whether I should be flattered or whether that's his standard sign off after a session. I bet he does get some takers, though.

'Thanks, maybe I will.'

Mel sidles up to us and flashes me a look. As I gather my things and we walk off, she leans into me.

'And who are you trying to kid? He's most definitely not your type.'

I laugh and shake my head. 'No, but he's perfect casting for the role of Jed. Maybe it's time I featured a cage fighter – what a challenge for my heroine.'

'Oh, don't! The thought of all these semi-clothed, perfect specimens around is just too much to take, as it is! Let's get out of here and grab a drink at the juice bar before we hit the showers and head back home.'

'Sounds good. Have you had a chance to go online at all since we arrived here?'

We stroll down the corridor and out into the open café area.

'Yes. And I've had a little email interaction.'

Her cheeks are glowing, but I can't tell if it's solely down to the workout.

I'm next in the queue and the woman behind the counter looks across at me with a smile.

'What can I get you today?'

'One Mango Vitamin Boost please.'

'Make that two,' Mel echoes.

'Take a seat and I'll be with you ladies shortly.'

We head over to a table and both flop down, rather gratefully.

'Well, are you going to share?'

Mel looks a little reticent.

'His name is Ross.'

I purse my lips, nodding my head in silent approval.

'He's quite sporty though and you know me, I'm not a spectator, that's not my thing. I will happily spend time working out in the gym, but standing in the cold watching a football match, or even watching any sport on TV – that's a no. But when I saw his photo there was something about him. He has a very friendly face. He's very tall so we might look like a bit of an odd couple and we've only exchanged one email so far.'

At five foot one Mel is a good two inches shorter than me. I think that's why we gravitated towards each other at school, commiserating while our peers were growing like weeds and outstripping us. We never caught up and those long legs we dreamt of having just didn't materialise.

Our drinks arrive and silence reigns for a few moments. As soon as the waitress walks away Mel looks across at me.

'So, this little period of writer's block is over?' I can see the concern she's trying to hide.

'Last night after dinner I went back to my room and wrote five thousand words before I literally fell asleep at the keyboard.'

Her eyes light up.

'Oh, Brie, thank goodness! Although you would have been more than welcome to move in with me if it had come to that!' she offers.

'I'll bear that in mind, thank you, my lovely friend. But for the moment I still have a publishing contract and an agent, so now I have to prove I'm over the hump.' What I should have said is *I'm over what ails my heart and I'm ready to get back to work.* The only fix for that is not to be writing a love story but to be living it.

4

My thighs are screaming but Mel goes on counting. How can she do this and talk at the same time?

'Five, four, three, two and rest.'

For a moment I can't speak.

'Did you feel the burn?' she enquires.

I burst out laughing. 'Feel it? I thought my muscles were on fire.'

'Well, it's true what they say – if you don't use it, you lose it. Spending lots of time in bed and then sitting for hours on end in front of the PC doesn't do your body any favours. Your system gets sluggish and you need to get the blood pumping to keep everything working properly.'

I must admit, I've never really thought about it like that.

'The solution has to be easy, Mel, as I have to fit it in around my work. You know me, I wake early and I'm straight on the iPad. When I'm writing the hours fly by, but as long as I know what I have to fit in and when, I can do it.'

Mel begins some gentle stretching exercises and I follow suit.

'Okay. So, we've set you up a routine which includes half an hour, three times a week on this new exercise programme. And you're still committing to your daily walk?'

I nod. 'You could set your clock by me.'

'Good. And I think now is the time that you should invest in a fitness tracker like this one.'

We stop for a moment and Mel proffers her wrist, demonstrating by pressing a button and flicking through some screens.

'This will be your reminder to make sure you keep up that daily count. It's gentle exercise but if you choose a circuit with an uphill gradient it really helps you to get the most out of it. Start off with say, five thousand steps a day, as your goal but aim to increase that to ten thousand. If you want to burn off more fat, then up the pace at which you walk, or adjust your goal. But it's a visual reminder and as you like to set yourself targets, I think it will work well for you.'

Hmm. 'That makes sense. And walking is a good activity for me as I can use the time to mull over what happens next in my work in progress. I can't do that when I'm having to count repetitions,' I admit, pulling a face.

'Whatever regime you take on has to work for you, or you'll give up. Actually, this little piece of kit will also alert you if you've been inactive for too long. See this bar at the top? It will turn red if you are immobile for an hour and that signals it's time to move around.'

That makes me smile. 'Yours isn't red and I bet that doesn't happen very often, anyway.'

She flashes her eyes. 'I do my fair share of sitting. But for you this is vital, given the nature of your job. Get up, walk around, grab a glass of water, whatever – just so you stretch your legs.'

'That works for me. In fact, I could walk around reading my iPad and proof checking. I often read chapters out loud to pick up typos. That food diary app you put me onto is working well, too. It took me a couple of days to really get into it but now it's brilliant. I log everything I eat and drink. Upping the water really helped and my energy levels have soared. I kidded myself it was just the comfort eating to blame, which didn't help, but my general diet before that wasn't good.'

Mel throws her arm around my shoulders, giving me a squeeze.

'You are what you eat,' she says, softly.

'I'll never go back to my old ways. This is so simple. When I type in a food item and see what's in it, I'm often shocked. The amount of cheese I'd nibble while making a spaghetti bolognaise is more than I'd sprinkle over a jacket potato now. I'd happily polish off what was left of a piece of Stilton while waiting for the pasta to boil. Now it's green pea or lentil fusilli for me and I love it.'

'Cutting down on the gluten helped, then?'

I pat my stomach. 'Look, no bloating. I mean I still have body fat but I was definitely bingeing on bread and pasta. Doctor Carter said gluten intolerance is quite common and frequent headaches, as well as bloating, are two of the tell tale signs. I just feel better having cut down in general and, ironically, I'm less hungry. I factor in my daily treat and, you know me, that means ice cream every single day.'

Her smile is broad.

'My treat is a toasted muffin with butter and jam,' she admits.

'Normally, talking about food would make me hungry and I'd dive into the cupboard to grab whatever was at hand. It's different now as I plan the whole day's meals first thing. I never get tempted to skip breakfast any more and that change alone means I don't need snacks between meals.'

'Well, you are looking and sounding so much happier, Brie. That's all that matters.'

I know what she's referring to. I haven't been online surfing my social media accounts, but I will have to return soon as I'm sure there are lovely readers who have left messages that need to be acknowledged.

This whole fiasco has been a wake up call in so many ways. And, actually, it's done me a favour. It wasn't just the Paul thing, but I was in a rut. When you make bad choices the only person who can turn that around is you.

'I owe you, Mel. This last two weeks haven't been easy and you've been so patient with me.'

'Hey—' she looks at me pointedly 'that's what friends are for. You've always been there for me and it's been kind of nice to be able to return the favour in a meaningful way. It has been a bit scary, though, as you aren't the sort to crumble and that was quite shocking the day of the *visit*.'

I nod, having to agree with her. It's only with hindsight I can see how appalled they must all have been when I answered the door.

'Denial is a strange beast but having tangled with it once, I don't want to go there ever again. I feel re-born. A bit like giving the cottage a spring clean from top to bottom and then seeing it with new eyes – all fresh and lovely. It feels good and even though I'm still carrying a little over an extra stone in weight, I'm back within the healthy range for my height – just. I'll chip away at the rest, slowly. The main thing is that I've reversed a dangerous trend that was putting my health in jeopardy. I stopped looking in the mirror and now I realise that was really stupid of me, because I was neglecting myself. That spa treat gave me back a huge dose of confidence at precisely the right time.' I stop, feeling a little tearful, and clear my throat. 'But look at me now!'

Lying in bed I gaze up at the ceiling and think about how lucky I am. How many people go through a crisis and have no one in whom they can confide? Human nature can be very wily at times. What made me want to run away from the truth when it was staring me in the face? I don't think it was laziness; apathy, maybe, because I felt like all of the sunshine had been sucked out of my life. After all, everyone was laughing at me, or so I thought at the time.

I remember my matted hair and those puffy, dark shadows beneath my eyes. And the breakout of spots, which I hadn't had for years. And my nails kept splitting. I could go on and on. All of the signs were there, and I chose to ignore them.

The last thought that runs through my mind before I sink into sleep is that if you can't be honest with yourself, you aren't *living* your life, you are merely *existing*.

5

My Fingers Are Flying Over the Keyboard

Who would have thought that writing two very different stories at the same time would be the motivator I needed to shake myself up? It's a daily challenge and it's fun. To enable me to split my day and refocus my mind for the switch, I'm now going for a run just before lunch. No more working in my PJs. Planning my meals and portion control, together with regular exercise, means I almost have a sort of waistline again instead of a doughnut ring. I'm feeling and looking better than I have in a long time.

Ironically, it turns out that sex is much easier to write than romance. Jed Jackman is the man Bella Hart is determined to tame. And he will end up falling at her feet. However, the enigmatic Ethan Turner is harder to read – precisely the opposite of the attention seeking Paul Turner.

I usually write in the third person. For some reason I'm writing the story through Ethan's eyes only and in first person, because he's rather cautious about discussing his innermost thoughts. So, instead I have to let the reader know what's going on inside that complex mind of his. Even after two very productive weeks I'm only a couple of pages into Ethan's story, whereas I have a solid, thirty thousand words written about Jed and Bella. It's going well enough now for me to produce a synopsis ready for my meeting with Carrie at the Eclipse restaurant in an hour's time. That, together with the first five chapters, should be enough to reassure her I'm back on track.

I take particular care when getting ready today as I feel I scared Carrie a little and she has been a tremendous support. My bank balance reflects her sterling guidance and she was right. I believe that without her steer I'd probably be working two jobs to make ends meet. Instead I have a steady stream of royalties coming in from my backlist and for that I'm very grateful. All I need to do now is to focus on getting that work-life balance right. Which is harder than it might sound. Closeting myself away to write is easy, whereas going out and mixing with people requires a lot of effort.

I'm still a little surprised each time I catch a reflection of the new me in the mirror, but I can't wait to see Carrie's reaction. And when I walk up to her in the very smart restaurant she does a double take.

'Wow! Mel said I wouldn't believe the change in you, but this is amazing.'

I catch myself doing the head turning thing, letting my hair swish across my cheeks for full effect.

'You're back, lady and with a real sense of style. And you're looking trim!'

'Almost a stone lighter already,' I confirm.

We hug, and I take the seat opposite her. It doesn't take long to peruse the menu and order a healthy salad.

'Right, tell me what's going on with you.' She leans forward, eagerly.

I place a manila folder on the table in front of her.

'Synopsis and first five chapters of Jed and Bella's story. I've also emailed it to you, but I thought you'd like to see it in print.'

The look of relief on her face puts me on a guilt trip.

'Well, I can't pretend I didn't have a few doubts there for a moment but it's great to hear you're back on form. And the other story?'

A little smirk begins to creep over my face. 'I think you were right. This is where my strength lies,' I tap my fingers on the folder lying between us. 'It's what I do best. Now I have a firm picture in my head of Jed, the cage fighter, the words are flowing. I have made a start on the love story with the heart meltingly gorgeous Ethan Turner, but it's slow going at the moment. It might be a while until I have anything at all to show you. If ever.'

The waitress returns with our salads and Carrie pours out two glasses of water.

'Who is your inspiration for Jed?'

'A guy named Rob. When Mel and I did the spa weekend he was the personal trainer who drew up my fitness programme. Arms like tree trunks and not an ounce of fat in sight. A good chat up line, too.'

We both laugh.

'I'd say it's good to see you back to your old self but there's something different about you, aside from the sassy new look.'

I'm pleased she can see the transformation and even I can now admit that I needed it.

'I might give online dating a go and get myself out there again. Mel has taken the first step and I know it was a big deal for her.'

Carrie looks up abruptly. 'Well, you need to take care choosing your profile name, Brie. And maybe don't disclose your real name at all until after you have one successful date behind you. I did tell you at the start that a pen name is often a good idea.'

My name is synonymous with sex, regardless of what I put in my bio, but I hadn't considered using a fake name in real life. I can't help wondering if this is more to do with the aftermath of the Paul disaster, though.

'I know I should have listened to you in the first place, but I was a very naïve twenty-two year old. It was a thrill seeing my name on the book covers. When I crossed over from writing contemporary women's fiction I didn't even give it a moment's thought. Poor Mum had such a shock when she read the first book I wrote after you became my agent. Dad still hasn't read any of them.'

'Precisely the point I was trying to make at the time. I don't see the harm in using a pseudonym if you go ahead and give it a whirl, though. You can reveal your little secret if you find someone you really hit it off with.'

I'm beginning to think she's right. Would Paul have dated me if he hadn't instantly recognised my name because his sister had read and raved over my books? Looking back now, I doubt it.

'Anyway, there are a few things I need to discuss with you. First, it's time to update your author photo and show off the glamorous new you. Do you want to arrange that, or shall I?'

I continue munching on lettuce, shaking my head from side to side until I clear my mouth.

'No, it's fine. I can sort that. I'll use the guy who did my last lot of shots.'

'Good. *Cosy Living* are going to do a double page spread on you and will be giving away copies of your latest novel. I'll send over the details and someone will contact you directly to arrange the interview.'

Inwardly I groan. To enable me to have an interesting chat for a feature I need to be living an interesting life. I stare at Carrie, with a dubious look on my face.

'Oh, come on, you can find something to talk about.'

'I guess the intervention wouldn't be a good idea?'

She gives me one of her unforgiving looks. 'No.'

'Okay. How about a spa weekend and the fact that everyone enjoys having a little makeover every once in a while?'

'Ooh, great idea! Maybe I can get the spa to join in and offer a free weekend away, or something. Email me the link to their website and I'll get onto that, the magazine would love it.'

She doesn't miss an angle or the potential to grab an opportunity.

The avocado and herb salad is delicious, but I've had enough. These days I listen to what my stomach is telling me, rather than eating every little morsel out of habit. I push the plate away and as I do so, a woman approaches the table.

'I'm sorry to bother you, but now you've finished eating can I just say that I love your books, Ms Middleton. I only wish I had one with me, so I could get your signature.'

The lady is probably in her fifties and I can see by her demeanour that she's a real fan. It's moments like this that remind me what it means to write. It's not about statistics but the readers who invite my stories into their lives.

Carrie has already pulled a copy of my latest novel out of her bag and passes it to me with a pen.

'Oh, that's amazing, thank you so much!' The woman is delighted. 'I'm Eve, by the way. This is such a thrill for me.'

Heads are turning in our direction and probably for the first time in a couple of years I don't feel like shrinking away. I push my shoulders back and keep my head high. I'm proud of what I've achieved now that I'm back on track.

'And I have to say that you are much more glamorous up close than you are in your photographs.'

An image flashes up in my head of the shot where I was getting out of a taxi exposing a wide expanse of white thigh, clearly dimpled with cellulite. I almost shudder at the memory. Instead, I smile and hand Eve the book. She hugs it close to her body, before walking back to her table and the gentleman sitting there, who is patiently waiting for her. I wonder if he realises what his wife is reading when she's lying next to him in bed at night? That thought raises a chuckle.

'Now isn't that a boost to the morale? You turn down so many opportunities to get out there and meet your loyal readers. I know you don't want to hear this but for the next book your publishers are planning an extended book signing tour. I thought I'd mention it now, so you can psych yourself up. Oh, and I have an idea that might help liven things up for you a little. Something you could also regard as doing me a bit of a personal favour at the same time.'

A personal favour? That's a first for Carrie.

'Fire away.' I can't wait to hear this.

'How do you fancy going to Italy on a writing retreat? It's in a villa in the hills above Lake Garda. Stunning views. Flights and accommodation are free in return for taking part.'

My brow lifts in surprise. 'Lake Garda?' I frown at her, wondering where this random idea originated. 'Taking part, you say?'

For the first time in memory, Carrie is squirming a little in her seat.

'It's for a period of four weeks. The villa is owned by Arran Jamieson and every July he runs four one week long retreats for writers of all abilities. People go along because they've hit a wall and need some quiet time away from any distractions, or are newbies writing their first manuscripts. You'd be replacing Kathy Porter, the renowned historical romance author, who was going to help Arran and, in particular, run one of the sessions.'

I must look stunned, because Carrie immediately puts up a hand appealing to me to wait and not jump in. July? That's only a week away.

'I know it's short notice because you'd be flying out on Friday, but I genuinely believe this will be mutually beneficial for you *and* Arran. He can only accommodate six people at a time, so that's eight of you in total. He provides breakfast but for lunch and dinner guests get a discount at a local restaurant, which is a five minute walk away. Arran's sessions on the writing process itself and the wider, technical aspects such as building a website and social media presence have gained him a solid reputation. Each morning he runs a three hour workshop. The rest of the day attendees are free to write, go sightseeing, or take part in informal chats to discuss best practice and generally talk shop. Kathy was down for a session on how to make characters leap off the page by tapping into their emotions and portraying real life relationships.'

I let out a rather loud 'hmm.'

'It's Lake Garda – four weeks of guaranteed sunshine and a change of scenery will do you good,' Carrie adds, quite forcefully.

His name rings a bell; Kathy, I know quite well from various events I've attended in the past. The name echoes around inside my head and I know I should be able to conjure up a face. Jamieson… Jamieson – got it!

'He presented and co-wrote the TV series *Inventions That Changed the Way We Live Forever*. He's written a few history textbooks, aside from his usual military fiction,' she informs me.

I remember watching some of the episodes; he's a history buff and it was an interesting series looking at different time periods. Basically, it was about how daily life changed with the advent of new discoveries and inventions. I've never read any of his novels though, as military fiction isn't my thing.

'And this would be doing you a personal favour because…?'

Carrie looks directly at me.

'As you know, Kathy has been in the game a long time and her workshops have inspired a whole generation of new writers. I was the one who introduced them, and this would have been Kathy's third year helping Arran. However, a broken ankle means her foot is in plaster and travel is impossible. I think this is a great opportunity to remind you how skilled you are at your craft and helping others is always the best boost to one's confidence. Plus, it's a bit of a holiday, too.

'The personal side to this favour is that Arran's current work in progress is based on the true story of a young couple who fall in love, only to be separated by war. He sent me the partial manuscript as I'm going to be representing him on this one and while it's up to his usual high standards there's something lacking. His skills lie in the detail and technically he can't be faulted; but within a harrowing story of life and loss during the Second World War, the love story itself lacks depth. Kathy was going to spend some time with Arran to look at re-working the love scenes. Just to add a little more emotion and realism so the reader can really connect with the poignancy of their situation.'

Critiquing another author's work isn't something I feel comfortable doing, least of all with the very formidable, and scholarly, Arran Jamieson.

Carrie is staring at me.

'It would be easy for you, believe me. It's a heart-rending story and the setting, the action and the plot are spot on. But the love scenes are mechanical and rather cold. I know it and so does Arran. You'd be doing him a huge favour, well, two favours in fact.'

Carrie wouldn't ask me if she didn't think I was up to it, but do I want to step outside my comfort zone and be exposed to such a daunting experience?

Lake Garda. I imagine my romantic lead character Ethan Turner standing and looking out across the rippling blue water as the sun glints upon it, turning it into liquid silver.

'Okay. But I'm repaying the favour you've done covering for me and this is a one-off. I am not going to be the backup for future emergencies when it comes to Arran Jamieson's writing retreats. Understood?'

Carrie nods, raising her water glass and I reluctantly raise mine to chink.

'Here's to a wonderful July in a stunning location,' she grins, looking suitably relieved. I can't imagine there were many fall back options open to her, or Arran, for that matter.

But everything happens for a reason, or so they say. Maybe this will also be the key to unlocking Ethan

Turner's heart and my love story will begin to flow. If I can't make two characters fall in love when they have Lake Garda as their background setting, then there is no romance left in my soul. As the characters' love for each other grows on the page, I'm hoping that it will also keep my dream alive too.

Sex sells, but in my heart, love rules. I hope that somewhere out there is a man capable of seeing the person I am beneath my authorly exterior. Someone who understands what love means, and that it isn't simply diving between the sheets in a lustful frenzy. I'm talking about enduring love that is so much more than the physical side; it's about instinctively knowing what makes the other person happy and putting their needs before your own. Lover, friend and confidant – the one who is your inspiration and the person around whom you build your future. That's not too much to ask, is it? Well, whatever… but I refuse to give up hope.

6

No More Excuses

'That's just the sort of challenge you need,' Mel confirms, looking pleased for me. 'It's time you ventured outside your little comfort zone. And Lake Garda – wow, I'm envious!'

She's sprawled across the sofa opposite me, recovering from our five mile walk. If I'm going to be slipping into one of those strappy little summer frocks I've packed ready for Friday's departure, then the effort is going to be worth it.

'Hmm. I'm still not totally convinced though, as what Carrie rather diplomatically left out was the fact that I might well have been her only option. How many people can fly off for the best part of a month at such short notice? Only someone without a man or children in tow, that's for sure!'

Mel frowns.

'Yes, but it had to be someone with the necessary skills for the task, too.'

'Agreed. But Arran Jamieson and I have nothing at all in common other than the fact that we are both writers. Oh, and now we have the same agent, of course. Kathy is well respected throughout the industry because she's been teaching creative writing for many years. I can imagine the two of them getting on very well together. I'm a little nervous about Arran's reaction when he hears who the stand-in is going to be. I think I'm probably a good ten years younger than him and I doubt we have many writing friends in common. And Carrie has asked me to assist him with his latest writing project; there are a few lack-lustre love scenes that need a little work,' I grimace.

'You've had no direct contact with him at all, then?'

'No, nothing yet. Carrie confirmed the flight times and said Arran will be in touch about picking me up from the airport.'

'So, he's a history buff, you say, and he presented a series on TV? How old is he?'

'I don't know. Late thirties or early forties? There's a YouTube video they made as a pilot for the programme; give me a moment and I'll find it.'

Not wanting to go into this situation blind, I've done a bit of online research about Arran. He's very personable, obviously, because you don't get a job as a TV presenter unless you are watchable as well as knowledgeable. He has charm and oodles of it, but he isn't afraid to speak his mind. Particularly on Twitter, I notice, where he's very vocal about his pet topics.

'Here you go.' I start the video clip and place the iPad on the coffee table between us, turning it round so Mel can watch it. I sit back for a few minutes, watching her reaction.

'He's younger looking than I was expecting!' she exclaims, a small smile spreading over her face. 'You made him sound a bit dull, just now. Lucky you, he's a real gentleman. And pretty fit. That haircut doesn't do him any favours though, which is a real shame but there's definitely a shade or two of David Gandy about him. He's wearing a wedding ring, I see. Will his wife be there at the villa?'

He's so animated when he talks and clearly he's passionate about history. As for the ring, well, I hadn't even noticed that. And David Gandy? I peer at the screen, squinting. Hmm… maybe. I pull back, rather sharply. Broody is the term I'd use and I guess there is a certain something that makes him watchable.

'I don't know and that's not really relevant, anyway,' I reply in a matter-of-fact tone. 'What I need to know is whether he thinks this is a good idea or not. I can handle running the workshop, no problem at all, but as for helping him out, that's another matter entirely. You need to be on the same page as someone conceptually to work on editing a manuscript. For the writer that means listening, taking on board ideas and then testing them out. I'm afraid that most of us have quite fragile egos; each story you write is like sharing a part of you, what's inside your head, with the world. It can be quite painful to have someone pull it apart unless you have the utmost respect for them and trust that their expertise will make your story better.'

My real concern is that although Kathy might be physically hampered at the moment, that shouldn't stop her working with Arran online. Or Carrie, for that matter. So what is Carrie not telling me and what is Arran's real problem, I wonder?

'So, have you packed your suitcase yet?'

I shake my head, taking a sip of my coffee.

'No, well, partly. I'm sort of hoping Arran declines Carrie's offer, even at this late stage. I know four weeks in the sun would be lovely, but I don't really need the hassle. Especially now I'm back in my stride and I want to meet the original deadline for my next book, if I can. Besides, Carrie says I have to do an extended book signing tour once it's out, so that's more than enough excitement on the horizon. Oh, and I'm doing an interview for *Cosy Living* tomorrow. Fortunately, it's via Skype but a photographer is coming here to take a couple of shots of me at home in the picturesque Forest of Dean.'

'And all of that is happening before you're due to fly out in five days' time?'

I replace the empty mug on the coffee table between us, then switch off the iPad.

'Yes, assuming I do fly out on Friday, of course.'

Mel is wearing a slight frown. 'You're going to miss my first date. Saturday night, I'm meeting up with Ross and we're having dinner together.'

'That's awesome news, Mel! Obviously, the email exchanges are going well.'

Her cheeks are beginning to colour up a little and she looks away for a moment, uncomfortably.

'Well enough. He's twenty-seven and he's a graphic designer.'

'Oh, another techie person, then. Right up your street.' Mel is the IT manager at our local school. She was the one who helped me set up my author website and social media platform.

The screen on my iPad lights up and I see it's an email from the man himself, Arran Jamieson.

'Well, talk of the devil! I need to read this email. It might save me finishing off that packing.'

Dear Ms Middleton,

Thank you for stepping in to take over after Kathy Porter's unfortunate accident. While I'm not personally familiar with your work, Carrie tells me you will do a great job of running the character development workshop.

I'll make sure it isn't too onerous and you will have plenty of free time to relax and write.

Your flight arrival time is 9.25 p.m. on Friday evening and I'll be at the airport waiting to drive you back to the villa.

Regards,

Arran Jamieson

There's peace and there's war – in between is a battleground

I read it out to Mel.

'Does it sound a bit… curt, to you? Like he's been talked into it? And there's no mention, at all, of his manuscript. Perhaps Carrie re-thought that one.'

Mel raises one eyebrow and I turn the iPad around, so she can read it for herself.

'It might have been nice if he'd said he was looking forward to working with you, or something, but then I suspect he's a bit formal given his academic background.'

I still think there's a dig in there when he says, '*I'll make sure it isn't too onerous…*'

'Guess I have to finish packing that suitcase, after all. Oh well, maybe the chance to soak up a little sunshine will revitalise me.'

Mel starts laughing.

'You'll be much too busy showing Arran how to plumb the depths of his emotions.' She grins back at me, trying her best not to laugh out loud.

'Well, according to him there's still going to be time for some relaxation, so I guess he won't be needing that much help. But we digress, weren't we talking about Ross?'

Her face falls a little. 'I'm nervous about our first meet-up. I know on paper it seems we have a lot in common. It is nice that we both have a bit of a geeky tendency, but there has to be a catch. He's good looking, if his photos are anything to go by, easy to talk to and has a good job. So why hasn't someone snapped him up?'

I chew my lip, mindful of the need not to deter her in any way, but he does sound too good to be true.

'You need to keep an open mind, Mel, and give him a chance. He's probably thinking the same thing about you. What happened with Justin wasn't your fault and maybe Ross will be able to empathise with that sort of situation. Or perhaps his focus has been his career; look at me, I still haven't found *the one*, probably because most of the time I'm too busy to look. But eventually even the most driven of people find that loneliness is a feeling that catches you unawares. You reach a point and suddenly you see there's something missing from your life, so you do something about it.'

She nods. 'I guess you're right and I'm looking for problems before we even begin. But after Justin's behaviour I'm going to be on my guard. I wish you were going to be around, though.'

'I'll have my phone with me so text me as soon as you can. You'll be fine, just relax and see what happens.'

We stand and hug goodbye; I hope this Ross isn't hiding anything because Mel deserves a guy who will really appreciate how loyal and kind she is; from the little she's said, they at least share some common interests.

'Travel safe,' she whispers, before drawing away. She looks me straight in the eye, frowning slightly. 'And text me when you're at the villa. Once you're settled, I want to know every little detail.'

How ironic that here we are, both about to set out on a new adventure. One which has a dual edge to it – there is a sense of excitement, but there's also a worrying sense of uncertainty.

7

A Busy Week and I'm on a Roll

'Hello, Brie, I'm Heidi Hoffman. It's so lovely to meet you. Do you mind if I record this interview as well as making a few notes as we speak?'

I was rather hoping it would be Heidi because I've read some of her interviews and she seems to be focused, but fair. It's so easy for things to be taken out of context and even when the journalist is friendly, interviews can veer off at a tangent. But I've done so many it's no longer daunting; what *is* daunting is the fact that I lead a very quiet existence and that won't sell magazine copies. But I love my life, temporary blips aside. All I need is to find my knight in shining armour who also happens to think curling up on the sofa and watching a chick flick is a good night in. My lips start to curl up and I turn it into a welcoming smile. So far, this week has gone well, and this is the last hurdle to jump.

'Lovely to meet you, too, Heidi. Sorry about the limited availability but I'm off to Italy tomorrow.'

'Oh, no problem whatsoever. We've just received the photos that were taken yesterday at your home. That's a beautiful cottage you have there. I'll send you copies of the two shots we're going to use in the article. Carrie has arranged for a free weekend pass for two people at the spa and we're giving away a dozen copies of *Loving a Stranger*. So when's the next book due out?'

I settle back in my seat, feeling comfortable and relaxed. That's the beauty of doing an interview via Skype – although I did tidy up my desk a little. But I have no idea why I felt the need to do my hair and make-up, except that it's all about image. I'm sure Heidi has interviewed a lot of writers and she knows the score.

'My writing deadline for the first draft is the end of October and it's due for release in early January.'

'Ooh, I can't wait. I've read every single one of your books. Can you give me a teaser for the article?'

I'm flattered; journalists will pamper your ego to get you to relax but she sounds like a genuine fan.

'Well, I can't give much away at the moment, but what I can say is that the main character is probably going to be a cage fighter.'

Heidi is scribbling away.

'My heart is pounding as I'm writing,' she laughs. 'A cage fighter? Where did that idea come from?'

'Channel hopping one night on TV. It was hard to watch actually, and yet it was compelling. Raw aggression can be scary to witness, but all I could think about was the dedication and fearless mental attitude. The other side of that has to be extreme, so Jed is quite a passionate lover.

He's just more committed to his sport and his physical needs, than he is to his emotional side.'

She stops writing and looks directly at me.

'How real are your characters to you and do you always have a clear picture of them in your head?'

'Definitely. Jed was inspired by the guy who did my training programme at a spa weekend recently. I admire people who take their fitness to the max. Life is too short not to give your all to whatever you choose to do.'

There's a pause while Heidi is bent over the notebook in front of her.

'It's been what, a little over a year, since your split with the very talented and gorgeous Paul Turner. Are we likely to see you out and about again any time soon with another man on your arm?'

A lump rises up in my throat. Damn it! Of course, she was going to touch on that as I've virtually been in hiding since my personal life made the gossip columns. It doesn't look good; it looks as if he broke my heart. He didn't – he simply dented it. The meltdown was all my own fault.

'When you have a demanding career, that must always come first, I'm afraid. Maintaining a successful relationship shouldn't be all about juggling two very full diaries and trying to make the impossible happen. My commitments for the next year mean I have a series of challenging deadlines to meet but maybe after that, who knows? It might be time to ease off a little.'

'It's a shame it didn't work out between the two of you. I don't suppose there's any chance of you getting back together?'

She must be joking.

'Sadly, that's a firm no, I'm afraid. I'm lucky enough to be living my dream and I realise that this is a time when I have to be focused. I'm able to do that thanks to the wonderful readers who keep me writing because they continue to buy my books. And not forgetting the amazing reviewers who spread the word, too. That's a two way commitment. I've no plans to change my lifestyle drastically, in the near future. But sometimes it's nice to reinvent yourself a little. The spa break was a little breather before a huge peak in my workload and I feel refreshed. It was nice to take some time off with my best friend, Mel, and be pampered. As for the long term future, who knows what will happen?'

Heidi studies my face for a moment.

'Well, I'm glad to hear it's not a knee-jerk reaction to the dreadful trolls who hounded you. That must have been a terrible experience and all credit to you, Brie, for getting through that unscathed. You certainly look *glowing*, that's why I thought maybe there was a new man in your life.'

The way she emphasised that word tells me she wanted to say *thinner*. Okay, lady, I'm going to stop you right there.

'The stigma around weight is a very dangerous and potentially psychologically damaging issue. When unqualified people choose to call someone out in public, whichever end of the scale they are at, it shows an intent to invoke a reaction. Whether it sparks off a sense of shame, humiliation, or plain old anxiety, it's thoughtless. In that situation, I think more people should consider suing to compensate for the suffering that follows, don't you?'

That stops her in her tracks and she nods politely, so I continue.

'I feel that the pressure these days is to be seen to have everything. The reality for most people is that is seldom the case. And you can't engineer the timing of every aspect of your life. You work with the opportunities that come your way and when the time is right, everything else will slot into place.'

'So, the message to our readers is to relax and let life happen?' She sounds a tad sceptical.

'What I'm saying is find something you love doing and work at it, rather than focusing on body issues, or peer envy. Successful people are passionate about what they do and they never give up. Work with your natural skills and take the opportunities that come your way; that's how to turn the dream into a reality. It involves sacrifices, of course, but that's the price to be paid.

'I believe it's important not to compare yourself to other people in any aspect whatsoever. Each one of us is unique within our shell and we will all, invariably, be at a different point in our lives. If a man comes into my life then fine, but I don't need that to make me feel complete. I'm the one who makes my life what it is and while I'm happy and busy, I feel fulfilled. I think people often forget to count their blessings for what they have, instead focusing on what they don't have.'

I hope she doesn't twist any of that because the moment I finish speaking I realise it sounded a bit preachy. I meant it to sound humble and I hope she doesn't see it as a red flag.

She's writing quite intensely again.

'This trip to Italy, is it work or pleasure and how long will you be away?'

Watch what you say, Brie.

'A little of both. It's a writers' retreat so I will be running a workshop and there will be some informal sessions. It runs throughout July.'

'Sounds interesting. What part of Italy?'

'Lake Garda.'

'Oh, stunning setting. Anyone else attending whom our readers might know?'

Awkward. If I don't mention Arran and he finds out he might be offended, but then would he read a woman's magazine?

'I'm filling in for another author who is unable to travel. The course is run by Arran Jamieson, a very notable and successful author, documentary presenter and historian.'

Heidi's head jerks up, her pen still in her hand.

'Arran Jamieson? That's quite a mix, putting the two of you together. My boyfriend reads his books. Military fiction isn't my sort of subject matter, I'm afraid. Still, I suspect the attendees will write in a wide range of genres, so being at opposite ends of the spectrum is useful.'

Heidi is simply mirroring my own sentiments, but I can't divulge the reason why I was drawn into this, or the fact that I don't think it's a good idea.

'I was happy to help out and am really looking forward to getting some writing done while I'm there.'

I'm ready to draw this interview to a close now. I know that Carrie has given Heidi a lot of information about the spa and I sent along a couple of photos that Mel took of me on the day. Together with the book blurb and the cover of *Loving a Stranger*, that should give her plenty to fill two pages. I'm about to thank Heidi for her time, when she looks up at me, rather pointedly.

'Once the attacks began to wane, you did a very good job of keeping your personal life out of the press, Brie. That must have put enormous pressure on you, though. Does the chance of being recognised ever make you withdraw, simply because that's the easiest option?'

I don't like the word *withdraw* thrown in there quite casually. It's a subtle dig implying I was hiding myself away. Which is exactly what I've been doing.

I suppose it was the shock factor that turned it into a big deal so quickly. No one ever expected me to date a rock star, as my escorts at parties and functions are usually colleagues from the publishing industry. Whenever I do TV or radio interviews I always steer away from talking about my private life and focus on my writing career. Over the years, reporters have accepted that as a given. Up until I began dating Paul I was very much in the swing of socialising in literary circles, which I'd been doing for a number of years. I chose companions who didn't mind seeing their photo staring back at them online or in a gossip magazine, and my personal life was very private indeed. But Heidi has done her homework on me and it's useless to pretend that I haven't had a low profile since Paul. Who wants to go to a party when there's one burning question on everyone's lips? The problem with seeking publicity is that you can't choose to gloss over a question simply because it doesn't suit you to answer it.

'No. I've been working on another book project which is very close to my heart, in addition to my contractual obligations. In one respect, my personal life has had to take a back seat for a while. If the project sees the light of day, then it will have been worth the sacrifice.'

Heidi looks interested and I jump in quickly to avoid a new line of questioning.

'If it comes off, then I'll make sure you will be the first to know. You can be the one to break the news!'

She looks delighted and I hope I've diverted a potential disaster here. Give a journalist a glimmer of getting a first and it will colour what they choose to put in print. Upsetting me might mean losing out on a potential coup.

'Wow! Thank you, Brie. I hope it goes well, then. And thanks for an amazing interview. Our readers will be fascinated at this insight into the daily life of a writer who really turns up the heat and has us drooling over a steady succession of ripped guys. I do hope your workload eases off soon, so you can get back to grabbing some fun again.'

I nod and smile. 'Me too, Heidi. All work and no play is sometimes the price we have to pay for following a dream. Hopefully it will soon be time to party again!'

As a writer your life is out there because that's what self-promotion is all about, but sometimes you are required to get a little creative. Anyway, I'm sure I'll be attending a party at some point in the future, even if it's just another book launch extravaganza organised by my publisher.

8

Jetting Off to the Sun

While I'm killing time at Gatwick airport, Dean, my lovely photographer friend, has sent through some proofs for me to select a new photo for my press pack and jacket covers.

There are four and I click on the first one; it opens, and I scroll across them all quickly to see if one jumps out, but I can't decide. I know Carrie will love them, but I'm still adjusting to the *new* me. Which is a bit of a thrill actually, and very empowering. I look slightly edgy with this new hairstyle and the expression on my face is one of a strong and determined woman. Which I am, but I look a little aloof. A sort of *don't mess with me* vibe going on there. Admittedly, on the day of the shoot, last Tuesday, I was feeling a little concerned about the upcoming interview with Heidi. My self-defence mechanism is to draw on that mask, my game face as it were. But in truth, any one of the shots will work so I forward them on to Carrie to make the final decision.

It's time to saunter past the bookshop and see if I can pick up one of Arran's novels. As I trawl along the shelves, I see there are three of his books in stock and I choose his latest title, *Men of Steel*. Of course, I can't walk away without doing a little book spotting of my own. I'm delighted to discover that *Loving a Stranger*, which has been out for nearly three months now, is number two in the 'Top Fifty' display. On an adjacent shelf I find three of my other titles amongst a line-up with a 'What's hot' banner above it. Hmm… not bad, Brie.

It never gets stale, seeing my books on the shelf in bookshops, or getting a new review. And yes, discounting the trolls, the bad ones do hurt. The worst I've received so far was just the one word 'Rubbish!' The exclamation mark wasn't necessary, I reflected, while my heart silently wept. I was so upset that later in the day I revisited it and clicked on the reviewer's name. I discovered that Ms Booklover had only posted the one review to date, which sort of made a double joke out of choosing that ID as she certainly didn't love my book! So, what did that mean? She tried one book, which happened to be mine, and it put her off reading for life? It served to teach me a lesson which was that some opinions are more valuable than others. Sitting there, a lonely one star among hundreds of four and five star reviews – many by serious book reviewers – it was obviously some poor, angry soul venting. Maybe she happened to download my book when she was having a really bad day and the story hit a raw nerve. Or maybe she has a lot of aliases and gets a kick out of being a rain cloud to spoil someone's day. Or maybe she compared her man to my hunky hero and felt life had cheated her, deciding there and then never to read a book again. I'll never know for sure.

But it is hard to develop a thick skin, which is what you need to do as an author in order to survive and keep writing. Accepting that not everyone is going to love your work is as tough as someone telling you that your baby is ugly. It's the price you pay for being in this game. You make yourself a sitting target with no right of reply because everyone is entitled to their own opinion. Especially if they've paid good money for something they don't enjoy. After all, the ninety-nine pence could have been spent on a chocolate bar, guaranteed to give a satisfying sugar hit every time!

I make a conscious effort to replace my frown with a friendly smile as I pull out my credit card to pay for Arran's book. The sales assistant behind the counter raises an eyebrow.

'It's a good book,' he adds enthusiastically, as I swipe my card.

'Well, I'm hoping to get it signed by the author himself.'

He raises his eyebrows. 'That's amazing. I've never met an author in real life. I suspect they don't do ordinary things like the rest of us. How the other half live, eh?'

I nod, trying hard to hide what is fast becoming a silly grin as I walk away with my purchase.

With an hour to go before boarding I pull Arran's book from my bag and leaf past the title page and copyright details to glance at the acknowledgements. An ammunitions expert, a retired Navy seal, an air-sea rescue pilot… not one single mention of anyone who doesn't have a working credit alongside their name. I know that some authors have an incredibly long list of people to thank and you begin to wonder how they manage to get any writing done. They make it sound like they spend most of their time talking to, or lunching with, their super-supportive gang.

But Arran doesn't seem to have anyone close to thank for being there throughout those anxious writerly moments. I skip forward to the dedication page and it simply reads: *In memory of those who lost their lives – heroes forever*. A poignant tribute and I find myself giving a nod of approval, then take a quick look around to check that no one noticed.

I have Mel, Mum, Dad and Carrie – all of them lend a listening ear at some point during the writing process. Outside that I have thousands of social media friends, so obviously they get a one-liner mention, then maybe one or two people if I have to do detailed research relating to a specialism. For instance, for my current novel I have a Skype interview with real life cage fighter, Jordan Lewis, scheduled for next week. He'll get a mention in the acknowledgements, together with the usual thanks to the people who make it all happen at the publishing end. How can you possibly write a book and only thank the people whose brains you pick on the research side? Moving on, I see that there's a short prologue before Chapter One.

Sometimes the darkness of a cloud covered night sky is so dense it blots out everything, except the constant flashbacks of dirt-streaked faces screaming in pain. But the pitch black shadows are a comfort to a soldier like Brett, and he welcomes it. In two minutes and thirty-three seconds he will slit a man's throat and think nothing of it, before moving on in search of his next target. Tonight, the body count will be high.

This is going to be a long journey in more than one sense of the word.

The plane lands at Verona airport on time and fortunately I manage to get through passport control quite promptly, given that there are a lot of families on the flight. It's late and the younger travellers are understandably tired and grumpy. Before I know it, I'm wheeling my two large suitcases out onto the concourse, the heat hitting me instantly. Arran Jamieson hurries forward to take one of them from me.

Well, at least he's a gentleman and, oh my, there is a little David Gandy thing going on there. His cursory 'hello' instantly transports me back to watching him on TV, but today he's casually dressed in jeans and a short-sleeved, check shirt. He's a lot more muscular in real life and I'm thinking that Arran has changed a little since the *Inventions That Changed the Way We Live Forever* series aired. Now his dark brown hair is longer on top, a mass of curls and I presume that's why the back and sides are shaved very short. Previously it was all short and it made him look like an army recruit on boot camp. As we wheel the cases to his car he asks about the flight and I tell him it was fine, just a little noisy. Once the suitcases are stowed away, he walks around the car to open the front passenger door for me. I realise we haven't shaken hands or anything, and I wonder if that's because he doesn't feel comfortable with me, or whether he's simply nervous. I hope neither is the case, as we're going to be spending a lot of time in each other's company.

We set off in total silence. I rack my brains to think of something innocuous to say.

'Is it far to the villa?'

Arran continues to look straight ahead as we filter out onto a busy road.

'Villa Monteverdi is about a fifty-five minute drive. It's set in the hills above the lakeside town of Salò, which is known for its boutiques and restaurants. It's a little over a seventy kilometre drive.'

It would have been nice to have received the information pack he sends out to the attendees, because I really don't know what to expect. I don't want to distract him by asking questions and he does seem to want to concentrate on the road. I can fully understand as night time driving isn't easy even when the roads are quiet. I decide to settle back in my seat and try to relax. In my head I'm piecing together the reasoning behind Ethan Turner's trip to Italy, where he will meet the very outgoing and decidedly quirky Izzie Martin.

A writer can easily fill an hour quite productively without needing to touch a keyboard because it's all about the thought processes. When Arran suddenly begins speaking again, I glance at the clock on the dashboard, surprised to see that we must be very close to the villa now.

'I expect you're tired after the travelling.'

I'm wired, not tired. 'No. My body clock is still saying that I'm an hour behind, anyway. I often write through the night, too, so it's been a long time since I kept normal hours.'

'This is it,' he interrupts, easing the car in through an open gateway. The tyres crunch on a gravelled drive as we pull to a halt.

Arran immediately leaps out of the car, but it's clear it isn't to open my door when I hear the click of the boot opening. Swinging open the passenger door and stepping out, the air is warm as I inhale. I pause for a moment to suck in a deep breath and it's like smelling a bouquet; a blend of perfumed notes that give an overriding impression of a luscious, floral backdrop. While there is a lot of ground level lighting, given the lateness of the hour what I see is mostly determined by shape. But surrounding the rear of the white painted villa I can make out an extensive garden on the gentle slopes of a hill. The incessant chirping from the cicadas is like a sound track, only broken by the sound of a car driving past the gate.

Arran is already carrying the cases over to the path and I hurry across to take one, conscious they are rather heavy.

'Welcome to Villa Monteverdi, Brie. I hope you are going to enjoy your stay here.'

'Thank you, Arran, I'm sure I will.' I hope I sound positive and not as dubious as I really feel.

I follow him along the sloping path, the lighting good enough to gain an impression of the landscaping either side of me. I catch the heady perfume from a bougainvillea intertwined around a tree to the left hand side of the large, oblong building in front of us. Even in the gloom, the pop of colour seems to glow against the almost indistinguishable mass of foliage.

Arran stops to retract the handle of the suitcase and unlock the rear door. It's a three storey villa and I glance up to see that the first and second floors have wrap around balconies. He carries the case inside, taking a moment to switch on the lights before I follow behind him, crossing the threshold. Finding myself in quite a wide hallway, immediately to my right is a large plant standing in a nook to the rear of a staircase leading to the first floor. Our footsteps echo a little as we walk parallel with the stairs and then turn to begin the ascent. The suitcase is heavy, and I struggle a little, but Arran doesn't seem to have any problem whatsoever with the one he's carrying.

To my dismay we aren't stopping on that level but carry on along the landing to the next flight of stairs taking us up to the top floor. Well, at least the views will be good.

'There are eight double suites in total. Each room has a walk-in wardrobe and an en-suite. The rooms on this side of the villa are a little larger than on the other side because the building is staggered on the front elevation. I've given you one of the larger rooms. I'm in the room directly below yours.'

He swings open the door and we step into a short corridor.

'Bathroom to the left, wardrobe to the right,' he calls over his shoulder. As the room opens out he stops to set down the suitcase he's carrying.

I'm relieved to put mine down as the handle is beginning to bite into my hand. Arran walks across to turn on the bedside table lamps. It's a very large, airy room with the balconied windows extending around two walls, giving it a dual aspect. Floor to ceiling white voiles are pulled back, allowing a glimpse of the rear garden which, with the little bursts of lighting, looks very atmospheric and rather pretty.

'What a lovely room. The villa is beautiful, Arran.'

'I count myself as very fortunate to live here. It was designed to accommodate a large family but it's only full when I'm running the retreats.' The irony reflected in his tone is rather poignant. I hadn't even glanced at his hand, but I can see now that it's ring free.

We stand, looking at each other uncomfortably.

'If it's not too late, would you like to join me on the front terrace for a drink?'

'That would be lovely, thank you.'

'If you retrace your steps it's the door to the right just beyond the stairs in the lower corridor. See you in a little while.'

He exits, and I walk over to the window to peer out. The balcony is a lovely idea and there is a frosted glass panel to one side, which is probably a divider between this and the adjacent room. I'm delighted to see a good sized, sturdy metal table and two chairs, which would be a perfect place to sit and write. At the other end the balcony wraps around the corner. Craning my neck to the side, I can see the headlights from a few cars as they drive past the gates, but aside from that the only lights are those in the garden itself. The terraced garden is informal, like a grotto with unidentifiable profiles of plants and shrubs giving an interesting contour to the landscape.

The room itself is spacious, airy and quite plain. With light cream marble floor tiles and crisp, navy and white pinstripe bedding it's very pleasant indeed. The bed faces the floor to ceiling glass windows looking out over the rear garden. On the far side of the bed that wall too is entirely made up of glass. With an elegant glass topped table either side of the bed sporting oversized table lamps, it's minimalist and chic. Very *boutique hotel* in style.

In the corner are two tub chairs and a coffee table; a pleasant seating area from which to enjoy the views in both directions. I discover that the bathroom has a bath and a separate shower, as well as a hand basin and toilet. The walk-in wardrobe is large enough for me to carry in the cases and stack them neatly beneath one of the hanging rails.

Taking a moment to freshen up I finish off with a quick brush of my hair, then make my way downstairs.

The door to the open plan kitchen-dining room is ajar. When I push it open, I walk into a very generously proportioned room, one wall of which is glass fronted and looks out onto a well lit terraced area. This is stylish, contemporary living and a sharp contrast to the cosy rooms of my sprawling, nineteenth century cottage.

'Perfect timing. What do you drink? I have most things.'

The shiny, sleek kitchen units are an interesting mocha colour which goes perfectly with the pale cream marble floor tiles running throughout the property.

Arran swings open a cupboard door to reveal a mini cocktail cabinet, including a wine cooler.

'Do you have any rosé?'

'I have a local rosé, Chiaretto, which is made from the same grapes as the ruby red Italian Bardolino wine. I can recommend it: it's dry, clean and fruity.'

'Perfect, thank you.'

'I think I'll join you. I'm a night owl and rarely get to bed before 2 a.m. I think a lot of authors develop irregular sleep patterns,' he adds.

I glance up at the clock on the wall and am surprised to see it's only ten past eleven.

'When will the group arrive?'

I stand watching as Arran loads up a tray with small plates of olives, cheese, some cooked meats and a basket of bread. He adds some dipping oil and balsamic vinegar then turns to face me.

'Lunchtime tomorrow. If you can bring the wine and the glasses, I think we're all set.'

Tucking two placemats under his arm he lifts the tray effortlessly, and makes his way to the half open sliding door leading out onto the terrace. As soon as I step out into the night air my eyes are drawn to the left, where a blue-tiled pool is all lit up. The surface of the water appears to shimmer as the pool lights pulsate.

'Wow, that's some pool,' I remark but as I pan around, my gaze settles on the view in front of us.

'Is this your first glimpse down onto the Città di Salò?' When he says the name in Italian his voice takes on a very charming accent. But then his voice is an important part of his profession as a presenter.

Reflecting upon the changes in his appearance since I last saw him on TV, particularly that haircut, I think the new style softens his overall appearance and makes him look younger. And a little less stuffy. But then, he's at home and clearly he's relaxed.

'Yes, it's breathtaking, even though it's merely a shadow against the sea and the sky at this time of night. All those twinkling lights make it look like a necklace, suspended against a dark blue background. How far away is it? I'll be honest and say that I didn't have time to research the Lake Garda area as I've been so busy. I wasn't sure exactly where on the lake the villa was located. I've been to the Amalfi coast and visited Rome but haven't had a chance to venture further afield.'

When I finally stop speaking I'm a little breathless; I realise I'm letting my nerves get to me and to my horror I'm saying the first thing that pops into my head.

He pours a little wine into the two glasses and hands me one, holding his own up so we can toast.

'A warm welcome, Brie, and thank you for stepping in at such short notice. It is rather beautiful and I never tire of this vista. It's just over eight kilometres to the town itself, but you'll get to see it up close on Tuesday.'

His welcome sounds genuine enough and he seems pleased now I'm here; we chink glasses.

I stare out over the vast expanse of the lake, way below us, with nothing to obscure the view. Savouring a mouthful of wine, I'm impressed; it has a crispness that makes it both light and refreshing. I can't help thinking this is surreal when you consider I'm used to being at home in my PJs, writing late into the night.

'Lake Garda is much larger than I thought it would be. It seems to go on endlessly.'

Arran nods, swallowing a sip of his wine and placing his glass back down on the table in front of us.

'Please, help yourself. I hope you aren't averse to eating cheese late at night. This is a locally produced Casàt, which is aged in oil and is a little spicy, and that's Tremosine. It has a soft texture and a delicate, yet fragrant taste. This is a salami made from beef, known as Pozzolengo, and then my favourites, Lonzino, a pork salami, and Cotechino which is a cooked pork sausage meat.' He passes me a plate before continuing. 'Yes, the lake covers 370 square kilometres. The town of Salò below us is located at the foot of the San Bartolomeo mountain which rises up to our left.'

Looking at the food it seems I'm hungrier than I thought, and I glance at the bread rather longingly. Do I want to feel ill tomorrow, I ask myself? Instead, I decide to take a small sample of several items, including the Tremosine, which has a soft texture, add a few olives and reach over to the bowl of fresh fruit to fill my plate. I can see Arran watching me with interest.

'Why was it named *Garda*, which I assume means guard?' I enquire to divert his attention.

'Yes, place of guard or place of observation. It is thought to have been named after the town of Garda, which at one point in its history had a fortress. It was important because of its strategic position occupying the south eastern shores. But the Venetians destroyed the fortress and took control of Lake Garda for nearly four hundred years. The lake was formed one and a half million years ago, when a massive piedmont glacier flowed down from the Brenta Dolomites to cut through and gouge out the valley. It's axe shaped and we're situated on the western edge of the widest part.'

The cheese is delicious, and I chew quickly, not just because I'm hungry, but because I have another question.

'What's a piedmont? I'm familiar with the word but not in the context of a glacier.'

He smiles, but it's a warm one and not a deprecating one.

'It's what happens when a steep valley glacier spills out onto a flat plain; an overspill, is probably the best explanation. When we visit Salò you will see how the promenade curves around the lake; it's rather wonderful, even though I'm biased because this is my home for a large part of the year.'

Arran is much easier to talk to than I'd imagined he would be. He seems comfortable enough in my company and I feel very relaxed.

'Carrie says you write romantic novels and that might come in handy. One of the first batch of authors arriving tomorrow is a romance writer too. I did look you up online and it said you write about *sassy females and hot, hunky guys*. I'm assuming there's a distinct line drawn between romance and erotica?'

I didn't like his tone when he repeated my byline as there was a lift of amusement in his voice, but I decide to give him the benefit of the doubt.

'There are lots of different interpretations, but I like to keep it simple. Erotica is when the sex is the basis of the conflict; sex being the central theme. Romance covers a wide range of storytelling; from sweet and simple, boy meets girl, to a love story which happens to feature sex and where the heat level is turned up a little.'

'Heat level?' He raises an eyebrow.

I ignore the question and help myself to some more olives and a slice of salami.

Arran tops up our glasses and I can feel him watching me.

'Your bio said your first novel was published when you were only twenty. I don't mean to be rude but that's a tender age at which to be writing full on sex scenes.'

Is he trying to insinuate something here? Well, I think that is a rude statement to make and it's intrusive. Fictional stories aren't based on first hand experience and the art of lovemaking isn't rocket science. Maybe my positive first impression of him was a little hasty after all and the more I get to know him, the less I'll like him.

'You're assuming everything I write is from personal experience?'

Touché. He looks shocked by my forthright response and quickly shakes his head.

'I wasn't… I mean, maybe I should rephrase that question. Was it difficult to get into a genre where the readers' expectations are so high with regards to one particular aspect of a story? You hardly had much in the way of life experience when you began writing.'

I burst out laughing. If he's trying to insult me then I'm not going to take him seriously.

'I pride myself on always meeting my readers' expectations,' I reply, playfully. 'But initially I wrote contemporary women's fiction about relationships and real life. Okay, the pursuit of true love was a part of that, but aren't most people looking for someone to love? After three books, and with Carrie in my corner, I ramped up the heat and here I am.'

'I gather sex sells, then?'

I can't tell if he's being sarcastic, or whether he's genuinely interested but his tone is a little disapproving to my ears.

'It does.'

'So, what is your definition of *love*.'

This is beginning to feel like the Spanish Inquisition; whatever I say is going to be the wrong answer because Arran Jamieson clearly doesn't take romance seriously, full stop. Well, two can play that game. I don't have to explain myself or pander to you, Mister. So now it's time to put on my game playing mask.

'I *love* being an international bestselling author. Enough said.'

He goes quiet, pretending to concentrate on eating but I notice he's only toying with the food on his plate. Even though this conversation is beginning to irritate me immensely, it's beginning to feel like we're bantering. As if he's playing with me. There's an understated coolness to his manner that's not unattractive. He has that slightly broody, enigmatic quality which is rather magnetic to watch in action.

'Ah, sidestepping the question. You don't seem to take sex seriously, either.' Arran's voice is tinged with amusement. It's not that I don't take either seriously but I certainly don't have to explain myself to him!

'For a lot of people sex is just about pleasure. It doesn't mean anything deeper and as long as it's between two consenting adults who aren't in a committed relationship with someone else, then where's the harm in it?'

I know that I'm coming across as an advocate of no-strings-attached sex here and as someone who writes solely for the money, but neither one is true. I write because I think a lot of people need a hero in their lives and some never find one. And writing is my guilty pleasure, not simply an occupation, more so than chocolate even. But he's pressing my buttons. It might be tiredness making me grouchy, but I stand up, more than ready to bid him goodnight. Besides, if you need to ask someone to define love, then you sure as hell won't be able to grasp the answer.

'Thank you for picking me up from the airport and for supper, Arran. Is nine in the morning a good time to make myself available?'

He stands, making no attempt to either shake hands, or hug.

'Nine o'clock is fine. I'll run through the week's agenda with you. Goodnight, Brie; sleep well.'

9

A Frosty Start Despite the Sunshine

I only drank a couple of glasses of wine last night, but I awaken with a cracking headache. Then I realise I'm probably dehydrated and I head downstairs to grab some water. As lovely as the room is it's lacking a few things. Like a drinking glass, for one, and it feels bare rather than minimalist. There isn't really anything to personalise the room and it lacks any hint of a feminine touch. It's curious because I thought Arran was married.

When I walk into the kitchen his back is towards me and he's singing to himself under his breath.

'Good morning, Arran.'

He spins around and has the audacity to look me up and down before replying to my greeting. It seems my simple, knee length floral dress in bright reds and pinks has invoked a reaction and I struggle to hide the beginning of a smile that starts to tug at my lips.

'Good morning, Brie. What would you like for breakfast?'

'I came down for some water, actually. But I'd love a coffee too, if it's not too much trouble and I'll grab a couple of pieces of fruit.'

'How do you take it? Americano, espresso, cappuccino?' Arran asks, as he reaches up into the cupboard in front of him.

'Americano, no sugar, thank you.'

He pops a coffee pod into the machine and presses the switch, then turns to grab a bottle of water from the fridge.

'That's not much of a breakfast,' he replies, handing them over. 'The fridge is always full, so help yourself whenever you want. I only stock breakfast foods and snacks, aside from drinks, as the restaurant a short walk down the hill saves the hassle of cooking. You're not one of those fussy dieters, are you?'

It sounds accusatory.

'No. I just watch what I eat and avoid gluten whenever possible as it gives me headaches.' I'll leave out the bloated stomach and the flatulence bit. But just thinking about it, I have to stop myself from grimacing. Fortunately, his back is towards me as we're speaking.

'How did you sleep?'

In fairness I slept well, waking at 5 a.m. to begin writing. I'm not ashamed to admit that I vented my annoyance through my characters and Izzie has just put Ethan in his place *big* time. But a lot of love stories begin with characters who don't instantly fall in love. It's the same in life, isn't it?

I suppress a sigh. If Arran is going to be difficult then I'll just put up a wall around the real me and keep him very firmly on the other side of it. He's obviously very well off and mixes in different circles but I won't tolerate anyone talking down to me.

'Very well, thank you. I'll be back down in an hour. I have a chapter to finish off, first.'

It's only just after eight so I have plenty of time.

He glances at me, a slight frown on his face.

'I didn't realise you would be working this morning. It was rather a late one last night after a day of travelling. I'm… um… sorry if I said anything to upset you. You left rather abruptly.'

Now he wants me to ease his conscience.

'Don't worry about it, Arran. I get that sort of reaction from a lot of people who don't read the genre in which I write. I was tired, but I'm used to surviving on five hours' sleep every night, so I'm well rested this morning.'

He'd made me feel uncomfortable and I'm determined not to let that happen again.

'Good. I'll see you in a bit, then. I'm going to grab some breakfast and begin setting up the tables outside on the terrace. The group will arrive at around twelve thirty. A minibus meets them at the airport, so we have plenty of time to get things ready.'

Last night he said nine o'clock and I don't intend on coming back down until then, even though he sounded a little disappointed I wasn't going to join him for breakfast.

With another three thousand words added to the manuscript this morning, I turn off the laptop feeling content. Sometimes it's good to write when you are in a different frame of mind because you take that emotion and plough it into your storyline. Poor Izzie is left waiting alone at a restaurant because Ethan had an emergency at work. He didn't remember their date until several hours later, when he arrived home tired out and a little stressed. She's mad at him and this morning it was so easy to write that dialogue and the accusatory back and forth of their first argument. The conflict is building between them but it's time to start peeling away the layers and find out why.

I was disappointed with Arran last night because my first impression was that I'd been too hasty in assuming he'd be a bit standoffish. Then he did a total turnaround and seemed to want me to justify my work, as if he didn't consider romance to be a valid genre. He might be younger than I thought he was, mid-thirties I'd guess now I've seen him up close, but his attitude was tinged with disapproval; it was a reaction one might expect from a much older man. I also can't stand writing snobs. Besides, it's an insult to romance readers all around the world.

I'll give him his due though, he does carry off that broody, slightly intense *smoulder* so well. As someone who spends a lot of time creating characters who give off the same vibe, I know that's precisely what makes them so irresistible. If they were happy, chatty people they'd be boring.

My phone pings and it's a reply from Mel. I texted both Mum and Mel when I arrived last night. Mum responded immediately. Naturally, I was expecting to find a text from

Mel awaiting me when I woke at five this morning but there was nothing. I'm just relieved to hear from her now.

Sorry! Very late night on Skype with Ross. We talked for hours and now I really can't wait until our date tonight! Glad the flight was uneventful and hope you have a good day today. Best of luck and don't be nervous. Speak soon because I can't wait to hear all about it. M x

I feel excited for her. That first buzz when you meet someone who catches your attention is electrifying and it's a shame it's a short-lived thing. It's meant to be replaced with much deeper feelings and emotions, of course, but I've yet to experience that first hand. Mel already has, but who could have guessed Justin would turn out to be a love rat?

It's two minutes to nine and I make my way downstairs and out onto the terrace. Arran has set up a row of small wooden tables and butted them all together to make one long one. It will probably seat over a dozen people quite comfortably, so it's going to be plenty big enough for eight. He's just installing a second parasol in a vibrant blue as I walk through the door.

'I'm almost done here.' He slides the parasol into a slot in one of the tables and turns the winder to open it up. 'I need to pop into the office to get the paperwork; shall we do the tour of the ground floor, so I can show you where everything is kept?'

I nod and follow him inside.

He looks very casual again today in slightly baggy jeans and a navy, short-sleeved cotton shirt. Arran is most definitely an attractive guy to look at and he can be charming, but there's something missing. There's no sense of genuine warmth to a voice that has such a… direct, and brusque tone. It reminds me of Richard Burton's voice from a black and white clip I watched, many years ago. He was performing Shakespeare and hearing him speak gave me goosebumps. The passion came from the gritty, clipped pronunciation of the words to which there was no warmth attached whatsoever.

With Arran, I can't put my finger on what isn't quite right – it's as if he's wary of me. I wonder if that's just around me, or women in general? He could be a man's man, I suppose, but he definitely isn't the matey sort. Well, I'll soon find out when the others arrive.

Arran leads me out through the kitchen-dining room and across the corridor into a huge sitting room, which looks out over the pool and the lake. In front of this side of the villa the luscious, Mediterranean vegetation has been kept low-level, unlike the other side where there are some tall cypress, lemon and olive trees partially obscuring the view.

The room has five large, off-white leather sofas arranged around a coffee table that's about six feet wide. It's a statement piece of polished glass set over a large chunk of stone. Obviously, his intention is to encourage informal discussions. This is a room that makes a statement, with an unbelievable view of the mountains to the front and side of the villa. I notice there's no TV, although there is what looks like a projector mounted quite high on the wall above a doorway. The air conditioning throughout the villa is quiet, but in here there is a definite low humming sound.

My eye is drawn to a very expensive and ultra modern walnut sideboard. The grain in the wood is beautiful and standing on short, chrome legs, it's aesthetically pleasing to the eye.

'That's a Wrensilva HiFi audio system. You can play everything on it from vinyl to plugging in an MP3 player. The sound quality is amazing, and it links to speakers out on the terrace.'

It's an expensive piece, that's for sure and, clearly, he's a man who appreciates music. I do a half turn and follow Arran in the direction of the back wall, where he swings open the door located directly below the projector. 'The study is in here.'

Like the sitting room, it's another dual aspect view but this time onto the rear and side garden. My room has the same view. An oversized desk butts up against the wall of glass and I wonder if the beautiful greenery is a welcome distraction for Arran when he's writing those harrowing scenes in his novels.

I'm two thirds of the way through his book and while I admit military fiction is never going to be my chosen reading matter, I respect his meticulous attention to detail. I've learnt a lot about the tactical side of a battle and how troops are deployed. I just didn't need the blood and the gore to be quite so explicit, as my own imagination would have easily filled in the gaps.

His desk is neat and well organised; the kit looks expensive and his monitor is almost the size of a small

TV screen: the sort that allows you to work on several documents simultaneously.

When I spin back around, I'm surprised to see that the wall behind us is a library of vinyl records. I haven't seen one single book anywhere in the villa and in this, his private space, his most precious possessions are records?

'An interesting collection you have there, Arran.' I have no idea how many records are there, beautifully lined up in purpose made racking set back within the wall itself.

'My grandfather on my father's side was a conductor and musical director; his name was Quinn. He was born in Scotland but brought up in Surrey. He studied in Vienna, before moving to Italy and was celebrated for his podium skills and embracing a wide range of musical styles. He was a noted interpreter of the music of Mozart, Strauss and Wagner. He led many of the world's greatest orchestras in his time. Sadly, he's been gone a few years, but I still miss him.'

I can see by the look on Arran's face that the thought of his grandfather really affects him.

'You were brought up on classical music and opera then?'

He nods. 'My father loves music, although both of my parents are retired medical doctors.'

'That must have been quite an inspiring childhood, surrounded by a family passion for music and being brought up in such an academic environment.'

He looks at me sharply, as if I've annoyed him.

'I follow my own path in life. After gaining a PhD in social history I studied interactive media at York University.

The project I worked on ended up being developed into a TV series, which started my career as a presenter.'

I know, I've watched a few episodes. I don't say that out loud, obviously. I wonder why he's so tetchy? My question wasn't offensive in any way at all. I wonder if his parents' expectations for him were different, although clearly, he's done very well for himself. He leads a privileged lifestyle.

'That's quite an achievement. Where did your interest in warfare and military history come from?'

I can see his discomfort growing and wonder if I should back off, but he didn't last night, and I can't see any harm in my question. I'm interested to know his background.

'I had a nanny, her name was Hope; sometimes we went to visit her father who told us stories about the Second World War. I came to realise why she'd been given that name. He was a brave man with a drawer full of medals, and yet he was very humble. He served his country and lost an arm while doing so. Anyway—' Arran looks at his watch 'time is flying by.'

I understand that being a doctor is a very noble and demanding career but if you have children you have to set time aside for them. To have two parents focusing solely on their careers would surely make any child feel they take second place. Still, it depends on the circumstances. It is noticeable there are no family photos around the villa, and yet he said he spends most of the year here.

Arran walks into the sitting room, after grabbing a box that was sitting on his desk. He leads me in the direction of the hallway. Adjacent to the door to the rear garden there is a cloakroom with a hand basin and toilet. Then we head back into the kitchen and a door in the corner takes us into a laundry room, with a pantry leading off it.

'The only restricted area to guests is my study. Feel free to use any of the facilities. If you'd like to listen to a vinyl record, I have a catalogue of titles and I'd be more than happy to put something on the turntable for you.'

'You don't have a library, I notice.'

He peers at me over the top of the box he's carrying and smiles. 'I'm saving that as a surprise for when our guests arrive later.'

IO

A Conundrum of Sorts

Returning to the kitchen area, Arran asks me to grab two bottles of water from the fridge. He turns on his heels and makes his way out onto the terrace. Curiously he carries the box around to the far side of the table, while I take the seat directly in front of me, facing him and the view. I can't help wondering why he did that; it seems odd. Perhaps he's being polite by putting his back to the stunning scenery.

'Pass me your phone and I'll put in my number. If you need anything at any time you can text me.'

I watch as he taps away, before handing it back to me. Then he slips the lid off the box and extracts a few printed sheets of A4 paper.

'The itinerary is quite straightforward as each week has the same agenda.' He hands me a couple of sheets of paper. The first page shows the entire month split up into days of the week. In each box is a short description of the daily activities and at the side a list of each week's attendees.

'When the group arrive, I usually give them half an hour to settle into their rooms and then we convene back here for a buffet lunch. Antonio, from the local restaurant, La Pergola, will arrive with a waitress to lay out the food in the dining room sometime between noon and 1 p.m. On the second sheet is a floor plan of the bedrooms, with the guests' names written on them. It will be quicker if we split the group into two to escort them to their rooms. I'll do the first floor if you can take the top floor.

'Once everyone is gathered around the table we'll have a leisurely lunch sitting out here while people introduce themselves. It's a format that seems to work well.'

He looks up at me for the first time, as if suddenly wanting to seek my approval. I give him a casual smile and then focus on the agenda.

'Sunday is a free day and very informal, to allow the newcomers to settle in and get to know each other. The five main sessions run from Monday to Friday and each one lasts around three hours, starting promptly at nine o'clock. You're down for the session on Tuesday.'

I glance at the workshop titles.

- Monday – Style, Structure and Plot
- Tuesday – Make Your Characters Jump Off the Page
- Wednesday – Surviving Writer's Block and the Editing Process
- Thursday – Book Blurb, Synopsis and Pitching to an Agent/Publisher
- Friday – Your Author Platform and Marketing Essentials

'You'll notice that there are two organised tours; one into Salò on Tuesday afternoon and one to Verona taking up Wednesday afternoon and evening. Following on from the workshops I'm flexible about arranging one-to-one sessions. The take up for that varies; some prefer to fit in as much quiet writing time as possible. I'm assuming you'll be open to handling any one-to-ones requested with regard to characterisation issues?'

'Of course. I only have one prior commitment I must honour this week and that's a Skype interview at three o'clock on Friday.'

'Good. I think we're sorted, then. Is this a publicity interview?'

'No, research. I'm talking to Jordan Lewis, you might have heard of him.'

Arran looks at me, shaking his head. 'The name doesn't ring a bell.'

'He's a cage fighter and one of the top names in his sport.'

The look on Arran's face is priceless.

After that we lapse into silence and I crack open my bottle of water, taking a few mouthfuls just for something to do. At least there is plenty to distract the eye and I turn my head away from Arran and gaze out at the sparkling blue lake. It's already hot even though the sun is still low in the sky and I pull my sunglasses down from on top my head to reduce the glare. The sun's rays seem to envelop me, sparking a surge of energy. It's one of those days when it feels good to be alive. The warmth seeps through to my core and I feel at peace; content. It's been a long time since I felt this way and could take a moment to actually appreciate it.

Arran busies himself filling a stack of folders with a writing pad, some leaflets and a pen. He doesn't seem to want any help, so I get up and walk across the terrace, stepping down onto a large grassy area sloping down to a low wall.

All I can hear are the birds, the occasional rasp of a cicada somewhere close by, and every now and again the rumble of a car engine slowing on the road that winds down the hill. The view out over Lake Garda is indescribably beautiful and I know that even a photograph wouldn't quite do it justice. The distance and depth of the scene in front of me makes me feel like a dot on the landscape. If I was down there looking up, I might even be a little afraid of standing here, on an outcrop of rock, perched halfway up such a commanding and steep hillside. And yet, I don't get the feeling that the villa and its gardens are clinging on – it feels more like they're nestling against the terrain quite happily.

The bonus of a villa set up here in the wooded hills is the panoramic view and Arran's description of the shape of the immense lake springs to mind. It is indeed long as it stretches out ahead of me and looking down over the wall as the hill falls away, the lake widens considerably into something that does resemble an ancient axe head. But some of the outcrops of rock jut out far enough to obscure sections of the view around the lake itself.

I hear the distant roar of a plane flying high overhead and it reminds me that the villa will soon feel a lot livelier than it does right now. I turn to see that Arran has finished assembling the packs and has disappeared. He's put everything back inside the box, which is now tucked away beneath the table. I guess it's time to get in some steps then; if I do a couple of circuits of the garden now I can hopefully fit in a longer walk later.

Arran is all smiles and handshakes as he greets his guests when they alight from the minibus. The driver ferries their bags inside, leaving them in the hallway as Arran escorts everyone out onto the terrace. I follow on behind, bringing up the rear.

'This is where we're going to be conducting the sessions this week and gathering for lunch in about half an hour. We'll do the formal introductions then. If Rick, Tom and Will would like to follow me, and Silvia, Kris and Yvonne go with Brie, we'll escort you to your rooms.'

I don't know if it's a coincidence that there is a male and a female floor, or that the group is a fifty-fifty split. Carrie said he had a waiting list, so presumably he can pick and choose his attendees. I wonder why he doesn't run more courses? But then I suppose there are several strands to his career and it must be a constant juggling act.

The general buzz of chatter as the attendees grab their cases and we negotiate the stairs, is lively. Everyone is on a high and excited about the week ahead.

Silvia and Yvonne are probably in their early forties, but Kris is a few years younger than me, I'd say at a guess. After consulting the floor plan and showing Silvia and Yvonne to their rooms, I lead Kris into the room adjacent to mine. As she follows me in through the door and we get that first glance out over the front of the property, she stops to gasp at the view.

'Awesome! And I can't believe I'm face to face with *the* Brianna Middleton. It doesn't get any better than this! You look so different to the photo on the back of your book. You're much slimmer and your hair is so stylish now.'

She looks like she's having trouble containing her excitement as she drops her case onto the floor with a clatter.

'Oops, sorry about that. Are you here all week?'

I give her a reassuring smile. 'Yes. Kathy Porter's foot is in plaster so I'm the stand-in.'

'It feels wrong to say I'm delighted about that, but you know what I mean. Poor Kathy and all that, but wow! I mean wow! Getting writing tips from my favourite author is going to blow my mind.'

Well, it's lovely to receive a positive reaction but I'm beginning to wonder what I've let myself in for as I beat a hasty retreat. Rejoining Arran downstairs in the kitchen he's laying out a tray of glasses and a selection of cold drinks.

'Is there anything I can do?'

'No, I'm almost done here. Oh, there's the doorbell. If you can let Antonio and his staff in, then we can retire to the terrace and leave them to it.'

The smiling face and babble of Italian that greets me when I swing open the rear door takes me by surprise. I know a couple of dozen words in Italian at best, from my previous visits. I do, however, know how to apologise for my lack of fluency.

'*Buongiorno. Mi dispiace non parlo molto bene l'italiano.*'

'Good morning to you. Is not a problem. I am Antonio.'

I usher in the team of three, standing back so they can carry the platters through to the kitchen. After all, they've done this many times before.

With the villa feeling more alive, I feel less daunted by the prospect of what lies ahead. The amount of alone time I'm likely to spend with Arran from here on in is probably quite small and that's a welcome relief. My phone pings and as I yank it from my pocket I see it's from Carrie.

I hope all is going well. He's an interesting guy, isn't he?

A horrible thought flashes through my mind. Did Carrie talk me into this because she was trying to set us up? Is this some ghastly attempt at matchmaking, because I'd mentioned the online dating thing? If that's the case, she's way off mark. My fingers fly around the keyboard.

He's tetchy and arrogant but I can rise above it.

That'll stop her in her tracks and it puts a wicked smile on my face.

11

Arran is a very considerate host and the buffet lunch is a real feast, from the Caprese salad, with mozzarella, tomatoes and fragrant sweet basil, to the unusual, pumpkin based pizza dressed with caramelised apple with a hint of cinnamon and topped with Parma ham. Then there are platters of bresaola, air dried salted beef, moist slices of porchetta, and boneless roast pork stuffed with fennel – all to be followed by tiramisu! It's a real taste of Italy and my stomach grumbles just looking at it.

I'm careful over what I choose, though, and keep the portions small. To be honest, no one notices whether you take one small scoop of dessert, or a huge dollop. However, I will pass on the tiramisu today and help myself to a low-fat yoghurt from the fridge instead. But I intend to taste everything, simply reining back on the items I know should be eaten in moderation.

There's nothing better to get people talking than to share food. Doing introductions during the meal makes it much less intimidating as everyone continues to eat and drink throughout the process. You don't feel quite so firmly in the spotlight. Arran begins.

'First of all, I would like to welcome you to Villa Monteverdi and what I hope you will find to be a most encouraging, informative and relaxing writing retreat. Right, I'll kick this off. I write under my own name and I'm the author of five history textbooks and eight novels; I'm also a TV presenter and historian. I hope everyone will enjoy participating as that's the key to getting the most out of the week. But please, only share what you are comfortable with and I ask that anything that is said remains confidential and is not repeated to anyone outside this group. It's important everyone adheres to that principle so that we can all relax and speak freely.

'I will be distributing information packs containing the agenda for the week and details about the area. The two tours listed on the agenda, as with everything else, are optional and together with transport, are included in the fee you have paid. Dinner can be taken at the local restaurant, La Pergola, where prices are very reasonable, and I think you can tell from the standard of the buffet that the food comes highly recommended. If you want to venture further afield there is a full list of restaurants a short taxi ride away inside your welcome pack. I usually book a table each night for La Pergola and if you wish to be included please indicate on the sheet of paper you will find each morning pinned to the wall in the kitchen.'

Arran stops to check everyone has what they need and seems content, so he continues.

'Breakfast is self-service; the fridge is always stocked with plenty of fruit, yoghurt, cheeses and cold meats, so please help yourselves at any time of the day or night. A wide variety of chilled drinks can also be found in the fridge, with spare supplies in the walk-in larder. A plan of the ground floor is in the pack, as are instructions on how to use the washing machine and tumble dryer. Oh, and the code for the WiFi.'

He pauses, probably going through a mental checklist.

'Anything I've forgotten will be in the pack. You'll excuse me if I start eating but I'm starving.' There's nodding and a little ripple of laughter.

He looks directly across at me.

'Hi. I'm standing in for the lovely Kathy Porter, following her rather unfortunate accident. My name is Brianna Middleton, but please call me Brie. I've recently begun writing my thirteenth novel. I'm just an author, I'm afraid.' That garners quite a peal of laughter and I look back at Arran, surprised to see he's frowning. I figured I'd try to inject a little humour. I wasn't making fun of his style and I hope that's not how he's interpreted it.

'And *what* a writer of romantic fiction,' Kris jumps in.

I give her a warm smile and then I turn to look at the man sitting next to me and give him an encouraging nod.

'Hi everyone. I'm Rick Preston and an avid fan of Arran's. It's taken me nearly six years to complete my first manuscript, which is a story based around the Cold War. It's a spy thriller with lots of action.'

Rick is quite a tall, wiry guy and it's obvious he's very excited about the prospect of having his first manuscript ready to go.

Next to him is Kris.

'Waves from me, I'm Kris Lacey, with a "K". I write romantic fiction WAG style. My first book is being published in four months' time.'

Kris is an inch shorter than me but probably three dress sizes bigger. She has one of those happy, rounded faces and I bet her head is full of questions as her enthusiasm brims over.

There's a lot of nodding of heads in between the eating.

'My turn. I'm Silvia Day with an "I" and not a "Y". Can I just ask Kris what *wag* means?'

Kris breaks out into a broad smile. 'Wives and girlfriends of sporting personalities, Silvia. Lots of glitz and glam and money; not always a lot of common sense.'

'Oh, I see.' Silvia winks at Kris, laughing. 'Well, I'm not sure some of my characters have very much of that, either. I write about the 1920s; purely fictional but inspired by some of the stories passed down in my family. It seems my great-grandmother was a bit of a party animal and we have some delightful photographs to prove it.'

She's lovely. Very elegant, classic good looks with shoulder length blonde hair, immaculately straightened and perfectly made-up. We all look up in interest, even Arran.

'I'm Tom Carpenter and it's great to be here among fellow writers. I began writing about six months ago, so I only have half a manuscript so far. Believe it or not, it's a romantic comedy. What do I know about romance? Well, probably not that much if I'm being honest but that's why it's going to be a comedy... of errors, most likely!'

I can already tell that Tom is going to be the comedian of the group. He has a face guaranteed to make you laugh because it's so expressive. I would guess that he's in his mid-forties, but his forehead is heavily wrinkled because his eyebrows keep shooting upwards at the end of every sentence he utters. This man seriously needs to learn to use his hands to express himself, as the Italians do, to give those muscles a break; but I guess it's his facial acrobatics which help create that characterful persona. I find myself chuckling away and he gives me a cheeky wink in return. I immediately look towards the person on his right for fear I will burst out laughing.

'I'm Yvonne Stone and I write historical fiction. I have three published books and I've recently signed another contract for my next two novels. I do find writing rather a solitary pursuit though, and that's why I thought this retreat would be a perfect working holiday.'

Yvonne and Silvia are going to get on very well together, I think. I should imagine they both come from upper middle-class backgrounds, although Silvia does have a surprisingly wicked glint in her eye.

We all turn and look at the final attendee with interest.

'Bringing up the rear, I'm Will Peterson. I have two self-published novels and I'm hoping to try to polish my latest manuscript enough for my agent to pitch it to a publisher. If I can get up the courage, that is. I'm actually a vet, so while my stories are fictional, the day job provides the inspiration. And the humour, if you're into farmyard muck, of course.'

I like the look of Will, he seems to be the sort of person whose style is rather laid back. He'd be great to have around in an emergency, exuding a very calm and patient vibe. He has hazel eyes and his hair is probably no more than a quarter of an inch long all over. It makes him look outdoorsy and he's sporting a natural tan that probably means he's quite fit; I suspect he's a jogger. And I suppose it helps to be quite muscular to handle livestock; his work will involve a lot more than dealing with small, domestic animals who fit nicely on the vet's examination table.

Arran gives Will a nod then wraps it up.

'I can't stress enough that this week is as much about the informal discussions that will break out amongst you all, as it is about the morning tutorials. Both Brie and I are free to arrange one-to-one, hour long sessions if you want advice on your work in progress, or if there's a particular problem you would like some help with. If a number of you want to delve further into a specific topic, then we can arrange an ad hoc session. Is everyone happy with that?'

There's a chorus of general affirmation.

'I'm about to look at setting up a website, Arran, so I'm particularly interested in the topic covering the author platform. How detailed is that? I'm quite IT literate in general but I'll be honest and say I don't have a clue where to start.' It's nice to hear Rick acknowledge the help he needs as that will allow Arran to tailor the session.

Arran looks around at the group. 'Anyone else looking for guidance in that area?'

Kris and Yvonne raise their hands.

'Great. Well, maybe we can get together on Friday afternoon, continuing on from the morning session which will link in to this topic. Maybe have a two hour lunch break and then retreat to my study so I can go through what to do in greater detail? I also have some step-by-step instructions I can print out in addition to some general advice. How does that sound?'

Three heads nod and I can feel the excitement building. When you get a bunch of creative people together we tend to feed off each other and writers, I've found, are such a supportive network. I guess it's because we spend so many hours alone with a keyboard and a screen. Fictional characters are great but sometimes it's nice to be around people who understand the angst of being a writer and can actually talk back to you. This might turn out to be more fun than I thought.

'If everyone has finished eating, let's do a tour of the garden. Ah, right on cue. Everyone, let me introduce my housekeeper, Elisabetta. Usually she's here from around nine in the morning until lunchtime. If you run out of towels or have any special requirements then please do let her know.'

I did wonder who kept the villa looking so immaculate. Elisabetta is very pretty and quite young; wearing a white T-shirt and a pale blue tabard over a pair of black trousers, she looks very efficient. I'm sure she keeps Arran on his toes and doesn't suffer any nonsense.

'Hi, lovely people. Hope you enjoy your stay.'

There's a chorus of 'hi' back. As people stand, taking Arran's lead, she approaches the table to begin clearing away.

'Right, we'll start with the view.'

Arran leads us all down to the next level, where he points out various landmarks and gives a general talk about Salò itself. I wander off to one side, checking out some of the planting. Kudos to the gardener because everything is beautifully tended.

'If we head off now in the direction of the cypress trees, there is a hidden section of the garden I'd like to show you all.'

The path snakes a little as it heads off in the direction of a single line of trees running at an angle to the villa. At first glance it appears to be the boundary of the garden. However, although the path stops we follow Arran across the grass and, filtering between the tall trees, discover there is another building which is totally obscured by the greenery. No one would know it was here. It's surrounded by clusters of lemon and olive trees resembling a small orchard.

The stone building is the size of a small bungalow and behind it the hill rises up quite steeply; it's a wall of solid rock. The front façade is all glass with a wide veranda running the entire width of it. Behind the glass are tall, white wooden shutters blocking out the sun.

'And this,' Arran says, tapping a four digit code into the key pad on the door, 'is the library.'

Once inside he tilts the louvres enough to let in plenty of light while keeping the sun off the bookshelves, which extend across all three walls from floor to ceiling.

We all stand there, staring up at thousands of books, in awe. Some of these, on the very top shelves, are very old indeed. There are six winged back chairs set in pairs and one leather sofa.

Arran waits by the door until everyone is inside and then closes it.

'The room is climatically controlled via an HVAC system which handles the heating, ventilation, air conditioning and humidity. The door must remain closed at all times, to help preserve the books. When leaving please ensure the louvres are closed. The access code is in the pack for those who wish to use the library. Please feel free to read any of the books you find on the shelves, but I ask that you keep them within this room. Some of these books belonged to my grandfather and great-grandfather, and have a lot of sentimental attachment for me.'

Gazing around, there is a very wide selection here, including textbooks and various genres of fiction, as well as biographies. Shakespeare is quite prominent, just above eye level on the back wall. But there's also a shelf for Jane Austen and Ian Fleming sits alongside Ken Follett in a section that is alphabetical by author name.

We're all wandering around, name spotting.

'The grounds are lit at night and the internal light switches are located on the panel inside the door. It's just after two thirty now, so I think the rest of the afternoon should be quite informal. Some of you may wish to take a siesta in your rooms or do some writing. Alternatively, you can use the pool or sit and chat on the terrace. Do pop in and check out the sitting room, where there are some very comfortable sofas. I suggest we meet up again at six o'clock on the terrace for wine and nibbles, and a little authorly chat before dinner. I'll put the information packs out on the table, please do grab one. Don't forget to look at the list of restaurants within walking distance or a short taxi ride away. I'm happy to phone around and make arrangements to book tables once I know everyone's preferences. I'll see you all later.'

Arran leaves and I'm not far behind him, heading back to finish reading his novel. An alcove at the side of the villa looks inviting and it's in the shade, at the moment, so it will be perfect.

'I'll see you later too, guys.'

Walking back to the villa I reflect upon the fact that we could easily have sat around all afternoon chatting, but Arran is a man who likes his privacy. I guess that makes two of us.

12

Life Isn't Easy Whether You are Fictional or Real

War is a tough subject matter at the best of times, but the horrors of trench warfare in the First World War is hard to comprehend because it was so very horrific. I find the telling of this particular story emotional because of the lack of emotion in the text. Men fight for the cause, conditioned not to question but to action the orders from above. Because Arran's novel focuses on the technicalities of war, there's little about the backgrounds of the people involved. I am moved to tears by several scenes in this book and it isn't just when someone dies or is badly injured. Sometimes it's because I can feel a sense of the inevitable. Many will return home, but will never be the same again – either in mind, body, or both.

Maybe it's because I find war depressing and a waste. Naïve, I know, because without the wars that have been fought we wouldn't have our freedom. In a way this fictional story is really a history book. But this would appeal to me much more if I knew a little about the lives these brave men had before they found themselves shipped off to fight. Most will have left loved ones behind and that's the real horror story waiting to be told, in my opinion. But there is a whole legion of fans who wouldn't agree with that thought. My father would love this novel, and I must ask him if he's ever read any of Arran's books.

I read for two solid hours, a lot of that time pacing back and forwards to rack up my step count for the day. When I turn that final page, I need to lighten my mood, because my heart feels wrung out. The truth is that when it comes to war no one is really the victor because of the enormous sacrifices involved.

Heading back to my room, I pick up the laptop and open up my love story. So far, I have the first chapter with the hero, Ethan Turner, struggling to find time in his busy life to date. When he does make an effort, he finds the small talk of two strangers getting to know each other rather tedious. Something inside him is gnawing away though, making him feel uneasy. It's loneliness but he doesn't recognise it; he just knows it's a feeling that is alien to him.

Aside from that, I have several chapters written that jump forward in the story to after he has met Izzie. And I have a whole series of romantic little clips that made me rush to my laptop in a typing frenzy. Somehow, I need to pull this together cohesively now and begin to weave in some clues about the workings of Ethan's mind and his emotions. I never realised how draining it is to write in the first person when the character is so intense. And he won't easily surrender his thoughts to me. What I'm doing is forming the character, piece by piece, but it's all coming together in a very random way. I never work like that and maybe it's because emotionally I'm still not in the best place. I decide to fill in the blanks, beginning with the key chapter where Ethan flies to Italy. He's spending the summer there, looking after a villa owned by his boss while he designs a new software programme. He jumped at the chance to get away from a life that made him feel he was living on a treadmill.

This is where having Mel as a friend will come in very handy – all the technical info I need will be on tap. It's the perfect vehicle to get him to Lake Garda.

Once the missing section is written, I can turn my attention to Izzie. I begin, not really knowing what I'm going to write. I simply sit quietly staring at the screen for a few minutes, thinking of her. Suddenly, her voice is in my head and my fingers do their thing. She's fun, flirty and chatting with a girlfriend. And then the perfect idea occurs to me. Izzie is going to be the boss's daughter and she's stuck at home because she's broken her ankle. With her parents away on a business trip followed by a holiday in the Far East, there is plenty of time for this romance to blossom. Thank you, Kathy, for being my inspirational turning point. I do hope you are healing well, dear lady and be assured, I won't be revisiting this experience, so your job is safe!

Feeling rather pleased with myself, I turn my head to look out over the rear garden. I catch sight of Silvia and Yvonne making their way up the gently sloping terraces, stopping to admire some of the plants. They're chatting and laughing quite animatedly. I wonder what Kris is doing and hope she's not feeling left out. It's funny how people tend to pair off; Kris and Tom might get on well as they both exhibit a sense of humour but Rick and Will? I'm not so sure. Rick would, I think, like to dominate Arran's time; clearly, he's a great fan and hungry to do something with his first manuscript.

I took to Will instantly. He isn't quite as outwardly charming as Arran, but he comes across as being a very friendly and modest sort of guy. I'm sure as a vet he's a consummate professional so maybe he's still at that stage where he's slightly apologetic about his writing. Most of us feel like that at first, as if it's not quite right to say you are a writer until you've proven yourself in some way. But I found that modesty in him rather endearing.

My phone rings, making me jump.

'Hello.'

'I thought it was time I gave you a call, can you talk?'

I didn't have a chance to look at the caller ID, just assuming it was going to be Mel, but it's Carrie. Which reminds me, I must ring Mum.

'Yes. We're having some free time before the first evening meal.'

'Good. I hope you're writing. I was a little worried by your comment *tetchy and arrogant*. Is it that bad?'

I laugh. I knew that would worry her. 'Yep. Unfortunately, I think we sort of got off on the wrong foot but I'm hoping things will be a lot easier now everyone is here. It was a bit intense, just the two of us last night. It's a great little group though, and no over-the-top personalities to threaten the balance. And with two people who have a quiet sense of humour simmering away in the background, that always helps. So, I'm relatively happy.'

She sucks in a breath.

'Hmm… I really thought you two would get on rather well. Has he mentioned his manuscript at all?'

Oh, this isn't just Carrie on a guilt trip then.

'No, and I'm certainly not going to be the first one to raise the topic. He is a bit prickly at times. Is that why Kathy isn't working with him on this? Or you, for that matter?'

There's silence on the other end of the phone for a moment.

'Definitely not. You know that it's easier sitting down with someone to discuss different ways of handling a scene. You're the perfect person for the job, Brie, and I have every confidence in you. The reason for the call is to say that I've chosen the photo, although you were right and there was little in it. It's a great new look and I've already sent a copy to *Cosy Living* for the article.'

I'm glad she mentioned that.

'Is there any way you can ask for a draft copy?'

'You're not nervous about it, are you? You said it went well.'

'It did, but I'd like a chance to read it through before it goes into print. She… um… mentioned Paul.'

'Oh, right! I'll see what I can do. In the meantime, you work your magic. You can charm anyone, Brie, if you want to, and Arran will thank you later.'

I splutter, half laughing and half choking.

'I wouldn't bet on that, Carrie. And I seriously doubt sitting down and discussing it will work in this case. If he approaches me, I will probably just do a read through and make my suggestions, then it's down to him if he takes my advice on board. That's the best I can do given the situation.'

'Beneath that stern exterior there beats a heart; he's just been through a horrendous time this past year following his divorce. It came after two years' separation and a lot of acrimony going on the entire time. His ex-wife's mother is his mother's best friend and his family haven't taken it very well.'

I suppose that might account for it then. Maybe I unwittingly said a few things that put him on the defensive and I need to be more careful.

'Thanks, knowing that helps. I'll do my best, but I can't promise any more than that.'

I'm a little late getting ready and when I head downstairs everyone is already there except Arran himself. Feeling a little awkward that our host is nowhere to be seen, I kick off the conversation by asking where people write and encourage them to share their writing routine.

Kris is happy to begin, and I excuse myself saying I'll fetch some wine and the glasses. I hurry back inside and head up the flight of stairs to the first floor. Arran's room is directly below mine, so I wander along the corridor towards the rear of the villa. Placing my ear against the door I can hear a raised voice, but it's muffled. I head up to my room, where the sliding door to the balcony is slightly ajar. Remaining out of sight, but within earshot because he's standing directly below me, I catch a glimpse of him holding onto the rail with his phone to his ear.

'I told you that's just not possible, Harriet. I need this place, not least because it's a part of my business and it's my home.'

Everything goes silent for a few minutes.

'That's unreasonable and you know it. I'm late and I have to go. You can hassle me all you want but I can't conjure that sort of money out of thin air.'

There's a pause as she replies, and his next words are explosive.

'You're joking! What sort of a woman are you?' With that it all goes quiet and I think he ended the call abruptly.

I rush back downstairs as quietly as I can, head into the kitchen and begin loading glasses onto a tray. Mere seconds later Arran appears, looking a little flustered.

'Oh, thanks Brie, I fell asleep and forget to set my alarm. Here, I'll take those if you can grab a couple of bottles of wine from the fridge. I'll come back for the wine coolers. Maybe start with one red and one white?'

I follow him out onto the terrace and Will offers to open the bottles while I enquire who wants what. I begin pouring and when I look up Arran is at my elbow.

'I forgot you've developed a taste for Chiaretto,' he whispers, a small smile flickering around his mouth.

'Thank you.' I look at him, surprised he gave it any thought. 'Anyone else prefer rosé?' No one is interested so I fill two glasses and pass one to Arran.

We take our seats and I follow Arran's lead as he raises his glass in the air.

'Here's to a great week with lots of sunshine, hard work and plenty of wine!'

For one moment I think he's going to drain his glass, but he stops himself short, looking like he needed the alcohol to steady his nerve. When he looks across at me his face is composed but his eyes seem to be searching mine. I give him a smile of encouragement.

'Right, is everyone decided on their chosen venue? Let's make this simple – hands up for La Pergola.'

It's unanimous. He picks up his phone from the table and dials.

'Hi, it's Arran. Can we have a table for eight, please? What time is best for you? Okay, that's fine, thank you, Antonio.'

'They have a party of twenty arriving at eight o'clock so does anyone mind if we head up there shortly after seven? It's a bit early but at least we won't have to wait long for our meals. It's a family run restaurant and very popular with the locals. Don't forget tomorrow at breakfast to put your name down for your chosen restaurant in the evening. I'll make the necessary arrangements for around eight o'clock. I do suggest you vary it, as each one has a slightly different ambience but it's entirely up to you guys.'

He sinks back in his chair, downing the remainder of his glass of wine and I reach out to pour him another. We exchange glances and I wonder if he realised I was upstairs listening to his conversation. If he did, he's not embarrassed or angry, he simply looks defeated.

Like the true professional he is, he soon rejoins the banter before anyone notices anything is wrong. When we set off on the short trek to the restaurant, Rick immediately engages Arran in conversation. The rest of the group fall in behind in single file; the road isn't busy but everyone is keen to take in the surroundings and we lapse into a companionable silence. It's a gentle downhill stroll which takes about ten minutes but coming back doesn't promise to be quite so kind on the calf muscles.

La Pergola is very pretty, with well manicured flower beds and neatly clipped hedges surrounding the car parking area to the front. With a covered veranda visible to one side, we step up into the wide, wooden porch and Arran leads the group inside.

It's a long, narrow building with one line of tables either side and a central gangway. The décor is very rustic, with stained oak floors and white painted, floor-to-ceiling wood panelling on the walls. Oversized mirrors on alternating sides make the space feel much wider than it is and with two rows of frosted white globe lights running the entire length of the room it feels light and airy. There are probably fifty plus tables in here and already well over half of them are taken. There's quite a family atmosphere with children of all ages and the air is filled with boisterous chatter, mostly in Italian. The overall impression is that this is a really busy restaurant indeed.

I'm bringing up the tail end of the group and suddenly we come to a halt but I can't see what's happening at the front. Only a few moments later we're moving forward again and when we stop, a gorgeous Italian waiter is pulling out chairs ready for us to be seated around a circular table. He oozes charm and his smile is enough to make any woman's heart flutter. I lower myself into the last available chair, trying not to stare at him.

'Don't you simply love the atmosphere in here?' Silvia asks in a low tone as she leans in to me.

I nod, a little dismayed to see that Rick has bagged a seat next to Arran. On the other side of Arran is Will, but he's already deep in conversation with Kris. Poor Arran, this probably isn't going to be a relaxing evening meal at all but an onslaught of questions as Rick picks his brains.

All I can do is to relax and make sure everyone else has a chance to join in to make Rick and Arran's intense conversation less obvious. For the most part the group manage on their own with only the odd steer required from me. But when it's time to head back to the villa I'm more than ready to say goodnight to our tired new arrivals. It isn't long before I'm alone in the kitchen, grateful to be off duty.

13

Is the Whole World Spinning or is it Just Me?

Automatically, I begin clearing up the glasses and empty wine bottles still cluttering up the table on the terrace. Three trips and it's done. I figure Arran isn't going to want to come down to this tomorrow morning and it's pleasant enough out here with a slight breeze cooling my skin.

If I go up to my room I'm going to write and I'm not really in the mood for that right now. Instead I go back inside to grab a clean glass and a bottle from the fridge. I'm careful about what I drink, rarely exceeding two glasses of wine, but tonight I need something to make me relax. I didn't realise how mentally exhausting it would be hosting a group of strangers. Being two down for most of the evening with Rick glued to Arran's side, it left me to keep five people happy and I wasn't prepared for that.

'Do you mind if I join you?'

I turn to see Arran walking towards me with a glass in his hand.

'I thought you'd gone to bed.'

He takes the seat next to me, flopping down into it as if he, too, feels drained.

'I had a text I had to respond to and anger is something best dealt with in private.'

I lean forward to fill his glass.

'Bad news?'

He nods, but doesn't speak. We settle down in our chairs and both end up resting our heads back to stare up at the velvety sky.

'That's one mass of stars. I didn't realise there were that many, actually.' The number seems to grow as my eyes become accustomed to the inky black background.

'There's hardly any light pollution up here. They're always there, you just can't see them this clearly, but the sky is perfect tonight. In fact, bring your glass and follow me.' He grabs the bottle of wine and jumps up out of his seat with a sudden burst of enthusiasm.

We amble along the path, past the cypress trees and the hidden garden and wend our way up around the side of the villa. There are fewer lights at the back of the house, and fewer still the further we walk. At the far end of the garden there's a nook where the rocky hillside has formed a shallow cave. It's only about three feet deep and five feet long but under the overhang nestles a rattan sofa.

'This is more comfortable and looking out from here you'll notice even more stars. The terrace lighting at the front doesn't help but I can't risk people stumbling around in the dark and falling into the pool.'

I nod, thinking what an intrusion it is to invite a group of strangers into your home. Arran refills my glass.

'I noticed that you didn't eat much in the restaurant and I'm sorry I left you holding the fort so to speak. I'm very grateful. Are you hungry now? I could certainly murder something snackish.'

I give him a forgiving smile. 'It's a bit late but I suppose it will soak up the alcohol.'

He gives me a grin and eases himself up out of the sofa. I watch him disappear into the semi-gloom, wondering if this is a good idea, or not.

There's a sudden buzz in my pocket and I pull out the phone to see there's a text from Mel – at last!

OMG what an evening! Ross is such a kind, gentle and thoughtful guy. There has to be a catch, Brie, because it seems too good to be true. We're seeing each other again tomorrow night and I can't wait. How's Lake Garda? I hope you can ring when you have a spare five minutes. I'm dying to know what Arran is like and how you're getting on with him. Take care, lovely! M x

Does there always have to be a catch? Mel is being cautious because of what she's been through, but it would be wonderful if life decided to give her a break. I hate to think the past will colour her judgement of Ross without even giving him a chance to prove he's a very different sort of man. Although, a part of me is glad she's treading carefully because I'd hate to see her get hurt again. It's an age old dilemma.

As for how I'm getting along with Arran – the answer to that is still in the balance. His outwardly charming persona and smooth voice is a professional veneer but who knows what really lies behind that? I feel that his impression of me is based on assumptions and he's not really giving me a chance. And I'm conscious that I'm retaliating quite a bit, which is equally as pathetic and unfair of me. *Come on, Brie, you know better than that. Give the guy the benefit of the doubt or the next four weeks will be living hell. You're coming out of an overly sensitive phase of your life and now you're in danger of going in the opposite direction. That's hardly fair on Arran.*

I type a quick response to Mel to let her know how pleased I am for her that it's gone well and will be in touch soon to find out more.

Then I sit back to think about Arran. But before I can assemble my thoughts he's back, carrying another bottle of wine and two huge bags of nibbles.

'I'm not that hungry,' I laugh.

'You said you weren't a fussy eater. They're for sharing and they're gluten free,' he throws back at me, settling down and letting out a groan as his body relaxes back into the cushions. Well, that was thoughtful of him.

We each take a bag and begin munching. After a few minutes we swap.

'I prefer these,' I whisper, wondering if our voices will carry.

'Don't worry, the wind's in the opposite direction so no one can hear us and besides, we're far enough away from the villa not to be seen or heard. I know exactly what you're thinking. The peace and quiet is nice.'

'It's stressful for you, isn't it?'

Our eyes meet, and he raises his eyebrows, letting out a low sigh.

'I have no choice. This fiasco began three years ago. And it's about to get much worse.'

I'm not sure if he's talking to himself or to me, his voice is so low. I put down the cheesy snacks and pick up my wine glass.

'I'm here if you want to share more than just the snacks.'

He turns to look at me again and this time his look is apologetic. His eyes show me a vulnerability I haven't seen so far.

'It's a saga worthy of a long running series. You could end up being sorry you asked.' Again, a weary sigh escapes from his lips and it's awful to hear because he sounds so very demoralised. 'My ex-wife, Harriet, left me three years ago. Well, she physically removed herself and whatever she wanted from the property. In reality, we hadn't been functioning as a couple for quite a while before that. I was extremely busy at the time and it seemed easier to give her what she wanted, which was a trial separation. So, I rented an apartment for her at Sirmione, which is on the southern shore of the lake. She has friends there and to be honest I was relieved to put some distance between us.'

He presses back into the deep cushions and stretches out his legs in front of him. I don't say a word, because I feel it's not necessary.

'Money seemed to be going out as fast as it was coming in so that's why I began running the courses. A lot of the projects I work on pay well but it isn't a regular income.

I get a large cheque and then maybe nothing for several months. The royalty cheques for the books come in every six months and for the time being, at least, that's all I can bank on.'

I don't understand why his ex-wife is still demanding money from him.

'But you're divorced now so all of that is settled, isn't it?'

'Yes, and no. I was stupid, and I gave her, I don't know how much exactly, maybe a hundred grand during that first year in rent and expenses. Then I realised that although it was well and truly over, she never was going to file for divorce. So, it was down to me. The lawyers thrashed out a financial settlement. Our two families live a stone's throw away from each other in Surrey and we'd purchased a four bedroom house there as a holiday home. The only other asset was this villa, which belonged to my grandfather and was bequeathed to me. That's a long story in itself; when he died my father hadn't spoken to him for nearly twenty years. But I spent every summer here with my grandfather from the age of thirteen.'

Arran pauses to take a hefty gulp of his wine and top up our glasses.

'What does Harriet do for a living?'

He gives a bitter laugh. 'She doesn't earn a penny, she does voluntary work. That's wonderful, of course, but someone is required to foot the bill for her lavish lifestyle.'

'You didn't have children?'

'No. Harriet wasn't at all interested and it wasn't a burning issue for me. So, basically, I had to agree a big settlement or pay her a smaller sum and ongoing maintenance to support her for the foreseeable future. I went for the settlement, even though I wasn't sure how exactly I was going to get the money together. She will remarry, of course, but not until someone very wealthy comes along. That's sad, but true. Believe me, I still think I made the right decision.'

I'm appalled.

'We sold the house in Surrey and I gave her my share of the handsome profit we made, then I cashed in some shares and emptied my savings accounts. When I handed it over there was still a hefty shortfall. Ironically, it's because of this place. It's a valuable property and it never occurred to me to protect my ownership of it. So even though I owned it before we were married, she could claim a share of it.'

'That hardly seems fair given there are no children involved. I think that's appalling.'

His expression is one of acceptance.

'It's the law. The court looks at the husband's and the wife's personal incomes, their assets and the standard of living during the marriage. They make the award on that basis. A legal charge has been put on the house until I've paid her the remainder of the lump sum owed. I have to make regular bi-monthly payments, plus interest accruing, and if I default at any time then the villa will be sold from under me.'

I know what's coming but I hope I'm wrong.

'At the moment I'm struggling to make those payments. I've just scraped enough together to meet the payment due last month. Sadly, as it stands now, I can't say for sure that I'm going to be able to make the next one. I made the mistake of asking if she'd allow me a little flexibility but I think she has one aim. And that is to take this place away from me because she knows it's the only thing that has ever meant anything to me.'

My heart is in my mouth. The only thing?

'But you loved each other in the beginning, surely? Doesn't that mean anything to her?'

'I thought it was love, but it's very obvious to me now that she was a different person back then. I didn't fully appreciate what a very determined woman Harriet can be. When she sees something she wants, she can be very persuasive. She convinced me we were the real thing but, sadly, her enthusiasm waned very quickly once we were around each other all the time. It turned out that I wasn't ambitious enough for her, you see.'

'That's sad. I mean, it wasn't you who changed, it was her by the sound of it.'

He shakes his head, sadly.

'I know, but it was a huge shock realising so quickly that it was all a big mistake and I didn't know how to handle it. So I tried to keep the peace in the hope that things would improve. Love isn't something that looms large in my family. It's all about doing the right thing, having a routine, not letting anyone down and being responsible. As a child if I fell over and hurt myself my mother would say I was clumsy, but then she wasn't around much to witness that, anyway. So, I did what I've always done and I simply put up with Harriet's outbursts and moods. Until, eventually, it all fell apart.'

'I'm sorry to hear that, Arran. A marriage shouldn't be like that. And a child deserves to be loved, as well as provided for – money can't buy that.'

'My grandfather loved me. But the antagonism between my father and him made life very difficult at times. Still, maybe Carrie will succeed in getting me a sizeable advance for the next novel. The manuscript needs a little attention but she's already talking to two publishers about it, so at least there's a glimmer of hope. It's based on a true story.'

He leans forward, staring at the ground. This must be the manuscript Carrie was referring to.

'Is it a lot of work to polish it up?'

He gives me a sideways glance.

'When I asked you to define the word "love" I wasn't being flippant. I was genuinely interested in hearing what you have to say. The story begins with a couple who have a brief affair before he's goes off to fight as a soldier in the Second World War. That happened a lot and wasn't unusual as it was an emotional time. People grabbed what comfort they could, the likelihood of death hanging over everyone from the constant bombings at home, as well as on the battlefield. It's clear she will wait for him until the war is over, if necessary.

'Obviously, it's predominantly about the battlefield. But Carrie says the love scenes fall flat. I need to get it sorted as until she's in a position to submit the manuscript to publishers, nothing will happen and the clock is ticking. Obviously, this is a new genre for me and it's going to be a learning process to get the balance right. Wanting to broaden my appeal is one thing, but Carrie says I need to do a better job of portraying the emotional turmoil away from the battle zone if I'm going to attract a new publisher and a new audience.'

He's reaching out to me and I'm touched because he needn't have shared the details of his dire personal situation.

'I'm happy to take a look and make a few suggestions if you're open to that.'

His eyes search my face.

'The sex scenes are cold, Carrie told me. "Lacking in depth and emotion" were her exact words. I've tried to re-write the scenes but it's beyond me. I'd be grateful if you could check it out.'

'Email me the file and I'll make a start tomorrow morning. I've never been one to have a Sunday lie-in, anyway. Will you need me there for your first session on Monday?'

'No, but I would like to sit in on yours on Tuesday morning. Carrie says I can learn a lot from you.'

Our eyes are locked, and I drag my gaze away on the pretext of needing a little more wine in my glass. I'm not sure how many glasses I've had but I'm wonderfully warm and fuzzy. It's a pleasant feeling. Sitting back and closing my eyes for a second I feel as if everything is moving but when I open them again it's fine. How very weird. Maybe I need some more of those nibbles. I'll just up the amount of steps I do tomorrow to compensate. Besides, sometimes a little reward is in order when you're being very good, despite the temptations around you.

14

Paying the Price

Buzz. Buzz. Buzz.

What is that awful droning sound? I pull the pillow further down over my head in a desperate attempt to blot out the noise. The sound seems to be reverberating around inside my skull, as if a manic bee has flown into my ear and it's painful. Then I realise it's an alarm and someone has, thankfully, just turned it off.

Someone has— 'Oh, shit!'

I drag the pillow off my head and squint, the brightness sending little waves of pain shuddering throughout my entire body. I look up to see a shocked Arran staring down at me and he's naked. I squirm around and realise he's not the only one in a state of undress.

'Look, it's not what you think, Brie. Nothing happened. We were both just a bit—'

Memories of us both collapsing on the bed come racing back.

He puts up one hand, palm facing me as if he's defending himself. The other hand is trying to hide his tackle. If I wasn't so stunned this would be quite funny. Arran looks mortified.

'I need to shower and get downstairs. I'm not being rude, really, but my head is thumping and if I don't get some painkillers inside me pretty quickly I won't be able to host today's informal gathering.'

He turns, all modesty forgotten, and heads into the en-suite, leaving me in a daze. Everything is blurry because of the pounding inside my head and I remember that's why I usually stick to just the two glasses of wine. It's been a long, long time since I over-indulged and I'm mortified, unable to comprehend what Arran must think of my behaviour.

Okay, damage assessment. I've seen Arran naked and we slept in the same bed, or we both passed out on the same bed is probably a more accurate description. No harm done; we're both embarrassed and we were too drunk for anything to have happened, even if we had wanted it to. This would have been a total disaster if one of us had been sober, but that wasn't the case. At least that makes me feel a little better.

As soon as I hear the shower running I ease myself out of bed and quickly throw on my clothes. Quietly creeping out onto the landing I scurry, unseen, up to my room.

'People do stupid things when they're drunk, Brie, and that's how mistakes are made,' I whisper to myself. 'But you're old enough to know better, my girl.'

This isn't an excuse, but it's a comfort knowing that it's out of character for Arran, too. Maybe it reflects the fact that we were both stressed and over-tired; too exhausted to sleep and needing something else to knock us out. 'That will not be happening again,' I mutter as I head into the shower.

Turning the knob all the way round to the blue dot, I let out a shriek as the icy water hits my skin. Once I've adjusted to it, it's wonderfully refreshing, even though my teeth begin to chatter a little. It isn't only my head that is aching, but my whole body. How do people do this on a regular basis? Goodness knows how I'm going to function today and then my memory kicks in. I vaguely remember promising to look at Arran's manuscript this morning and that might just be a lifesaver. Stepping out of the shower I wrap a towel around me and scrabble around in my bag for some tablets. Then I text Arran.

Send me that manuscript before you head downstairs. I'm going to skip breakfast and make a start. See you later. Hope your headache isn't quite as bad as mine.

Seconds later he replies.

It's probably worse but I deserve it and sorry to hear you're suffering too. I'm ashamed, but thank you for being a listening ear. MS on its way together with a photo of Arthur and Rose. They did eventually marry. Arthur returned to the UK when he was shot, but he ended up losing his arm. I'm off to play host. And thanks, Brie, for everything.

So, it's the story of his nanny's father, the hero who returned. I pull on some underwear and slip on a silk wrap. It's almost seven thirty and I'm eager to make a start. As the painkillers haven't quite kicked in yet, I'm going to lie back on the bed with my iPad on my knees until my body begins to recover a little.

There's a gentle tap on the door and I groan as I slide myself gently off the bed and into an upright position. When I swing it open there's no one there but I glance down to find a tray bearing two bottles of water, a low-fat yoghurt and two apples. I smile as I bend to pick it up but that's soon wiped off my face when a shooting pain stabs me in the back of my head. Okay, tilting is not good.

Moments later I'm opening Arran's email and downloading the attachments. I click on the photo first and when it opens my eyes instantly begin filling with tears. Zooming in, there's a handwritten date on the top right hand corner. The nineteenth of September, 1939.

It's Arthur and Rose standing close together holding hands, Arthur resplendent in a navy suit and Rose looking very sweet in a pale grey, lacy dress. They're glancing at each other, so their faces are in side profile and the happiness jumps out and grabs my heart. The horrors of battle are yet to inflict any damage on Arthur and I swipe away my tears angrily, hating the thought of war. How hard was it to smile when they had no idea if they would ever see each other again? Imagine making love knowing it might be the first and last time?

Guilt consumes me for the way I take everything for granted. Things that are only possible because so many men sacrificed their lives during the Second World War to secure freedom for their country. No homage could ever be enough to repay the debt. It was a generation of strong, noble, young men and women who somehow managed to grab some happiness while living through six long years of hell.

I crack the seal on a bottle of water, then stand, pacing back and forth as I begin reading. Carrie is right, the opening love scene doesn't jump off the page. I hope there aren't too many scenes like this one because if this is typical then it's going to involve a lot of work. Ironically, Arran has cracked the sexual tension and it's powerful in one way. It's more graphically descriptive when it comes to the physical act than I would have expected from him. He isn't a prude, that's for sure, but the imbalance caused by a lack of any real emotional impact makes it all seem very mechanical. Almost as if it were a release of sexual frustration, rather than an expression of their love for each other.

There's no sense of what must have been precious moments of intimacy, made special because they had such little time together to demonstrate how they felt. Knowing the clock was ticking and the minutes were slipping away, must have been agonising. It represented time spent in each other's company that they might never get again. It could have been their first and last time alone together.

I turn on track changes and highlight the first two chapters, my heart sinking a little. But after that I'm hooked as Arthur's story unfolds. The references to Rose are few, except for the brief letters they write to each other but often those arrive in batches, after days on the move for Arthur.

There's a sharp tap on the door and it opens, Elisabetta's head appearing around the side of it.

'*Mi scusi*. Sorry. I come back later?'

The bed hasn't been slept in, although it's very clear I've been lying on top of it. I can see Elisabetta looking puzzled.

'Oh, I have a headache, so I made the bed and am doing some work. There's no need to clean in here today, but thank you, Elisabetta.'

'Si. No problem. Feel better soon.'

I'm sure I'm not the first visitor who drank too much the night before and ended up staying in their room the following morning. I might be the first who didn't actually *sleep* in their bed though.

My phone rings and I see it's Mum. Oh no, I've been meaning to call her.

'Hi Mum, how are you both?'

'We're good, but how are you? We've been worried. One text and then nothing. I rang Mel and she reassured me you were fine, but I wanted to speak to you and check for myself.'

She's right and I've been remiss.

'I'm sorry, every time I've thought about calling you something has cropped up and I've had two very late nights. I have this morning off but I'm working on someone's manuscript.'

'Oh, I didn't mean to disturb you, darling. But it is nice to hear your voice. How is Lake Garda and is the heat getting to you?'

'It's stunning, Mum, and I'm managing just fine. There are plenty of shady areas to sit and the rooms are air conditioned. The villa is beautiful, and my room has a balcony on two sides. The views are amazing. It's going to be a busy week though, by the look of it. Then we have the first changeover on Saturday and a whole new group of people arriving. I don't know how Arran manages to do this every year. It is a lovely bunch of people though.'

'You sound happy enough.' Her voice reflects her smile and, no doubt, her relief. 'And busy. I won't keep you, but you know where I am if you need me. We assumed no news was good news but it's nice to know for sure.'

I sigh, feeling like the bad daughter I am.

'It's easy to get caught up in things here and after such a long period on my own in the house it really is doing me good. But I am sorry, and I will ring later in the week for a proper chat. I'm working on a manuscript for Arran right now, and there's a tight deadline. I'll be working on it all day tomorrow, too. After that, on Tuesday we're taking a trip into Salò, which is the nearest town. That's after I've done my session, of course, and on Wednesday there's a trip to Verona, so we will be back late. I haven't had a spare moment since I arrived, and I haven't even been in the pool. You and Dad would love it here, you know. The setting is amazing and I'll send you a few photos when I get a minute.'

There's a laugh. 'Oh, so Lake Garda has captured my daughter's heart, then? I haven't heard you sounding so enthused for a long time.'

If I had the right man by my side then, yes, I could easily spend my life here. Who wouldn't be content to live amongst all this beauty? Chuckling to myself, I know that at least I've been blessed with enough common sense to know that some dreams just don't translate into reality.

'Mum, I have to go because inspiration is striking, and I need to get some words on the screen.'

'Go, write and make that author's manuscript come to life. Speak soon, darling, love you loads.'

Within seconds I'm on the laptop, my fingers are flying around the keyboard and I'm weeping as I type. I try to remember to keep stopping to drink some water as I'm dehydrated enough as it is. I'm feeling Rose's pain and love in equal measure and I'm grieving already, even though I know they will eventually be reunited.

There's another tap on the door and I glance at the clock. It's just after noon and I've been reading and typing for more than four hours. Arran's head appears around the edge of the door and he's wearing a sheepish look.

'I brought more water. Are you sick to your stomach?' He walks in carrying a bottle in each hand.

'No. I've been working. I haven't even stopped to get dressed.'

He glances at the loo roll on the bed and the scattering of crumpled tissues.

'I'm reading and tweaking the scenes with Rose. It's a wonderful story so far, Arran, and you've done a brilliant job. I hope you think the changes I'm suggesting portray Rose's character and emotions in an accurate way. Some of it is down to good old female intuition, but there are things that I believe, as a strong woman, she would not have left unsaid.'

He looks surprised. 'You've already edited some sections?'

'Yes. I've made major changes to two of the more intimate love scenes so far. I'm not sure how many more there are. I have taken a bit of a liberty and embellished a few of Rose's letters to give the reader a little more of her backstory. I know that as I was reading she was constantly in my mind and I wanted to feel her emptiness and pain. But you can reject anything you aren't happy with. I bet Carrie can't wait to get this one under contract. I think you will be widening your audience for sure as it doesn't focus so much on military tactics, as in *The Vengeful Enemy*.'

Arran leans forward to place the bottles of water on the side table next to the bed.

'You've read it?'

'I did, on the trip over and I finished it yesterday. I wanted to get a feel for your writing. I admit military fiction is not my usual choice, but I learnt a lot, although it left me with questions. My grounding in romance means I can't help but want to know more about the personal lives of the characters outside the plot. With this new one you've made quite a leap. You nailed the sex scenes, but you skated over the emotional turmoil of love under those circumstances.'

He smiles.

'Well, it's good to know I got something right. But I'm glad you're here to fix the bits that fall short.'

I give him a wry smile.

'It's your story, Arran, so my revisions might not coincide with your thoughts on Rose's perspective. But I think readers will expect to be given an insight into her emotional journey and how steadfast she was in her belief that Arthur would eventually come home to her for good. I believe it will help to give the story balance, but it's entirely up to you whether or not to take my suggestions on board.'

He shrugs.

'I can't be precious about this; you know your job and you sell a lot of books. I need to grab a big advance and that becomes more likely if a publisher can see that I'm able to seamlessly swap genres. I doubt I'll take exception to anything you re-write because I know it's a weakness in my writing. In this case you're the teacher.'

I look at him wishing he wasn't in such a dire position. Like Rose, I know it's too late to put a halt to what has been put in train and what lies ahead is going to hurt.

'That's kind but reserve your judgement until after you've combed through it. And run it past Carrie if you aren't sure. How did it go today, did everyone join in?'

'Yes. It went well; some of the group have already gone along to the restaurant for lunch. Do you want to grab something light out on the terrace?'

My stomach is rumbling but mainly because I've only had time to nibble on some fruit, although I have drunk two bottles of water.

'I'll throw on some clothes and make myself decent, then I'll be down.'

Our eyes meet and linger. I only hope Arran isn't having flashbacks of last night. I wonder who carried whom up the stairs? Or maybe we just clung to each other, trying not to make any noise as we staggered around. As Arran exits the room, closing the door behind him, I let out a loud groan. It was hardly professional behaviour, and this is work, not pleasure. Although having a hangover can't really be classed as pleasure, anyway.

Arran and I sit on the terrace to eat, although neither of us seems to have an appetite. I wonder why? He tells me about settling the group in and how they took turns to talk about their current work in progress and other things they'd written. He reassures me that our night exploits seem to have gone unnoticed.

'Lesson learnt,' he says with a wicked grin and then his face creases up.

'Shooting pains?'

He nods. 'Time for some more painkillers, I think.'

I look at him, shamefaced. 'Me too. Do you think the group would mind if I didn't circulate but head back up to my room to read some more of your manuscript?'

He raises both eyebrows, rather gingerly. 'You're keen. No, I'm sure it will be fine. Only Rick has asked for a one-to-one, so far. We're going to check out his opening chapter this afternoon: he's eager to hear my thoughts. I see a little of myself in him. I was impatient to make things happen when I first veered away from textbooks to write fiction.'

This isn't just about raking in an additional source of income, Arran really cares – and he has a lot of patience. I'm worried about my session on Tuesday as it will be a first for me. I'm used to doing talks in general and often get asked for writing tips, but it won't be the polished and honed performance Kathy would have given. Still, I've made a list of bullet points and to some extent I'm hoping the group will help steer where they want the session to go.

We take our plates back into the kitchen, as Elisabetta has already left for the day, and head off in separate directions.

15

Becoming an Arran Jamieson Fan

I can't wait to get back to Rose and Arthur's story. Knowing that much of what is written is probably close to the truth makes it compelling reading. I reach the part where Arthur is given a pass to return to England to marry Rose. They have five days together and after a quick trip to the registry office, and a buffet at the local pub for a dozen or so friends and family, they head off to Cornwall.

It's like a story within a story and a wonderful contrast from the previous scenes. It makes me wonder how soldiers managed to adjust after being in such a hostile, bloody environment exposed to all manner of horrors. They were often cold, wet and caked in mud – living life one single second at a time. The comforts of home must have seemed surreal and almost wantonly luxurious by comparison. But it serves to lift the story and gives the reader a welcome break from a painful reality. I know that I felt in need of a reminder that life could be good, and it emphasised what Arthur was fighting for – freedom.

My phone vibrates and it's Carrie calling.

'Hey, Carrie, how are you?'

'Good. I'll email over the draft of that article. I didn't realise you'd talked about Paul, but I think that might be a good thing. People will, no doubt, be interested in your side of the story and it reads well.'

My heart misses a beat. I can't worry about that right now, so it will have to wait until later.

'Thanks. I'm working on the edits as we speak, you'll be pleased to hear.'

'Please say you're talking about Arran's manuscript. I have two publishers eager to read it and I can't give them anything more than the synopsis – especially until that opening love scene is rewritten. Chapter one reads like a page out of a sex manual. I don't think Rose was like that; she was passionate, but it needs finessing.'

I start laughing.

'Already done. Arran hasn't seen any of my proposed changes yet, as I'll hold off showing him until I've gone through the whole thing. It's a brilliant story and I admire his talent. Rose touched my heart and I cried as I was re-writing the opening scene. I hope he approves.'

'Great! I knew you'd nail it. How soon will I get it?'

I'm guessing Arran has been talking to Carrie and is trying to push things along. I wonder how much she knows? A fair bit, I'd say, as she was the one who warned me he'd been through a harrowing time.

'I hope to get halfway through it by the end of the day. I've been working on it since seven thirty this morning with one short break. I will have to rejoin the group for dinner, but I'll make that as short as possible. Tomorrow I'll make myself scarce again and get as much done as I can. On Tuesday I doubt I'll get more than an hour to work on it. I'm running the session in the morning and in the afternoon, we're all heading into Salò. I think it might appear rather strange if I don't go. Wednesday is also a long day. We're off to Verona after the morning session and won't get back until late evening. It will be Thursday at the earliest before I will be able to pass it back to Arran, if it all goes well.'

'Great! Arran is keen to get it all wrapped up. Thank you, Brie. I know it was a big ask. I will be honest and say that I'm not sure Kathy would have been the right person to tackle this one.'

She sounds relieved.

'It's my pleasure. I hope you both think I've done it justice as the story around it is amazing. Knowing it's based on a true story really rams home the harsh reality of that period in history.'

'Well, I won't keep you. But before I go, how are things between the two of you now?'

I can't help thinking Carrie is hoping we'll make a connection on a personal level. And in a strange, rather unexpected way, I suppose that is the case. I'm discovering we have more and more in common as each day passes but fundamentally our approach to life is very different. In my heart I know that at some point I want to settle down and have a family. I have this romantic picture in my head of a sprawling old stone cottage with a flagstone floor, not the pristinely renovated one that I already own. My writing desk looks out over the garden and I gaze out to see a child playing with a cat. I would be happy splitting my time between family and my passion for writing. But I would also be content to put my work on hold for a while if the situation warranted it.

'Much better. We've found the middle ground between us and are a little more relaxed in each other's company.'

I'll omit the fact that we have shared a bed together as that might be a tad misleading.

'Great! Let me know Arran's reaction on Thursday. Happy editing.'

As I put the phone down I wonder if Carrie is ticking off two items on her action list. Sort Arran's manuscript and get Brie back out there. I can almost hear the sound of the electronic ticks filling the boxes. Maybe she wasn't trying to push us together and would be horrified to discover the awakenings of attraction stirring in the pit of my stomach. In my little daydream the man who is *the one* is never quite in the scene; he's in the shadows but he is there and that's enough to reassure me it will happen. I seriously doubt when it's time for the reveal it will be Arran's face staring back at me though.

I'm almost ready to head downstairs when I hear the scrunch of tyres pulling into the parking area. I look out and watch Rick, Silvia, Yvonne and Tom making their way along the path towards the taxi. They're all very jolly and I can hear peals of laughter. It seems there's a little dinner party excursion going on and I'm grateful Arran didn't make a thing of asking me if I wanted to be included. I wonder what Will and Kris are doing tonight? That could mean a cosy dinner for four at La Pergola. I'll be able to excuse myself as soon as we've eaten so I can come back and squeeze in another couple of hours work tonight.

I shower, wash and blow dry my hair, and apply a little light make-up, before slipping into a simple A-line dress in a pale blue floral print. I still don't have that sun kissed look but then I haven't really spent much time outside.

When I walk out onto the terrace Arran is sitting on his own with a highball glass next to him, reading his Kindle.

'Good evening. We're down to four this evening, then. Where are Kris and Will?'

He looks up, easing off his sunglasses to look at me.

'You look remarkably fresh and recovered. You just missed them; they decided to walk down to La Tagliata. I didn't make a commitment, so they aren't expecting us to join them. I hope that was alright? I… um… indicated that you had a bit of a headache. I had a vested interest in freeing up your time.'

'I think it's rather nice that the group are happy to do different things. It was hard work last night with everyone there. You were deep in conversation with Rick and I discovered that trying to ensure no one is left out is a real juggling act. With the background music adding another layer of noise to the general hubbub of conversations going on, I was quite stressed by the end of it.'

A slight grin creeps over his face. 'I know.'

I ignore the inference. 'Okay. So, what's the plan? I've allocated two hours for dinner and then I'm back to working on the manuscript. I promised Carrie I'd go through it with you on Thursday. I think she's counting on you to turn it around quickly.'

He nods, his expression now one of seriousness.

'Great. That works for me. I guess we'd better get off then, I'll give Antonio a call as we walk so he can get a table ready for us.'

I turn and step back inside as Arran locks the patio doors and we head through the hallway and into the rear garden. He nestles his phone between his chin and his shoulder as he locks the door.

'Do the others have a key?' I mouth, and he nods his head.

'Antonio, I'm heading up with Brie and hoping you can find us a table for two. Is that a problem?'

His face is animated as he listens to Antonio, whose answer seems rather long, but I can see it's fine.

'Thank you, my friend. Much appreciated.'

As Arran slips his phone into his trouser pocket he looks across at me.

'He said he'd find us a romantic corner. I didn't disillusion him; Italians are so hot blooded. Have any of your books been translated into Italian?'

I nod. 'Yes, six of them so far.'

'Ah, that accounts for it then. I think you might have a fan there.'

As we head out through the gates and down the hill, we walk in double file. There's no path but you can hear vehicles approaching in the distance because the traffic is light. It feels good to be out in the air after a day inside.

There are a lot of overhanging trees that help to diffuse the sun but there's no breeze at all tonight and I think longingly of the pool.

Everywhere I look there are explosions of colour; climbers taking over walls, shrubs and even trees. Then at the lower level, despite the lack of rainfall and the constant heat there is a profusion of flower heads. Pinks, blues, yellows, deep purple… a wild array with a backdrop of luscious greenery. The hillside looks like a never ending garden, amongst which there nestles an unknown number of homes and a handful of restaurants. Few can be seen, as they are so well hidden, but the clues lie in people's attempts to tame an area of garden or plant an orchard of fruit bearing trees. Where there's a slight clearing you can usually cast your eye around and spot a path, or even simply a gate.

'Are you looking forward to your session on Tuesday?'

Arran breaks our companionable silence as we approach La Pergola. He holds the door open for me to enter.

'I'm nervous. But I am looking forward to our trip out in the afternoon.'

'*Buonasera*!' Antonio immediately steps forward to greet us, bowing his head in acknowledgement and vigorously shaking hands.

'Come. I have a quiet table on the balcony. We are busy tonight but here you will be away from the music, yes?' Antonio talks over his shoulder as he leads the way.

We follow him down the long gangway in the centre of the restaurant, which is buzzing tonight, with most tables already taken; at the rear there is a single glass door leading out onto a wooden balcony. There are only four tables out here and we are the first to be seated. Antonio pulls out a chair for me then produces a lighter from his pocket, even though it's still a little bright to warrant a candle.

'As the restaurant is so busy maybe we should go with today's special? What do you think, Brie?'

Arran looks at me for approval and I nod my head. 'Great idea.'

'I bring you a nice antipasti platter for two, then maybe orecchiette with chicken meatballs, yes? Is best dish in the house.'

Both Arran and I smile up at Antonio. There's little point in trying to explain that pasta and I don't sit well together, and I don't want to make a fuss.

'Sounds wonderful, thank you,' Arran confirms and suddenly we're alone together on the balcony.

Our eyes meet and it's obvious we are both thinking about this morning in Arran's bedroom.

What was rather hazy earlier on is a little clearer this evening and I recall us both laughing as we collapsed on top of the bed. I remember saying, 'I just need to sleep. I won't stay long.' And then it was morning.

'Look, I know it's awkward and I can assure you I don't make a habit of over indulging. You are a guest at the villa and a peer doing me a big favour. I don't know what exactly happened if I'm honest, but I'm a gentleman first and foremost, I can assure you of that. I had no intention of taking advantage of you given the state we were in.' He sounds somewhat regretful.

'Um… the same goes for me, too.' I agree.

And I was sitting here thinking how romantic it would be if Arran said how lovely I was looking tonight. He's spoilt the moment now by spouting an awkward apology.

'We can't undo what's done, so I think maybe it's best to forget it, don't you?' I add.

He looks both surprised and relieved. 'That's very good of you to be so understanding, Brie. My reputation—'

'Is intact. I don't think either of us is very proud of how we conducted ourselves last night. We're clearly both under pressure and I know it's been a while since I was able to relax and unwind. Tonight I'm on the water though, as I have a manuscript to work on.'

His eyes haven't left my face and I'm surprised because suddenly he looks a little disappointed. Oh no! Is he offended now, thinking that was some sort of rejection?

'Good, um, yes, well… I'm glad we cleared the air. So, how are the revisions going?' His tone is edgy.

'As I said, Cassie would like me to be in a position to go through them with you on Thursday. It's achievable if I can work on it solidly tomorrow and then grab a couple of hours in between my session and the trips to fine tune the changes. I realise that will mean you've virtually coped with the group alone for two straight days, but it's the only way around it.'

He pours out two glasses of water, holding one out to me with a wry smile on his face.

'I think we can toast to that! It's a small price to pay. I really do appreciate what you're doing, Brie.'

Well, he's done with the awkwardness, so he can't have been too disappointed, can he? We chink glasses. 'Better save the thanks until you've read my suggestions.'

'I think I'm going to be wowed. I saw that you were crying as you were writing when I popped by to see you this morning.'

I nod, unable to pretend that wasn't the case because it was obvious with tissues all over the bed. Goodness knows what state my eyes were in.

'It's a powerful story, Arran.'

This time when our eyes connect I see something else there; a hint of sadness that touches my heart.

'If you'd met them, you'd understand just how powerful. Ah, here comes Antonio. I don't know about you, but I'm starving. What a day it's been.'

Amen to that.

16

Crying a River

I don't hang around after breakfast. I'm eager to set myself up on the balcony again so that I won't be in Elisabetta's way when she comes in to clean. Besides, it's lovely and cool here in the shade and there's a slight breeze going, which is rather refreshing. And I need the air. My stomach is angry with me this morning and it looks like I've swallowed a football. I chide myself that this is ridiculous and I'm going to have to explain to Arran that there are some foods I need to avoid.

However, I made a lot of progress last night as most of the chapters I read through were about the harrowing reality of war. This morning I keep looking at the photo of Arthur and Rose, drawing inspiration from it to add the emotion to those rather sterile love scenes. What is rather frustrating for me is that Arran has written very little about what happened to Rose when she was alone, because the story follows Arthur for the most part. It's the one thing that stands out as a major flaw in the storyline.

I decide I simply can't ignore this gut feeling that the reader wants to know more but it's not something I can write. This is, after all, based on a true story. So, instead, I draft out some suggested text for an additional chapter that Arran will have to flesh out by doing a little research. It will give at least a little insight as to what life was like in the UK for Rose. She would have been representational of so many women missing the love of their lives and contending with wartime conditions. She is about to discover that in the few months they have been apart Arthur has changed; he went away a boy and came back a man, already laden with memories that will haunt him forever.

With fierce determination she wraps him in her love as she tries to sooth his troubled soul. He feels guilt for stepping away, for leaving his comrades, as if he's shirking his responsibilities. Somehow, she instinctively understands that she must ground him in the present as he needs a break from the constant horrors of war. I want Arran's readers to be touched by that reality, too. I'm not unhappy with where I'm directing him to go and although I think it will challenge him a little, I hope he will understand where I'm coming from.

'*Mi scusi*. Is okay to clean?' Elisabetta steps out onto the balcony hesitantly. I hadn't even heard her enter. 'I knocked, no answer.'

'Yes, that's fine. You go ahead.'

'I make no noise.' She smiles at me warmly.

'You're very kind but I don't hear anything when I'm working.' I shrug my shoulders and she laughs.

'Is like Mr Jamieson. He work hard; nice man.'

He is a nice man, she's right. 'Very talented,' I add.

'Sad, he alone now. Lonely is terrible.'

She turns and begins to mop the floor just as my stomach gurgles so loudly it stops her mid-stroke and she looks at me aghast.

'Sorry,' I apologise, 'and I totally agree.' I can feel my face beginning to heat up as the trapped gas begins to rumble again.

Loneliness is terrible and isolating. Been there, done that and it's soul destroying. As I think about Arran I have a sudden flashback. Having seen a lot more of him than I bargained for, he didn't disappoint, and I can't stop myself from literally bursting out laughing. Fortunately, Elisabetta is in the bathroom now and doesn't appear to have heard me laughing out loud. Or, thankfully, the loud succession of burps I can't control, but afterwards my stomach begins to settle nicely.

Of course, I long to have a caring and loving man in my life; to meet someone who doesn't just want to jump into bed, thinking five minutes of foreplay is a romantic gesture! But if I'm being honest with myself it's been too long, and I miss that intimacy, too. It would be nice to fall asleep in the arms of a man again, after a night of lovemaking. Just to feel wanted, desired again, would be a confidence boost and tell me I haven't totally lost the ability to inspire someone. Maybe, before too long, I will meet the man of my dreams, a person who can live up to my hopes and expectations. But the longer I'm forced to wait, the more I'm beginning to think that either he doesn't exist, or maybe I should lower my standards. Maybe the Jude Law in my head is as fictional as my heroes. And that thought is rather depressing, to say the least.

I hate to admit it to myself but physically I find Arran very, very appealing. Suddenly the flashback I'm getting now isn't quite so funny. Did we end up kissing as we staggered upstairs, or is this manuscript and my imagination playing tricks on me? I close my eyes and focus on remembering but nothing more comes. *Okay, you're safe*. Imagination is a wonderful, but scary thing.

My phone kicks into life and makes me jump as it starts to skitter across the table.

'Hey, how are you?' It's Mel.

'I'm good. Well, I'm in heaven, actually. Ross is not only a lovely guy but he's fascinating, witty, kind and an IT genius.'

I sit back in my chair with a big grin on my face.

'He's impressed you, then,' I can't really hide the amusement in my tone.

'We do spend a lot of time talking shop, which I kind of guess would put a lot of women off. But not me, I love that we share the same interest. After seeing each other two nights on the trot we're going for the hat trick tonight.'

I smirk to myself. 'I had no idea Internet dating websites did such a great job of matching people.'

The silence that ensues is a little awkward.

'He's special, Brie. Besides, it's a more adult way of discovering someone new, that's all. You know quite a bit about each other before you meet for the first time and that's actually quite helpful.'

I'm astonished, not least because it sounds a little boring, I suppose. But then Mel has been very cautious since her break-up, even when it comes to considering a first date. I think she's only gone on two that I can remember, having turned down rather a lot of offers. It's her chatty nature and bubbly personality that does it but she's still very fragile. So, I suppose this approach had an element of safety to it. After all, if you go through the whole process of getting registered and looking at potential matches you are demonstrating a serious interest in finding a Mr Right.

'I thought you were worried he was too good to be true?'

She sighs. 'Yes, because I can't find any flaws. He's a softie and he made a home for two rescue cats named Bowie and Hendrix. They adore him, and you know what cats are like – they give love in return for love received. This morning I arrived in work to find my desk covered in flowers and a note saying he's counting down the hours until tonight. Seriously, my heart thuds in my chest whenever I think of him.'

I gulp. Mel sounds besotted and while that's amazing, it's a little worrying too. Every high has a corresponding low; let's hope the only low going on here will be the fact that it all feels a little… too easy. But he seems to be making up for that with romantic gestures, so I guess that says a lot about him. What is heartening, is that they are both going into this with their eyes wide open.

'I've dreamt of someone like Ross coming into my life for so long and now I have to keep pinching myself to check it's for real.'

'I'm thrilled for you, Mel, but please take it slowly. Take time to savour *the getting to know each other* phase, because new love is the best feeling in the world. Just don't rush headlong into it until that adrenaline high settles down. I'm sure he's the genuine article, but sometimes feelings dip after they soar. You know the score and it's still early days for you.'

I don't want to add negative words about past hurts, or future disappointments, or worse – having her heart broken if she steams into this new relationship with too much optimism. Somehow it feels all wrong to find someone from a list matched by a computer programme. If fate wanted your paths to cross, then wouldn't you just find yourself in the right place, at the right time? Justin trampled all over her heart and left her in pieces: I don't think she could go through that again.

'Trust me, Brie, I know what I'm doing. That's why we're taking it one step at a time. We talk openly and honestly about everything. In fact, I almost feel that I know more about Ross than I ever knew about Justin. Ross is really in touch with his emotions and says he isn't prepared to settle for anything less than total commitment when it comes to settling down. Anyway, enough about me. How is Lake Garda?'

I glance at the laptop screen in front of me. It seems love really is all around me, at the moment.

'Wonderful, although today I'm going to be doing a lot of crying, I think.'

'Whaaat?'

'Sorry, I was just thinking out loud. The pressure is on to boost the emotional content in the love scenes in Arran's manuscript, which is set during the Second World War. It's a heart-breaking story, even though it has a happy ending. I've been sobbing my heart out already. Arthur has just been given five days' leave to get married. Already the horrors he's witnessed have changed him. Can you imagine what that must have been like for his sweetheart, Rose?'

I hear Mel suck in a deep breath. 'That's so sad, Brie. Loving someone means when they're hurting, you're hurting too. Rose must have felt powerless when he was away fighting. Gosh, it's making my eyes well up as we talk. How is Arran?'

Another flashback. Oh no! I hope this isn't going to be a constant thing.

'He's an interesting guy, actually, just getting over a horrendous divorce. We… um… had a few drinks and he told me all about it.'

A little laugh travels down the line. 'A *few*, you say? That's not like you. I hope it ended well.'

I burst out laughing. 'If I could remember, I'd share the details. Anyway, stop it! He's nice and I admit he is very attractive but we're worlds apart on so many levels. Besides, once I run him through my suggested revisions he might never speak to me again.'

'Well, it's his loss if that's the case. I know you'll do a great job and have those love scenes leaping off the page. Hot and emotional is what you do!'

'Well, surprisingly all I'm adding *is* the emotion, he more than had the sex scenes covered. I'd give him ten out of ten for technique.'

We both start laughing and it's good to hear my dear friend so happy and light hearted.

'I know you're in good hands, then,' she adds cheekily. 'Don't go making assumptions. He might not be quite the staid academic you thought he was – so give him a chance.'

If Mel only knew, her eyebrows would shoot up into her hairline.

'I'm here to work and enjoy a little sightseeing, so I'm going to have to rely upon you to provide the tantalising little love updates. Anyway, it's great chatting but I must go. Until I get this done poor Arran has to cope with the group all on his own. Enjoy those flowers!'

'Oh, I will. Lilies are my absolute favourites and I have no idea how Ross knew that; he just seems to know everything. Speak soon.'

As the line clicks I find myself staring down at my phone. This Ross better be the real deal, or he'll have me to answer to!

I turn my attention to Rose, trying to put myself in her shoes. How would you go about comforting the man you love when his head is full of horrific memories of the battle field? He's stepped away for a short while, but he knows returning is inevitable. In between, somehow, they have to free themselves of the tragedy of war, so they can celebrate their love and their marriage. Even as I begin typing a tear is already running down my cheek. I want to give Arran a flavour of what he needs to add to bring this to life.

★

It's lunchtime and I watch as the group wend their way up the path towards the gate, no doubt heading for La Pergola. I notice Arran is missing so I save the file and put the laptop into sleep mode to saunter downstairs. As I walk into the kitchen Arran is preparing two plates of food.

'I was just about to text you. I thought you might want lunch in your room but I'm glad you're taking a break.'

His smile is warm and genuine. He seems relaxed.

'The first session went well then?'

He nods, finishing off the grape he just popped into his mouth. 'Mm. Always best to get the myths out of the way, first off. A writer's life is often a poor and a lonely one; few win the jackpot. We tackled the dreaded rollercoaster of emotions and how to keep on an even keel. I keep it fun though, for the most part, and cite a few stories of the overnight sensations who were writing for years before their books were noticed.'

'Keeping it real, then.'

'Yep. Can you grab that jug of orange juice and the glasses? I thought we'd wander down to the lower level and sit beneath the olive trees.'

I follow Arran as he carries the tray and as soon as I step out onto the terrace, the glittering blue water in front of me is mesmerising. No wonder Arran loves this place and the fact that he has fond memories of his grandfather's life here must make it hard to share with strangers. And yet he doesn't give that impression at all.

Settling down, we sit in silence for a short while, eating and surveying the garden. Birds swoop as Arran throws a little bread out for them and for me it's a welcome break away from the emotional trauma of this morning.

'How's it going?' Arran asks, as if reading my thoughts.

'You've written a compelling story and my stomach has been in knots with the harsh reality it portrays. But I've been trying to get inside Rose's head to tap into the emotional trauma and I hope you like what I'm doing.'

'I always think that plumbing the emotional depths is about telling, whereas I'm best at showing. Action, I can do, but getting inside the head to understand what's in the heart – well, I don't have the patience for it.'

What an odd way to put it. I can't help but frown and Arran turns to look at me, puzzled. 'I come from a family who don't express their emotions. My father made no time at all for his own father. He thought my grandfather was a sentimental fool for over indulging me during my summers here. My mother, well, she worked up until just a couple of days before both my sister and I were born. She was back to work less than a month later, apparently. I once overheard her telling a friend that she didn't have the skills, patience, or the instincts to raise young children. So, she handed us over to someone who did. It was Nanny Hope who was there to pick us both up when we fell over and dispense medicine when we were sick. But when she wasn't around it was a cold environment, very strict and where achievement was everything.'

He doesn't look, or sound, resentful or hurt. He's just telling it as it was, I suppose.

'Coming from a childhood full of parental love and affection, I find that tough to hear.'

'I suppose that's why I find it hard to understand this need to analyse every little emotion. Readers have imagination. Are the love scenes in the book as much of a let-down as Carrie has indicated?'

I stop eating, or rather, playing with an assortment of food I simply can't eat for fear my stomach will rebel again. Which truth do I tell him first?

'The passion between Arthur and Rose is clear and the physical aspects are handled well, you certainly didn't shy away graphically. I commend you on that – it needed to be treated in the same explicit way as the harrowing war scenes. And, after all, Rose was a virgin, so it was a huge turning point in her life to give herself to a man going off to war. But as a reader, increasingly I'm left wanting more. I feel I only have one half of the picture. What was going on in Arthur's head aside from the flashbacks you interspersed, where he was thinking about his training and wondering what was to come? How distraught was Rose when she lay in bed alone at night, thinking of him?'

Arran sits back, folding his arms across his chest and his body language signals he's uncomfortable.

'But aren't those private thoughts? Things people don't share?'

This was what I feared would happen. Why would he respect my views on his manuscript when to his mind all that matters is the telling of the story about men pitched against men in the battle for freedom?

'Some internalise it, but most people turn to their family and friends. I'm sure soldiers would have had moments when they needed to talk about home. And Rose would no doubt have had a friend to confide in. But it's the emotional aspect that makes all the difference between a sex scene and a love scene.'

He lets out a laugh that sounds more like a snort.

'Oh, come on, the scenes you write are hardly tame according to the articles I've read about you. Sex is sex, after all and it's driven by the chemistry of the body.'

You haven't actually read any of my books; that little voice in my head is clamouring to be heard but I resist the temptation. Now I'm annoyed – very annoyed.

'I write about lusty, consenting adults having fun and readers engage for the thrill; but the sex is only one small part of the story. Okay, so you're writing about the harsh realities of war, which is your strength, but this time it's based around a passionate love affair that lasted for decades. Remember you are trying to appeal to a much wider audience with this semi-autobiographical story of Arthur's life. A life that endures a war and the equally as cruel aftermath.

'That first time they made love, at the beginning of the book, he was going off to war the next day. Would strategic planning really have been in his head at all that night? If it had, as you showed it flashing through his mind, I seriously doubt he would have been able to perform any sexual act that night. Somehow, he would have managed to switch off and think only of Rose and grabbing their moment together. That is what makes for a powerful scene the reader will engage with and believe.'

His arms fall to his side and he looks suitably apologetic.

'Sorry, I should know better than to let my ego get in the way. I know that I need to find my feet as I widen my genre and accept that I have to expand my comfort zone, too. I need this contract and I am grateful for your guidance. I'm sure I'll get used to the idea of the emotional trappings of love.'

I accept his apology and feel for him, because he isn't doing this out of choice but necessity. And that's down to his ex, Harriet. I need to change the subject.

'The spelling of your Christian name with two r's is unusual, how did that come about?'

At that moment my stomach starts to complain. Loudly. I wince, putting my fork down on the table with a clatter and hopefully helping to disguise the sound.

Arran leans forward to grab his glass of orange juice and then settles back, looking at me with a wry smile as it's obvious I'm trying to change the subject. But I also need him to talk in case my stomach continues growling.

'My grandfather was Scottish but lived in Surrey from the age of twelve. My grandmother, Eilidh, was from the wonderful Scottish Isle of Arran. My grandfather lured her away to Italy, but he took her home to die there in 1993 after she was diagnosed with cancer.'

The sheer sadness of that makes my heart constrict and a wave of emotion passes over me. That's a love story worth telling, right there!

'How long did she live after the diagnosis?'

'Two months. He was by her side every single moment of every day. She was too ill to fly with a commercial airline, so he chartered a private jet to take her home.'

How can Arran tell me that without it touching his heart? He replaces his glass on the table and leans forward to grab a chunk of bread. When he sits back he looks unmoved, and I'm rather lost for words. I can see him thinking about something.

'I've told you my sordid little non-love story, but what's yours? It can't be easy dating when your fame goes before you.'

The comment is tongue-in-cheek and one I don't appreciate, but he's astute, I'll give him that.

'I don't need a man to make me feel complete. Besides, I'm too busy for the time being to even entertain the thought of a relationship.'

'I Googled you. Can't really imagine you with a rock guitarist, if I'm being honest.'

I can feel the heat rising up from my chest, as a sudden hot flush threatens to set my cheeks alight.

'Why not?'

He leans forward, spearing an olive and suddenly he turns around to look at me as if he's weighing me up.

'Don't get me wrong, I love a bit of rock music myself, but I should imagine that Paul Turner leads quite a wild life.'

'I've had my own wild times but that's firmly in the past now.' How can I sit here and lie like that? I trailed around as Paul's girlfriend for a while, watching people fawning over him and refusing to be treated like one of his starry eyed fans or to partake in some of the over indulgences on offer. It was a very pathetic attempt to prove something to myself and in the end it nearly pushed me over the edge.

And as for my boyfriends before my insane little interlude with a rock star, well, they were all pretty decent guys. Nothing wild to report there, either. But also no one I felt any long lasting connection to and I wonder now if that was a part of my initial attraction to Paul? Were my heroes unsettling me and I felt the need to step outside my comfort zone? I find that thought rather worrying.

'I did wonder why you were able to fly out here at such short notice. Obviously, I'm very grateful for that, but I'm a little surprised you don't have a guy at home pining for you.'

Is he being sarcastic?

'Guys come and go. I haven't yet found one worthy of keeping.' I sound angry but it's just the way the words come out because he's beginning to annoy me. Again.

'I had no idea it was a sensitive subject and I apologise if I've overstepped the mark. Really, I mean that. You were good enough to listen to my depressing story and I wondered if you needed a listening ear too.'

There I go, jumping to conclusions. He meant well, I suppose but he lacks… diplomacy.

'When you spend your days writing about heroes, it's hard to find a man who measures up.'

He stares at me, considering my words and then nods, a slight frown creasing his brow.

'That's one dilemma I hadn't considered. Is that your stomach I can hear?' he asks, shovelling another large piece of bread into his mouth.

'Actually it is, and I have a little confession to make. I'm going to have to avoid the pasta or I'll end up looking like a balloon.'

'Why on earth didn't you say from day one?' And then he begins laughing, in between trying to apologise profusely for finding my gassy predicament so funny.

Having been absent again for most of the day, I think I made up for a little lost ground at tonight's dinner. With everyone content to go to La Pergola it was quite a night. Arran fussed over me, explaining which items I might consider without *detrimental effect*, as he put it.

It served to reassure me that the group are happy and seemed to have had a great day with Arran. When we arrived back at the villa he suggested we all watch a film and it was a nice way to end the day.

An early night is just what I need to set me up for my session with the group tomorrow morning. Let's hope I can deliver and that I don't disappoint. Gauging people's expectations is difficult and rather daunting – the pressure is really beginning to build now.

17

Taking Class

This morning everyone is seated around the table on the terrace looking bright eyed and eager. The nerves are beginning to manifest themselves and to my abject horror I see that my hand shakes a little as I pass around some handouts.

'I'd like to begin this morning's session by saying that all views expressed are my own; people's opinions will differ and I'm speaking from my very personal experience of writing in the contemporary women's and romance genres.'

This is much worse than I thought it would be. All eyes are on me and I realise that this group reflects the whole spectrum from an unpublished newbie, right through to Arran, who is a recognised name.

'For the first hour we're going to run through a few fun exercises but please feel free to ask questions at any time. We'll begin by describing a character, in no more than thirty words, which will convey his or her age.

Then everyone has a go at guessing the magic number, give or take a few years. It serves to highlight the sort of information your readers will be looking for you to give them. But the answers also serve to demonstrate the level of detail required to give them a clear picture of the person you're describing. Often, it's not about the number of words, but the relevance of the words you choose to use.'

The exercise triggers a lot of very animated discussion and I'm pleased that everyone joins in with the chatter and the good natured laughter. The second exercise is about describing a famous person. Names and occupations can't feature in the descriptions. Everyone assumes it's going to be easy but often it's extremely hard to do. Then the team must guess the person's name. I'm clock watching, conscious of the time as there's still quite a bit to cover.

'If you're a plotter, then when you sit down to write you will already know your characters quite well. I often think that's more of a challenge than starting with a blank page and simply writing. I'm in the latter category and what appears on the screen is really a reflection of my thought processes as they develop. So I can't get ahead of myself because I don't know any more than the reader does, no matter what stage I'm at. We learn about the characters together.

'As a plotter you have to remember to see your characters through the eyes of the reader and the written word. You need to be very clear about what you have told them, as opposed to what you haven't yet revealed. For instance, if you haven't mentioned the fact that a character was married, and you start talking about their divorce, the reader could find this rather confusing. The danger is in a writer having such a clear picture of someone in their head that they forget to flesh them out in the text. One way to handle that is to have a characterisation timeline in the same way you have a plot timeline. I'm a great believer in keeping things simple and it's easy to run the two alongside each other.'

There's a lot of note taking going on and then I read out a few examples from some of the most famous authors of all time. Most of the second half of the session is spent looking at a character's backstory. We discuss different ways of revealing that, covering everything from the use of a prologue, to flashback scenes and timeslip.

'I have one final exercise you might find interesting before I bring this session to a close. But before we tackle that are there any other aspects of characterisation anyone would like to discuss?'

Kris catches my eye. 'I had a closed bedroom door policy when I wrote my first manuscript and because edits haven't started yet, I don't know if my editor will want me to spice it up a bit. That thought scares me a little because I'm writing about glamorous people and I know I've been avoiding the issue. I'm a bit worried about crossing a line too. You write about sex with ease and it never seems out of place, but I'm not sure I can do that.' Her cheeks are colouring a little and I understand her nervousness. I was like that when I first began.

'While my current novels do include sex scenes, those scenes do not drive the plot itself. It sounds very much like that's the case with the story you've written. Essentially, we're talking about relationships and how love changes people; sex is a natural part of that and it's fine to stop at the bedroom door. Not all readers want to read the detail, while others like a little frisson to jump off the page and then words like 'hot' or 'explicit' would be a part of the marketing campaign.'

Kris inclines her head. 'I wonder how many women out there put down one of your books on their bedside table at night and then roll over, quite happily, into the arms of their partner?'

Everyone laughs, including Arran, I'm pleased to note.

'Can I have a quick show of hands if sex features anywhere at all in any of your stories.'

Four hands rise in the air, two being lowered as quickly as they went up.

Rick is quick to jump in. 'As a reader, I think sex can really liven up a story and I don't see anything wrong with that. As a writer it poses a dilemma about how far you go. The female characters in my story are all hard nosed, domineering types as I've just been through a nightmare of a divorce. It's like getting my own back.'

I see one of Arran's eyebrows shoot up, but he says nothing and looking around I see a few uncomfortable glances being exchanged.

'I'm a single woman still and how would a lady know about such things?' Silvia gives a saucy wink. 'I'm joking, of course. I write about the roaring twenties. The hair went up and the knickers came down.'

That elicits a peal of laughter.

'Do any of you read men's magazines? I don't mean the top shelf stuff, but the popular monthlies?'

That draws a blank.

'The reason I ask that is because Arran asked me a very moot question the other day. How do I manage my readers' expectations when it comes to writing the sex scenes? The advent of *Fifty Shades of Grey* made some writers feel the pressure to add a touch of heat. I think that might be where you are coming from, Kris. As if something is missing, when that isn't necessarily the case.

'My advice is to first look at other novels in the same genre, so you can get a feel for what else someone choosing your book might also be reading. If sex is quite a dominant theme within other stories in your genre, then that is something to weigh up. But there are other considerations. Context is one. Unless you are writing full blown erotica, then a sex scene has to be relevant to the story and flow. If it doesn't add something in a meaningful way, like bringing two people closer together, or being a source of tension going forward, then consider why you're adding it. If in doubt, leave it out.

'Obviously, I'm not talking about the crime or thriller genres here, where violence and horror usually require actions to be taken to the extreme. But there's nothing worse than reading something that feels contrived. The other thing to remember is to keep it real. I mentioned the men's magazines because I regularly read them to keep up to date with what's current. The pressure is most definitely on for the guys to be well groomed, work out, dress well… and perform. Don't feel your hero always has to rise to the occasion, if you get my drift.

'In the same way that a heroine might not always be in the mood. If your characters frequently have sex and every occasion is a mind blowing experience, then consider how realistic it is and whether it's in danger of becoming too predictable. Whatever you do, don't divorce the emotion from the sexual gratification. Unless that's the point of writing the scene.'

Kris leans forward a little to speak. 'Do you always get it right first time, Brie?'

'Good question, Kris. And the answer is, unfortunately, no. A good editor is your best friend and saviour. When they do the first round of edits on your manuscript, known as the structural edits, any weaknesses in the storyline will be picked up. I've had sex scenes taken out and notes in the margin to say, "after a row like that they need to have make up sex", so it varies.'

I'm surprised when Arran joins in.

'Brie is currently helping me out with the editing of a few sex scenes in my latest manuscript. I thought I'd done a pretty good job, but my editor threw up her hands in despair. Because of the harrowing nature of the story, which is set during the Second World War, the characters are separated for long periods of time. For the few scenes where they are together it has to have impact. Her instruction to me was to ramp up the emotional tension. So, I called in the expert.'

He grins across at me.

As our eyes meet my stomach does a little flip. It throws me, and I feel flustered for a moment. I turn away, grabbing some sheets of paper and passing them around.

'Right, if we're all happy to leave it there, it's time for the last exercise. I want you to write down phrases you might use to convey a particularly emotional state. The categories are: anger, happiness, despair and optimism. As an example, you might say "he lashed out" when describing someone who is angry. But you could also say "his knuckles whitened as he grasped the chair tighter". We're going to explore ways of widening the vocabulary we use to give those phrases more impact. Let's say twenty minutes for this exercise in case anyone wants to stretch their legs first and then we'll reconvene for the final part of the session.'

A few already have their heads down and are writing, but Rick disappears inside the villa. Arran walks over to me.

'I'm going to get some more cold drinks for the table, want to give me a hand?'

'Sure.'

As we saunter along, side by side, I glance at him.

'That acknowledgement wasn't necessary, you know. You would have returned the favour if it was the other way around.'

He grins back at me. 'I think it's a good lesson to demonstrate. No matter what stage we are at with our respective careers there's always something to learn; some boundary to push to make our writing even better. We owe the reader that, at the very least.'

He's right and I wonder why I ever thought he was standoffish. It just goes to show the pitfalls of prejudging people. But then he is more relaxed with me today and his deep blue eyes reflect his lighter mood. The eye contact between us is easy and a little more compelling than it should be. I realise that it must be extremely difficult to let go of the worry over his financial situation, but he's good at hiding it. And I'm glad that he appears to be enjoying himself this morning.

We fill our arms with cans and bottles then head back out to the terrace. Suddenly the phone in my pocket pings. I put the drinks on the tray and retrieve it to see a string of texts from Mel. I switch it off, unable to hide a small smile creeping over my face.

'Everything alright?' Arran turns to ask in a low voice as he hands out drinks now everyone is back at the table.

'Fine. I hope I managed to deliver this morning. How do you think it's gone down?' I whisper back at him.

'Good. Interesting. I've enjoyed it and you've made me think about a few things. The sex isn't gratuitous in my story, is it?' I can see real self-doubt reflected in his eyes and that surprises me.

'No, it wouldn't have the same impact if it wasn't in there. It's merely a case of using the right words, in the right order – that's all.'

He begins laughing.

'I use a similar phrase when I'm in teaching mode.'

I hitch up one side of my mouth in a sympathetic half smile. I notice Kris, who has suddenly appeared at my side, is listening to our conversation as she waits to lean across and grab a drink.

I think this is something the whole group might be interested in hearing, as I can see the others tuning in.

'Arran and I are talking about the editing process with regard to his latest manuscript. The point of structural edits is to check for inconsistencies in the plot, timeline and characterisation. After that, line edits polish it so it's the best it can be. I know the feeling when my editor pulls something apart and I don't immediately see her point. Once it's re-worked the improvement is usually plain to see. It's very important to realise that this is a natural part of the process and your editor is rooting for you.

'Occasionally, though, I stand back and, if it's merely a difference of opinion, if I feel strongly enough about a particular word, phrase, or scene, then I stand my ground. I'd say that 98 per cent of the time I go along with the suggestions put forward though, because I know they are valid improvements. As a writer you benefit from the expertise of a good editor, but you must be careful not to let your ego get in the way.'

For the first time I see a frown on Kris's face.

'I'm dreading the editing stage and it's imminent. What if there are a lot of changes to be made? How long does it take?'

Everyone is now seated, and all eyes are on me.

'That varies. If there's a fundamental flaw in the plot, for instance, it can have quite an impact throughout the entire story. That's tough and it happens. You simply work through the manuscript methodically. Usually it's more localised and it's just a case of re-wording if something doesn't flow and it feels clunky, or awkward. Yvonne, is there anything you can add from your experiences? You're on your second contract now so you've been through the process a few times.'

She looks pleased I've called upon her to contribute.

'It was a shock at first as I assumed the fact that they'd read my manuscript and then offered me a contract meant it was perfect,' she exclaims. 'I was very proud of what I'd written and floored when I saw the extent of the changes. But one's writing develops over time and with experience; even I would pick holes in it if I were to read that original draft again. I'm learning all the time and using that to improve my writing going forward. The first time around what made it more difficult was that the timeline for my plot had become a little confused. When the structural edits raised that issue it took me the best part of a week to sort out the consequences. That was a huge lesson to learn. I haven't made that particular mistake again since.'

I'm not sure that has reassured Kris, but hearing about first hand experiences is invaluable to a new writer.

'Line edits will address formatting issues, punctuation, grammar and typos. Missing words, too, can be a problem as your brain will often fill in the gap for you, so the eye doesn't always pick it up. Especially when you become overly familiar with the text because you are constantly re-reading it.'

Will joins in.

'I have two self-published books and I can vouch for the benefits of working with an editor. I edited and proofed my first book myself. That was a big mistake and one of my first reviews actually listed some of the errors

I'd missed. By then I was just about to launch my second book, so I delayed it. I commissioned an editor to work on both manuscripts and now I'm reasonably happy with the results. I do find it daunting though, now I'm about to start submitting to publishers. How perfect does my manuscript need to be?'

I look across at Arran as this is a part of his next session.

'We'll be covering the editing process in more detail tomorrow morning and pitching on Thursday morning. The answer is that when you're submitting, it needs to be as good as you can make it. Be honest with yourself and if you need to employ someone to go through it to give it a polish, then it might improve your chance of snaring that contract.

'It's a fiercely competitive market whether you are self-published or traditionally published. Having a publisher has advantages. Not least because their experience and expertise will go into choosing the title and the cover, aside from providing the editing services and some level of marketing support. That will vary according to the size of the publisher and the popularity of the book. However, a lot of authors who are doing it themselves are making a good living and enjoy having total control. Can I ask why you chose to self-publish in the beginning, Will?'

He takes a moment to consider his answer.

'This might sound a little naïve. I'd written eighty-five thousand words and I was rather pleased with myself. A friend read it and said it was a good story. I didn't know any other writers and I Googled how to publish a book. I did look at a few publishers' websites, but it scared me off, to be honest with you. I had no writing history, I wasn't on Facebook or Twitter and still don't have a website. I figured they'd be unlikely to take my submission seriously.'

It's an honest response and Arran gives him an affirming nod.

'Fully understandable, Will. Thank you for sharing that with the group. Do you mind if I ask what your sales were like at the beginning? You don't have to give numbers, just whether it met your expectations or not.'

He bursts out laughing. 'Well, I'm only on Amazon, right now. My mother and my sister-in-law each bought a copy on launch day. I did, too. After that I think it took about six months to sell the next five copies. I've sold a total of 115 copies to date and have three reviews on the first book and five on the second. They're all five stars. Only one is written by a friend and it was an honest review.'

There's a lot of nodding going on and you can feel the support from the entire group. That's good because it means no one has unrealistic expectations.

'Actually, you've done well, Will, because without a strong author platform it's very difficult for readers to even know your books are there. So, I'm impressed. But there are things you can do to get the word out and we will focus on that in Friday's session,' Arran confirms.

We end up running over by half an hour, but everyone seems content. The workshops are tiring because it's a lot to take in and naturally there's going to be a wide range of interesting questions. But we're heading out to see the town very shortly and I think we'll all be glad of a change of scenery.

18

No Turning Back

The minibus arrives and it's only a short drive down the hill to the lovely lakeside town of Salò. As we drive through the heart of this charming hub of activity, it seems to be full of boutiques, wonderful restaurants and elegant bars packed with tourists. The driver pulls into a lay-by and Arran stands to address everyone.

'Okay guys, please grab one of these packs before you alight. We'll meet back at this spot at six o'clock. There's a map in here of the suggested tourist trail.' Arran holds up one of the small folders. 'If you follow the route it will take in most of the main sights. Well worth a visit are the cathedral, the building housing the famous town clock, and the square, home of the winged lion of San Marco. If you get adventurous and take the ferry to explore one of the other towns around the lake, then my mobile number is in the folder. Let me know if you are going to be late back and I can book a taxi to collect you from this point.

'If everyone is happy, I'll say *arrivederci* and enjoy!'

There is a chorus of '*grazie*' and it's interesting watching everyone split into twos as they all head off in the same direction.

'Any surprises there, do you think?' Arran asks, as I follow his gaze.

'Not really. Silvia and Yvonne clicked immediately. Kris and Tom might look an odd couple, but humour is the key there. As for Rick and Will, well, I think the conversation might be a little one sided at times. Will is rather laid back, whereas Rick's enthusiasm can be a little overwhelming at times.'

'You nailed it. I'm not unhappy with the way the group have come together though. It's not easy getting the right mix. Anyway, that just leaves us. I hope that isn't too daunting a prospect for you.'

I laugh. 'I'm in your hands. I'll be doing this four times over, so lead on. I guess we can take our time.'

Arran steers us through some pretty little back streets which are mainly residential, but it isn't long until we're at the water's edge. Surveying the curve around the lake and the wonderful, paved promenade abutting the shops and restaurants, it makes me catch my breath. Above us, the creamy stonework of the three storey buildings rise up in the shadow of the mountains beyond. Along the whole sweep of the lakeside walk, the wonderfully contrasting terracotta roofs, the pretty window shutters, and lines of colourful little row boats, are picturesque. I stop to take a few photos with my phone.

'This is stunning, Arran. I see what you mean about the head of the lake being axe shaped. It's vast, but on the other hand there's a real sense of the personality of the town and the thriving community as we walk along. I thought it would be more touristy and I'm relieved that isn't the case. I love the buzz.'

I watch as two cyclists pass by and then glance at the many wonderful lanterns, which must be glorious at night to dispel the shadows. There are sail boats further out on the lake and I strain my eyes to look way into the distance.

'Are you hungry?'

I shake my head. 'No, but I'd love a cold drink.'

'Follow me, then.'

We wander along to one of the small cafés until we find a table for two in the shade.

'I think this should do the trick,' Arran says, pulling out a chair for me.

The waiter appears and Arran orders for us as I take in the surroundings. There is low level chatter going on around us and a steady stream of people walking past. Cycling appears to be a rather popular pursuit. It's all very charming and lends a relaxing atmosphere to the beautiful setting.

A line of plant pots to my right send out a floral bouquet of perfumed notes. There's lavender, a very strong smelling bay which has been neatly clipped into a cone shape and a red geranium adding a bittersweet scent into the mix.

'My grandparents loved this part of Italy. It was second only to Scotland in their hearts.'

For a man who was given very mixed signals about love at an early age, the preciousness of what his grandparents had wasn't lost on him.

'You mentioned selling the house in Surrey. Do you have a place to stay in the UK now? I suppose your TV work is mainly London based.'

The waiter returns with two San Pellegrino Limonata, a sparkling lemon drink. He half fills the tumblers, leaving the bottles in the centre of our small bistro table.

'*Grazie.*' Arran gives him a nod.

'*Prego.*'

I watch, entranced, as the guy makes his way back to the bar inside. There's something about Italian men and the self-assured way that they walk. I realise Arran has that trait and maybe he learnt it here, on his summer vacations. Head held high, shoulders back and a lightness of foot that reminds me of dancing, of all things. Yes, purposeful but stylish and with a sense of enthusiasm. Goodness, you can tell I'm a writer.

'No, I don't have anywhere at the moment. It's going to be a problem, but I can't think about that just now. Thankfully there are studios all around the country, which is just as well as London is so expensive.'

'Well, if you are ever stuck and in need of a bed within striking distance of the Forest of Dean, I have a guest room that's seldom used.' He really is in an awkward position and I feel for him.

'Thanks, I might just take you up on that offer.'

He's embarrassed now, and I feel awkward. I think he mistakes my silence for reflection.

'Thinking about this morning? The first session is always the worst. One down, three to go.'

'No, it's fine. I just wanted to explain something. I've recently lost quite a bit of weight and I'm careful what I eat now. That's why I often pace around when I'm proof checking or reading.' I raise my wrist, jiggling my Vivofit bracelet.

'Oh, I thought that was a watch.'

'No, it counts my steps and while I'm away from home I'm upping my daily target to compensate for not doing any cardio.'

He stares at me, frowning. 'You're not overweight, Brie. Don't for goodness' sake end up like Harriet. I swear she's borderline anorexic and it won't take much to tip her over the edge. She looks at herself and thinks she's fat but she's unhealthily thin, given that she's quite tall. Why do women do that to themselves?'

Do I talk about the haters and the trolls?

I let my eyes settle on Arran's face. He's really concerned but all I can think about is the fact that he's very kissable. There's a loud ping and at first, I think it's my phone, so I drag it out, but Arran is already staring down at his mobile.

Clearly, it's a text because he scrolls down. And it's a long one. I watch his face and he's oblivious to the fact that I'm taking in every little detail. At one point he stops for a brief moment, his eyes flickering shut before opening again as he reads on. His head slouches a little as he turns it off, slipping it back into his shirt pocket.

I can see by the look on his face it's bad news. When he turns to face me, his expression is grim.

'Would it help to share?'

He takes a long, slow gulp of his drink before setting it back down.

'I'm running out of time. Harriet's solicitor has spelt out her terms if I can't make the next payment on time. Even assuming Carrie can get me an advance quickly, it's unlikely to be enough. In addition I have the running costs of the villa to cover and my next TV project doesn't even start recording until August. There's only one option left open to me. I have to go to my father and see if he'll help me out.'

Judging by the look on Arran's face it's a last resort he hoped he'd never have to contemplate. From the little he's said about his father I can tell that this hurts him, deeply. He looks disappointed in himself but it isn't his fault at all.

'Please don't take this the wrong way, Arran, but I have a little money put aside. It's sitting in the bank doing nothing and earning very little. Money has never meant very much to me and I know it would be safe with you. This situation you're in is an impossible one and I'd like to help if I can.'

Arran looks across at me and he clears his throat, visibly upset and pulling himself together before he speaks.

'It's incredibly kind of you, Brie, and please don't think I'm not very appreciative. But if I don't make this next payment she wants the lot, in one go – that's over half a million pounds. She's well within her rights to demand that. If only the darned villa wasn't worth so much. The only real option is to ask my father to buy a share in it to avoid it being sold off. But it has to be enough to pay Harriet every last penny the court says she's due, or I might as well give up the fight now.'

Arran is virtually crumbling in front of my eyes. He thinks she's won because his father can't be relied upon to do the right thing. How sad is that?

'Pathetic, isn't it?' He leans forward, resting his hands on his knees, his head bent over for a brief second before he raises it to look across at me. 'I'm a bit like you, Brie. Money isn't everything to me, but I guess it's a lot more important than I thought it was. My grandfather left the rest of his estate to my father; it was mostly cash and shares but more than enough to bail me out if he wants to. But it was the villa my father wanted, and he felt cheated. If I have to beg him to help me save it then that's what I must do.'

The colour has drained from his face and I think the shock is beginning to hit him hard.

'Look, let's go back to the villa. You need to get your head around the next step so you can get this sorted.'

He looks at me with sad eyes. 'I don't want to spoil—'

'You're spoiling nothing. I have work to do, remember? I can see the town next week, or the week after. It's not the end of the world. Come on.' I stand and offer him my hand. He takes it, hardly applying any pressure as he stands, but drawing comfort from the contact.

Arran pulls a handful of coins out of his pocket, placing them on the table. He waves to the waiter, then we head towards the door. The journey back to the villa in a taxi takes place in total silence after Arran sends a quick text to update everyone. I can't help but feel emotional on his behalf as I can see that this has rocked his world.

★

We head off to our respective rooms with hardly a word. Divorce law is an unknown to me. However, I find it mind boggling that both parties aren't expected to work to support themselves if they split up. Obviously joint assets should be shared, regardless of who worked and who didn't. Behind every successful man, or woman, as the saying goes. But having a share of pre-existing assets? And the court expecting one of the parties involved to maintain the standard of living for the other person *after* the divorce? That's insanity unless there are children involved, which is an entirely different matter.

After a few minutes I'm getting angry; throwing myself into the manuscript is the only way to stop my mind from whirling.

I keep a careful watch on the time, and when it gets to just after five, I stop, have a shower and change. The minibus will no doubt be heading back to town to collect the group and I have no idea whether Arran will reappear tonight. I fleetingly wonder if the driver has been informed he's picking up only six people now, but there's nothing I can do about that.

Wandering downstairs, it's quiet and I have no idea where Arran is right now, or even if he's in the house. Then I remember the library and I make my way outside, crossing the garden and keeping out of sight as best I can. I approach the building rather cautiously. Some of the louvres are tilted, so I know he's in there. Quietly, I head back to the house.

By the time the minibus returns it's a quarter to seven and people head straight off to their rooms. Arran's absence isn't noticeable, thankfully. Tonight, everyone has ticked the list to eat at La Pergola again and after that the plan is to laze around the pool. I ring the restaurant to book a table for six, saying that Arran is tied up on an important phone call and I have that manuscript to work on. No one seems too bothered as they've obviously had a good day and I think tonight might be a late one. There's a bit of a party mood going on, which is a great diversion. It's a relief in one way, although I'm not sure how Arran will feel about it if the noise level rises later tonight. As soon as they all leave, I head back across to the library.

Peering inside, Arran is sitting in one of the winged armchairs. I think he's reading a book. I turn the door handle, gently inching it open, and step inside. He immediately looks up.

'Sorry. What time is it?' As he says the words he checks his watch and jumps to his feet, sending the book crashing to the floor. 'Is everyone back?' He sounds appalled.

I bend to pick up what I can now see is a photograph album. A few photos have fallen out and I pick them and the album up, handing the pile to him.

'Yes. Don't worry. I booked the table, and everyone has gone off for a relaxing meal. I wondered if you wanted anything to eat? And to warn you that I think there might be a bit of a party going on tonight around the pool.'

He looks a little dazed.

'I see you put the lights on, thank you. Sorry, I sort of went into a bit of a freefall there for a while. I needed to reminisce. I'm not hungry right now, maybe later.'

'You haven't made the call yet?'

I can see by his face the answer is no. He doesn't respond but places the album on one of the shelves. Following him to the door, I wait while he shuts the blinds and then I close the door behind me, stepping out into the garden.

Feeling helpless to offer any sort of meaningful consolation, I say nothing. Once inside the villa, I follow Arran up the stairs and he disappears into his bedroom without a backwards glance. Hurrying onwards to my room, I go straight out onto the balcony. Sitting quietly, I avoid touching the laptop for fear of making a noise and alerting him to the fact that I'm here.

In truth I can't really hear anything other than a low murmur and he's probably sitting on the bed as he talks on the phone. Suddenly I hear an almighty crash and I run back into my room, fling open the door and hurtle down the stairs. When I throw open the door to Arran's room he's standing there with blood running down his arm.

'What on earth?' I stare at him in horror for one split second before hurrying into the bathroom to soak a towel in water.

When I return, he's slumped on the edge of the bed shaking his head and cradling his hand against his chest. Very gently, I ease his arm away from his body and he slowly uncurls his clenched fist. Glancing at the wall, there's a blood splattered mark and it's clear that his knuckles bore the brunt of his anger.

'My father won't help me. That man has no conscience whatsoever, just bitterness.' He spits the words out vehemently. It doesn't scare me, because he isn't angry and isn't resisting my attempt to clean up his hand. In fact, he's watching every move I make.

'Thank you, Brie. I'm sorry you're witnessing this mess I'm in. It's not fair on you and this wasn't what you signed up for.'

I shush him and continue wiping away the worst of the blood. The grazes are bad, and it takes a while for the bleeding to ease off. Gradually, I peel the cold compress away and it's obvious it's going to need bandaging.

As I look up, Arran's eyes meet mine. 'That was a stupid thing to do, wasn't it?' he admits. 'The medical kit is downstairs in the utility room. Do you mind sorting me out?'

'You stay there, I won't be a minute.'

I walk downstairs, trying to calm my wildly beating heart and return my breathing to normal. As far as I can tell he hasn't broken anything. I've moved each of his fingers without making him aware of my concerns. I can't imagine the amount of anger inside him to do something like that, knowing how much pain it would inflict.

Foraging around for the kit, I'm pleased to find that it's well stocked and I return to Arran's room, climbing the stairs two at a time. To my surprise he's on the phone, so I hover in the doorway until he's finished.

'… it's wrong to lose this place and he knows that. Thanks for the offer and I'll think about it. I'm not sure a quick fix is going to help but I appreciate that you're going against him. I know that won't sit well with you. I'm sorry it came to this. I'll ring you tomorrow and I hope he calms down.'

Arran stands, placing his phone on the side table before turning to face me.

'That, surprisingly enough, was my mother. Seems my father and I both needed to vent, only he didn't hit a wall. He just threw a chair across the room, but it smashed a window.'

He sits back down on the edge of the bed and I kneel in front of him, unwrapping his hand gently from the towel. After using an antiseptic wipe, applying some cream and then bandaging his hand, he looks at me guiltily.

What I see is such a well of emotion that I half stand to sit beside him on the bed. Suddenly, without any prior thought at all, I find myself throwing my arms around his shoulders and hugging him to me. His breath is warm on my neck and before I know it we're falling back onto the crisp cotton bedding and his lips are on mine.

My body feels like a firework has exploded inside me and there isn't a part of me that isn't tingling with expectation and anticipation. I pull at his shirt, while he eases the straps of my dress down over my shoulders and we adjust our position, frantically tugging to free ourselves of our clothes.

When our eyes meet, Arran's face is full of longing and something deep inside me begins to melt. I want to feel his body on mine and I don't care whether this is a good idea or not.

Arran pulls away, yanking off his trousers and boxer shorts, while I begin to slip my dress off and then I freeze. Looking down at my stomach it's still like a mound. A mound which wobbles like a jelly.

'What's wrong?' Arran asks, concerned. 'Is this a bad idea?'

I nod, then shake my head and he looks at me, confused.

'I'm not in the best shape at the moment,' I admit, lamely.

'Oh. That's not a problem. I understand.' He turns away, preparing to get up but I place my hand on his shoulder.

'Sorry. Just a little paranoia. I've been through a tough time lately, but that's a long story. My body shape is what it is and I'm just being pathetic.'

He rolls back in towards me, and I laugh as he playfully teases my lacy pants down over my hips one-handedly. Then he helps ease my dress up over my head. He runs his good hand over my stomach as if it's flat.

'You're beautiful, Brie, and that's a fact. Are you really sure about this? I don't want you to feel uncomfortable,' he asks, his voice husky and rather breathless.

'I'm sure,' I whisper as his mouth closes on mine.

He rather gingerly continues to explore and suddenly I don't care about the jiggly bits because he seems totally oblivious to them. As his arms wrap around me, I'm otherwise engaged and I'm having my David Gandy moment. Arran's body is firm beneath my touch and he smells so good.

I groan, unable to stop myself and he mutters, 'I hope that's a positive noise,' which makes me giggle.

It isn't long before words aren't necessary because already my legs are entwined around him, guiding him into me, and the ecstasy begins. But nothing that has ever gone before could have prepared me for the level and depth of passion this man has in his soul. And the tenderness, after such a shockingly violent display of temper, is a real surprise.

19

It's Time to Party

We lie in each other's arms, allowing our bodies to calm down from that gloriously heightened state of sexual bliss. Nothing makes you feel more alive, but something was very different for me this time. Before, I've always been left with a transient doubt, not quite a regret but a sense of having given something and hoping I won't regret it later. I have absolutely no regrets about having done the deed with Arran. And by the look of it, he has no regrets either.

'That was rather cavalier of me,' he admits. It's obvious we're both thinking roughly the same thing.

'You can lay the blame at my door.' I tilt my head up to look at him, so he can see I'm fine with it.

'I didn't think about—'

'I have an implant in my arm. Not that it comes in handy very often, I hasten to add.'

'Even with the famous Paul Turner?' He's trying to make a joke of it but I can see it's bothering him.

'I'm really not the sort of woman who usually acts on impulse. That's why Paul Turner and I split up. I didn't fancy adding my name to his list of conquests when it was clear he wasn't looking for a long term relationship. What he wants is an A-list celebrity dangling off his arm, preferably one who photographs well from every conceivable angle. And that wasn't... dammit!'

'What?'

'Carrie sent me the draft of a magazine interview where Paul's name came up. I meant to read it as I felt a little uncomfortable when the topic reared its ugly head. It'll be too late now to change anything. Well, Carrie wasn't upset by it so maybe I'm worrying over nothing.'

Arran gives me a gentle squeeze.

'It's not easy, is it? Publicity might sell books but it's intrusive. It curtails freedom and you never know when something is going to be blown up out of all proportion. I've ended up commanding your full attention, haven't I? You are such a surprising woman, Brie. I wasn't expecting you to be so interesting and genuine.'

His eyes are sparkling as he looks at me in a way I haven't seen on a man's face, ever. At least on a face that was peering back at me after having had sex.

'And I thought you were going to be intellectual and dismissive. Do you think Carrie knew what she was doing when she put us together?'

What am I doing? That's such a telling remark but it's with a sense of great relief that I can see he isn't fazed by it.

'I believe so. We're an unlikely pair, aren't we? And I hate to admit it, but I did inwardly groan when she put your name forward. I mean, I'm not undervaluing your work or anything, as you sell more books than I do. But I didn't think we'd have anything much in common aside from the basics of the publishing industry. Shows how wrong a person can be.'

I snuggle in closer to him, enthralled by the feeling of skin on skin. It's both comforting and thrilling at the same time. For the first time ever, I feel safe because I trust him implicitly. Uh-oh. Alarm bells start ringing. Isn't this exactly what I've just warned Mel about doing? That first rush when your mind is clouded by the chemical and hormonal effects of lust on your body?

'I need to shower and get dressed. I think one of us should be downstairs, ready for when the group arrive back.'

Reluctantly, I raise myself up on my elbows, preparing to jump out of bed. Arran places his hand very gently on my thigh and I gaze down at him.

'Do you want some company?' he enquires.

My head says no, enough, but my body is crying out for more. Dare I brazenly expose my entire body? It's one thing being naked lying down, another to walk around as if I don't care what I look like, because I do.

'Is this just sex, or is this something a little more?' It sounds blunt when I say it like that, but it's an honest enough question.

Suddenly Arran is sitting up next to me and he pulls me into his arms.

'I don't know what this is because it's a first for me. You seem to have gotten under my skin, lady. I'm not even sure

I'm comfortable with that. It sort of feels like I'm not in control any more. Maybe you've bewitched me.'

He drops his mouth down onto my shoulder, his lips soft against my skin.

'Okay. Seems like we have a bit of a *thing* going on here. And yes, I'd love some company. One of my favourite scenes to write takes place in the shower.'

Arran begins laughing. 'I hope I don't disappoint.'

Something in the pit of my stomach tells me he won't. And I'm beyond caring what I look like because Arran seems just fine with it.

We manage to head back downstairs a few minutes before we hear voices as the group follow the path down from the rear gate. There's a lot of laughing and high spirited banter going on. Arran takes hold of my hand for one brief moment, pulling me into him. His freshly bandaged hand lies at his side, bruised and no doubt quite painful.

'It's going to be tough keeping up a professional appearance around you, Brie. If I get it wrong, just let me know.'

I place my other hand against his chest, feeling the pounding of his heart and knowing mine is doing the exact same thing.

'We can do this, Arran.'

He kisses the tip of my nose before reluctantly pulling away. 'What do we say about my hand?'

I shrug, casting around for something that doesn't sound too lame.

'Why don't you say you slipped getting out of the pool and advise everyone to be careful. It's believable.'

He nods and suddenly everyone is piling in.

'How was the meal?' Arran asks, becoming the perfect host once more.

'Wonderful,' Silvia confirms, glancing quickly between the two of us. 'Oh, Arran, that looks bad. Whatever happened to your hand?'

My mouth goes dry under everyone's gaze.

'I slipped on the terrace after getting out of the pool. Stupid of me but it could have been worse. At least nothing's broken and it's just a graze, so people beware. Anyway, enough of my clumsiness. Anyone in the mood for dancing? Maybe we should push the tables to one side, set up a mini-bar and I'll get the music going.'

Faces instantly light up. It's not long before everyone, except Rick, is up and throwing themselves around to the strains of an Italian song I doubt any of us have ever heard before. After a couple of dances Arran catches my eye and nods, indicating in the direction of the library. He saunters off and I wait a couple of minutes before following him.

As soon as I pass through the line of trees and step out onto the grassy area in front of the library, he's there in front of me. We literally fall into each other's arms and he kisses me until I have to pull away to catch my breath.

'Do you think anyone has noticed anything different between us?'

'Only Silvia and she's a rather discreet lady by nature, I think,' Arran admits.

I shrug, and he slips his arms down around my waist, wincing a little as his bruised hand makes contact. I relax against him, thinking how wonderful it is to be in the arms of a man again. But not just any man. Arran is different.

'A party atmosphere must have been the last thing you needed tonight,' I whisper, looking up at him.

'Maybe it was exactly what I needed. Well, second only to that little surprise earlier on which served to raise my spirits no end!'

We laugh, conspiratorially.

'I've sort of put my problems to one side for tonight. It's not something I can easily solve. I need to face up to the fact that maybe there is no solution and I'm wasting my energy fighting the inevitable. My mother rang, that was the phone call when you returned to the room. She has money of her own and has offered to lend me the next payment to give me thinking time.'

Arran seems impressed by that but I'm not. Making him a gift of the money would have been a real demonstration of her support for him. What use is money sitting in the bank when you have everything you need, anyway? I know my mum and dad would give me their last penny without a second thought if I needed it.

'Will you take it?'

He loosens his grip and I tilt back a little, so I can see his face more clearly in the half light.

'I don't know. She said she would talk to my father when he calms down. I've never known them to have opposing opinions on something before. My mother isn't an emotional woman and if she thinks he'll regret his decision if I end up losing the villa, then that's quite a telling thing.'

I stare into his eyes, letting him see my concern. 'I meant what I said. I have a little over sixty thousand pounds in the bank if that helps.'

He tips his head back to let out a sigh that seems to come from deep down inside him.

'I don't deserve your kindness, Brie. But I got myself into this mess and I don't want to drain the resources of those around me who are kind enough to offer help. It wouldn't be right, and my conscience won't allow that. If it all went wrong, then you'd have to wait until I sold the villa to get your money back. That wouldn't be fair; this is my problem, not yours, or my mother's, for that matter.'

I huddle in close to him. If he won't take money, then all that I have to give him is myself as comfort and I know I can do that without reservation.

When we head back to mingle, everyone is tiring and the seats on the terrace quickly fill up. I bid them all goodnight, as Arran kicks off a conversation about place settings for a story. He's too wired to sleep and as the perfect host he wants to give his guests every opportunity to exchange views and share their experiences.

He catches my eye as I turn, and I close my eyes briefly, sending him a silent hug goodnight before I hurry up to my room.

Undressing in the dark, the cool silky slip feels decadent against my skin. Before I can jump into bed there's one thing I must do, and I sit down in front of the laptop to scan my emails. There's only one of interest and that's the one Carrie sent with the attachment from Heidi Hoffman.

Even before I click to open the document I have an uneasy feeling. It begins well. Then I groan out loud.

Commenting on the aftermath of her very public split from Paul Turner, Brie said she felt the need to reinvent herself. Sporting a vampish new hairstyle and fresh from the spa, she was glowing, but confirmed there is no new romantic interest in her life right now.

We touched on the subject of social media and the very real dangers of fat-shaming, in light of her recent experiences. Brie was very concerned about the resulting mental anguish and psychological damage that could result from bullying of this nature.

However, she was emphatic that her dramatic weight loss is part of a general move towards a healthier lifestyle. It is not as a result of having sunk into a depressive state of mind following those very personal attacks, or the break-up of her relationship.

Having recently had the pleasure of interviewing self-confessed bad boy of rock, Paul, it seems his reaction was a little different.

'Life's too short to get serious too soon. Case of the cover not reflecting the contents,' he told me, rather drolly, making a parallel reference to Brie's hot and sexy series. However, Brie confirms her body clock is not ticking and explained away her continuing low profile existence as solely down to pressures of work. For more news on that front, look out for a Brianna Middleton exclusive coming very soon to Cosy Living!

And now for the competition. Haven't read Brie's latest book? We have ten signed copies of Loving a Stranger to give away. Plus, one lucky winner will receive a voucher for a spa weekend for two. To enter, share the story of your love blues and what you did to pick yourself back up after hitting rock bottom!

What the hell? I grab my phone and my fingers click on Carrie's number the instant I read the last word.

'Hi, Brie. It's late for you to ring. I'm relaxing with a glass of wine. It's been a tough day. What's up?' I can hear the exhaustion in her voice.

'Well, I'm about to add to it. I've just read Heidi's article. She's twisted the entire thing about Paul. She has to change it, it can't go out like that!'

I'm aware that my voice sounds panic-stricken.

'Calm down. I read it through and thought it sounded okay. Your fans will love the snippet of gossip and she's clever. I'm sure they'll have both your and Paul's names on the front cover somewhere and online. Two big names, twice the hits.'

'But it makes me sound pathetic. Like I've spent the last year pining over him! He wasn't worthy of one date, let alone several weeks of my life!'

'You're taking this too personally. Readers will be combing your new book and wondering if the bad boy in the story is Paul, and you are simply using it as a vehicle to dish the dirt. Fans really want to know what went on and not simply what the papers were reporting. Boyfriend bashing sells, Brie. So does the name Paul Turner, because he's made a fortune out of his bad boy image. But we all know that's mostly hype to gain him attention; he simply has a good business head and knows how to play the game. You sort of knew that when you started going out with him. This surely can't come as a shock? And it isn't going to harm your reputation because it will sell books.'

I hold my hand to my head to stop the banging going on inside it.

'I don't subscribe to the *there is no such thing as bad press* theory, Carrie, because I don't want to set the trolls off again. I'm still getting hate reviews. And the competition adds insult to injury. Ethan Turner is the very opposite of Paul, because I write about heroes; not self-centred, egomaniacs out to make their fortune before they retire to a faraway place in the sun.'

There's a pause.

'Look, I'm sorry I didn't know you were going to be so upset about this, but I assumed you were okay with it. It's too late to get it amended now.'

I feel guilty as that is my fault for getting so caught up with everything else and forgetting to check it.

'Well, she's not getting the exclusive, then.'

I can hear Carrie spluttering.

'But, Brie... are you mad? The article is precisely why she has to have the exclusive on your next book.'

I'm treading a thin line here between what's right for my career and what's right for my personal life. Carrie obviously draws her line in a different place.

'She made it sound like I went to pieces because he ditched me over the fat-shaming frenzy, which isn't strictly true. In fact, I was the one who said I'd had enough because it was clear it wasn't going anywhere.'

Carrie clears her throat. 'You haven't been yourself for a while, Brie, and people have noticed that. Then you reappear looking very different. Things are almost back to normal, so why worry about it now? There's nothing you can do because you know it doesn't work that way. People will continue to think what they want, regardless.'

I don't believe she thinks my little episode was simply all about finishing with Paul!

'Well, I'm just going to have to show everyone that isn't the case in some other way then.'

'Fighting talk, I like it! Just make it newsworthy and it's a win-win situation. Sleep well, Brie. Everything passes with time, so don't let it get to you, but enjoy the spike in sales.'

I throw the phone down on the bed in disgust. Not so much with Carrie, because it isn't her fault, but Heidi knew what she was doing in twisting my words. Maybe she twisted what Paul said too.

In desperation, I grab my phone and text Arran.

How's it going?

He responds almost instantly.

They're beginning to wane, at last. You?

That raises a smile. He must be feeling shattered.

Rather humiliated. Just read that article. Pride comes before a fall and I've just face-planted.

Well, maybe more like having my legs swept out from under me.

Give me five minutes.

I swear it's less than two minutes before there's a gentle tap at the door and he's standing in front of me.

'I've left them tidying up. Do you mind?'

I watch avidly as he begins taking off his clothes. He watches me, watching him.

'Can I hop into your shower? I don't really relish the thought of walking down a flight of stairs naked.'

'Help yourself, it's your villa.' The moment I hear myself say the words I wish I could claw them back.

'Well, for the moment, anyway,' he mutters with an ironic smile, 'but thanks.'

He returns a few minutes later with a towel wrapped around his waist and looking meltingly hot. How is it that men walk out of a shower looking sexy and cute, whereas women tend to look like drowned rats with straggly hair?

'So, I assume you want me to read it and give you my opinion?' He stifles a yawn. 'Sorry, exhausting day and that balmy heat out there tonight doesn't help.'

I gasp at his words, and he begins laughing. 'It isn't often I have sex twice in one day with a woman who writes steamy romances. It's a lot of pressure.'

This time my eyebrows shoot up at his shameless references to our afternoon of love.

'It's not at all romantic for one's lover to talk about it. In fact, it's bad form!'

'My apologies. Today has been a rollercoaster ride of the worst kind, so I know you'll forgive me. And the last word anyone would use to describe me would be romantic. I don't believe in that sentimental stuff because I choose to live in the real world. Right, let me read this upsetting article.'

He digests every single word with a deep frown on his forehead. When he looks up, he stares at me, his expression hardly changing.

'Well, I think it makes him sound like a total idiot. Albeit a very talented one I used to respect for his undeniably brilliant guitar playing skills. But you were *fat-shamed*? What is that? You aren't *fat*.'

I glare at him. 'I will admit I was carrying a few extra pounds at the time. Most of our dates were events he had to attend and at first he enjoyed the fact that people recognised me. Even if that was by name, rather than by sight. Then some of his fans began targeting me with some very cruel comments on social media. At the same time a couple of awful photos of me went viral and the press loved it. They commended him on the fact that he wasn't concerned I wasn't exactly slim. "Generously proportioned thighs" and a "cuddly build" were two of the nicer terms used. Then his agent suggested I didn't accompany him on one of his red carpet events and I more or less told him exactly what I thought about that.

I was done with Paul's obsession with image and the way he made no attempt to defend me. So I went home having drawn a line under our non-starter relationship.

'The next morning he broke the news to the press, making it look like he'd dumped me.'

'Hmm... nice guy. Does it matter in the grand scheme of life? It will sell books and a lot of what is out there isn't true anyway. On a personal note, I'm relieved to hear he didn't sucker you into sleeping with him. That's probably why he wants to lash out; you could be his first failed conquest.'

I feel myself sag. That means Paul has an axe to grind.

'He can be charming and dazzling when he wants to be and he's actually a very intelligent guy. But it matters to me, Arran. Why do I have to be the butt of this? He's implying I'm boring. "The cover doesn't reflect the contents". That's a low blow and totally out of order after everything his fans put me through! He wasn't man enough to condemn their unacceptable behaviour.'

Arran is now sitting on the edge of the bed. His elbow is on his knee and his chin is lightly resting on his bad hand, which now bears a rather soggy looking bandage.

'Sorry, I'm sounding off and I know it. Here, let me ease that off and see how the wound is doing.'

I gently take his hand in mine and we exchange a meaningful smile.

'I could probably confirm that the cover does match the contents but sadly I haven't read any of your books. And I am ashamed to admit that.'

The look on his face makes mine feel even hotter than it already is, so I ignore his comment and focus on his hand.

'Well, the bleeding has stopped and it's scabbing up nicely. Maybe get some air to it and see how it looks in the morning.'

'Yes, nurse. How about diverting attention away from this article with something even bigger?'

I shake my head. 'I'm only halfway through the next book and it isn't due out until February. That's the breaking news Heidi refers to as my publishers are very keen to get some advance publicity, but it won't be until December at the earliest.'

His finger taps against his bottom lip.

'I'm thinking of something a little different. Imagine this headline. *What happens when Brie Middleton and Arran Jamieson get their heads together on a project – sparks fly!*'

I draw in a sharp breath.

'You wouldn't!'

'I would. For you.'

'But. But… we don't know what this is, exactly. I mean, what if it's a passing thing?'

His hand falls away from his chin and his back straightens.

'That's how you feel?' He sounds disappointed.

'No. No. This feels different, special. I wasn't sure how you felt.'

We stare at each other cagily.

'Damn it, I can't think past wanting you right now. But this is about more than that. I'm experiencing something new and I'm not even sure how to handle it, or what to say. I'm not messing with you, Brie. I just can't help myself.'

A hot flush is coursing through my body and I take a couple of deep breaths to stop myself from leaping across the bed.

'We need to keep our voices down a little,' I shush him, as I definitely heard a creak on the landing outside the door.

'I hate the thought of someone hurting you, so think about it. What harm can it do? It would certainly confuse the gossips out there.'

Walking around to him and lowering myself down onto the bed, our faces are merely inches away.

'I don't want to jinx this, whatever it is that's going on between us.'

He looks at me, one eyebrow raised. 'Well, you're the romance writer so I was rather hoping you'd explain it to me.'

There are no suitable words in my head, so instead I cover his mouth with mine. It lends a whole new meaning to writer's block. Maybe when it's all happening up close and personal it's not quite so easy to qualify.

As Arran lies back on the bed, pulling me on top of him, it could be a scene from one of my novels. This isn't what I'm looking for… is it? I want the romance and the whole feeling protected and adored thing, but the toe curling sex is such a temptation. I can't help myself either, so that makes two of us. But this isn't what I see when I dream of meeting the one I want to be with forever.

Okay Brie, so you simply step off the bed.

There's one problem with that simple solution. My mind doesn't seem to be connected to my body right now and the wires of communication must be a little mixed up. Instead I pull off my slip and pull Arran into me.

'Argh,' he groans deliciously. 'Do you know what you do to me? I could get used to having you around. You are making me crazy, lady! Ahh, can you do that again?'

I do it again. And again. And again. It seems when it comes to Arran I have no resolve whatsoever. He is my new guilty pleasure and I've turned into one of my lusty heroines.

20

The Charm of Verona

I wake just after 5 a.m., quietly sliding open the door to the balcony so as not to disturb Arran. If I work solidly through until noon, that will leave me an hour to get ready for the trip to Verona.

It's pleasant out here with a slight breeze distributing a waft of heady perfume that teases the nose. What I want is to saunter out and walk around the garden before anyone else is up but I'm a woman on a mission. If I can finish my work on this manuscript today, then maybe I can talk Arran into letting me take over tomorrow's workshop. He needs to focus on making those changes and getting it off to Carrie quickly, if there's going to be even a glimmer of hope of getting an advance in time to help him. Even if it's a staged payment, with a contract for more than one book, the trigger is upon receipt of a signed contract. But first Carrie will need something concrete in her hands to get that offer and prove Arran can satisfy a new audience of readers. It might help, if it isn't already too late by then.

The first hour or so is spent mainly reading, as Arthur manages to survive a particularly harrowing night. One of his fellow soldiers died in his arms and he cried, not just for the friend he had lost, but for them all, living or dead. I find myself having to wipe away my tears before the story moves on and becomes all about the lack of rations. Was there no end to the test life was throwing at them in their battle for survival? After a convoy of lorries are bombed, supplies run out and morale plummets in the inhospitable conditions.

'Hey, how long have you been out here?'

The tousled head that suddenly appears around the edge of the sliding door makes me laugh. Arran is naked, seemingly unconcerned that he's standing in front of a glass panel. I shake my head and try to keep my eyes firmly focused on his face.

'A little while and I don't want any interruptions.'

My eyes return to the screen.

'Oh. Okay. I understand. Room service will arrive shortly.'

Arran makes himself scarce and I'm too wrapped up in what I'm doing to take much notice. I don't know how much later it is when he reappears with a breakfast tray, placing it without fuss on the bistro table behind my laptop.

I'm typing and don't stop, so he leans in to kiss my cheek and then disappears.

A couple of hours pass and I'm conscious of noises coming from downstairs, but nothing really disturbs me. I stop for a quick shower and to throw on some shorts and a top, figuring that Elisabetta will be doing her rounds sometime this morning.

Grabbing a bottle of water from the bedside table, I return to my seat to tackle the final twenty per cent of the story. This isn't going to be easy reading.

'Right, Verona, here we come.' Arran slides the minibus door shut and turns to slip into the seat next to me.

The driver pulls away and Arran turns his head, leaning in and talking in a low voice, although with the level of general banter going on around us I doubt anyone could pick out his words, anyway.

'I could see you wanted to be left alone to concentrate this morning. It felt wrong, but I do appreciate you being so focused on my behalf.'

I can see his gratitude reflected in the look in his eyes. He's nervous and I realise it matters to him what I think, aside from the help I'm giving him.

'It's done. I sat and cried as Arthur arrived at the twelfth Casualty Clearing Station in Annezin, northern France. Was it really that bad?'

Arran nods his head. 'Yes. It was one of many front line medical units that were highly mobile. Each CCS would take in anything up to 250 casualties at peak battle times. On the day that Arthur was injured there were over a thousand men injured in just that one skirmish. A partial amputation had to be performed immediately he was brought in. Hard to believe these units were in tents and it wasn't until he was transferred to a Base Hospital, a few days later, that it became clear a further operation was required.'

Arran ended the story with Arthur boarding a ship at Dunkirk for the journey home.

'That was in late March of 1940, a month before Operation Dynamo began on the twenty-sixth of May. As we know, the Dunkirk evacuation of more than three hundred thousand Allied soldiers and the carnage that ensued will never be forgotten. In a way Arthur was lucky he was shot when he was – how ironic is that?'

'You do know that any publisher will expect a sequel, as you can't leave the story half told.'

Arran raises his eyebrows. 'I have the interviews and the photos. I'm just not sure I'm the right person to tell the rest of the story.'

I lean into him, maintaining eye contact. 'You are exactly the right person to tell the story. After all, you knew them both. Who better?'

He looks away, shrugging his shoulders. I reach out and touch his hand, figuring no one is really watching us.

'You did an amazing job. Really. It needed telling because it's the story of a brave man whose whole life changed because of his experiences, but it's also a wonderfully uplifting love story. I've simply tweaked it, that's all. And there's one chapter that I've roughed out that I really think needs to be inserted. I've given you the framework, but you understood Rose and I know you'll make it hers.'

'I don't know what to say, Brie, because "thanks" just doesn't seem to be enough.'

'If you let me take over the session tomorrow morning then you could spend the entire day on it. I can look after the group. Carrie can't do anything until she has the final version. It's in your hands now.'

Arran turns his head and rises out of his seat to address the group.

'I've just had my orders and I have manuscript duties tomorrow, guys. Brie will be taking the session on book blurb, synopsis and pitching to agents and publishers. I know you'll be in good hands.'

There's a cheer. 'See, they're fed up of me already,' he muses.

As he sits back down, Arran grins at me conspiratorially.

'So,' he says as he stretches his legs out as far as he can, given the confined space. 'You can get back to your own projects now.'

'Hmm. Well, I'm torn and trying to write two totally different stories at the same time.'

He looks at me, rather straight faced. 'You won't turn me into one of your characters, will you?'

I burst out laughing, settling back in the seat ready to enjoy the ride. Too late, the decision has already been made!

The journey takes about an hour and twenty minutes. The traffic flows smoothly and it's more or less a straight route on a very good road. It's rather relaxing to sit and watch the scenery whizzing past but I can't stop my thoughts from whirling. Arran is right and now it's time to turn my attention to my own work in progress. Friday afternoon I'm doing that all important telephone interview with Jordan Lewis. If I'm going to make the character of Jed Jackman leap off the page, then it means I need to understand the mindset of a real cage fighter. Research takes you to some strange places, that's for sure.

Several times on the journey Arran gives me a quizzical look. He's wondering why I'm so quiet, but I don't feel like joining in with the general back and forth banter going on. When my characters aren't battling for space in my head, the thoughts I can't seem to stifle all relate to Arran's situation. Not only is it none of my business, but there's nothing I can do to help him fix the problem. I simply can't believe he might end up losing the villa though. It's not right and it's not fair given the circumstances.

Arran's head is inches from mine as he leans in once more to whisper in my ear.

'We're nearly there. You've been deep in thought the whole time. I haven't said anything wrong, have I?'

'No, of course not. I needed some quiet time to brainstorm a few ideas. It won't be long before Carrie is asking me for an update on my word count, so I have to get my head around where the plot is going next.'

He shoots me a guilty look, but I give him a reassuring smile.

'What's the plan for this afternoon and evening?'

'A quiet saunter around the town and then we all meet up for a meal in the Piazza delle Erbe at seven thirty. I've had a word with the chef and he's going to make something special for you.' He grins at me. 'People usually split up and head off in different directions, depending on what they want to see. Verona's a history lover's dream but it's also a very beautiful city full of shops, markets and plenty of little places to stop for a coffee or a gelato.'

'Sounds perfect and thank you.' I'm not used to a man going out of his way to do something for me. It sends a satisfying little tingle running up my spine to know Arran cares.

As the driver negotiates his way into a narrow street he has no other option but to double park to allow us all to disembark. In doing so the street is suddenly filled with the sound of impatient car horns honking. I grimace as the noise seems to echo around us as we pile out onto the pavement.

'Ignore it. Italians like to express themselves. A few seconds and the road will be clear again.'

The minibus pulls away and after letting three cars pass we all follow Arran across the narrow road. It's only minutes until the world renowned Roman amphitheatre looms up, towering above the buildings on our left. As we turn a corner, suddenly the pavement widens out into a vast open area, mostly covered with intricate cobblestones laid in a shell like formation. I'm grateful to be wearing flat shoes as it would be a nightmare to walk on in heels.

Arran draws to a halt, and we cluster around him.

'If you can all grab one of these, the first sheet is a walking map around the town with the main tourist attractions highlighted. It's just coming up to two thirty, so you have five hours to wander around. Also highlighted is the main shopping area and marked with a big, red cross is the restaurant where I have booked a table for seven thirty at Bottega del Vino. It's literally two minutes from here and will mean it's only a short walk back afterwards to pick up the minibus. Alfredo will be waiting to take us back at a quarter to ten.'

Arran distributes the handout and surveys the group, who are already pairing off quite nicely. He seems content everyone is happy.

'Right, well, I'm going to show Brie around the area and impress her with my vast knowledge. But if you turn to the second page you'll find a potted version of that which I hope makes for interesting reading. See you all later. Any problems call me on the mobile.'

Arran looks at me, nodding his head in the direction of the towering building behind us. 'Step this way for the guided tour,' he says with a smile.

'Oh dear, is this going to be a history lesson?' I'm teasing, because I'm intrigued to see inside. From the outside, the two storey façade made up of enormous arches looks solid enough but there's no way to glimpse what lies beyond.

'Impressive, isn't it?' Arran's gaze flicks over my face, watching for my reaction.

'You can say that again. I know it looks solid but it's not complete and it sort of looks half finished.' Now I feel mean teasing him because I can't wait to see what's inside. I only hope I won't be disappointed.

'Ah, that's because what you are looking at is only the internal structure that holds everything up. The outer wall was made up of pink and white limestone; if you walk this way, a large portion of it remains standing.'

He leads me away from the incredible arched structure, which looks like some sort of crazy wedding cake waiting to be iced. But it's only the core of this monumental building. The scale is mind blowing and when we stare up at the only part of the original outer wall that remains standing, you get a real feel for the importance attached to this building.

It dominates the Piazza at this end and there must be well over a hundred people in small groups scattered around in front of it, all either gazing up in awe, or busy taking photos.

'There were three tiers of arches originally, but as you can see, only four of the arches on the third level have survived. But it's incredible, isn't it?'

I nod in agreement. 'Why has the interior remained in such a complete state, and yet the exterior has been decimated?'

'Several earthquakes, one of which destroyed most of the façade.'

We are inches apart, our heads tilted as we gaze up in awe.

'Come on, let's make our way inside.'

He takes my hand and then winces, slackening his grip a little.

'How is it today?' I ask, tentatively. 'You were lucky you didn't break anything, you do know that?'

'Yep, I know. It's just bruised. I want you to know that I'm not in the habit of lashing out.'

'I figured that out for myself, don't worry. It's hard not to vent when you are being pushed to the limit.'

We lapse into silence as we join the queue at the entrance. It moves forward slowly until, at last, we find ourselves entering a large passageway that skirts the entire building. Then we turn into one of the walkways leading us up to the core of the building. The pitted marble floor underfoot is flanked by cobbled strips and the vast walls seem to be made up mostly of a composite material.

'It's creepy in here. It feels claustrophobic, as if we're trapped. Like the air is closing in around us.' I'm conscious that sounds ridiculous as it's a tall corridor, one of many, like spokes in a wheel leading us into the actual arena area.

'The tunnels are wide enough to drive a gladiator's chariot through. For almost four hundred years they fought here, and this was home to the bloodthirsty carnage of the games. It's hard to believe it was entertainment, isn't it?'

As we climb a flight of stone steps and cross a platform which takes us up to yet another level, I try to imagine it packed with people: everyone pressing forward in earnest, eager to take their seats.

Even though up ahead I can clearly see an end to the gloom as we approach the exit, my arms are covered in goosebumps. Just thinking about the number of men who lost their lives here in such horrific and cruel conditions is making me feel slightly nauseous.

And then we re-emerge into a massive, sunlit, stone arena and the stifling, slightly oppressive atmosphere lightens. I wasn't expecting it to be so vast and it certainly exceeds my expectations. It's so complete and not merely in a state of ruin.

The beautiful blue sky above changes everything and that creepy, doom laden feeling leaves me.

'It's set up for opera season,' Arran confirms as we gaze down upon the large swathe of red seating that covers an extensive area of the arena in front of a lavish stage.

Scanning around the stone tiers circling the entire stadium, large banks of seating have been erected. It's broken only by the tunnel access points, which stand out as gaping, dark openings against the pale stone backdrop. We walk forward to step down between one of the original rows and it's quite a span.

'The four remaining arches of the fourth floor look remarkable from this angle, don't they? Originally this would have accommodated a capacity of around thirty thousand spectators.'

'Did they always fight to the death?'

'No. As with all sport there were favourites. The voice of the crowd could succeed in saving them on the day, even after a defeat. If the match was a good one, demonstrating great skill and bravery, then there was no shame in defeat. Although the high ranking magistrate *editor*, who sponsored the games, could choose not to endorse the popular opinion. But either way, the crowd would have been very vocal.'

Once more I feel that cold seeping into me, despite the fact this is now the home to lavish operatic productions. From the barbaric to the civilised... how time changes but the mark is still left upon it and, to me, it's tangible.

'Shall we move on?' Arran asks diplomatically, seeing that the experience has moved me, and I nod.

'I'm eager to see Juliet's balcony.'

He rolls his eyes. 'It's over rated in my opinion,' he bemoans.

'Oh, so the site of wanton bloodshed is a monument, but the inspiration for Shakespeare's heartrending *Romeo and Juliet* is hardly worth a glance?'

As we walk back towards the steps to make our way out, he begins laughing softly.

'I didn't say that, I simply think it's no big deal. This is an incredible testament to the Roman empire and history in general. Up against a mere balcony it's hardly a comparison.'

As we start the descent, walking side by side, I glance across at him.

'They were so young and it's a cruel end for lovers, thwarted by family rivalry.'

He at least manages to look chastised.

'Yes, sorry. Sad story, fittingly immortalised by Shakespeare, of course.'

He's trying to sound genuine for my sake but it's insincere. He managed not to roll his eyes for a second time, but I could tell it took a concerted effort not to do so. I reward him with a pleasant smile, thinking that I'll be glad once we're outside in the square again.

Crossing the Piazza there's a constant stream of people walking in both directions. We follow the wide, paved walkway flanked on one side by tall, rather elegant lamp posts and on the other by an imposing array of buildings.

At ground floor level most are shops with emerald green sunshades extending out above us and casting some very welcome shade.

From here we head into a knot of smaller streets, off which run a series of lanes. The buildings are beautiful, reflecting the era of Renaissance romance in all its glory. Verona exudes a sense of passion for life and a love of all things that make the heart swell, whether that's history, architecture, food or, of course, music. Any country so in love with opera has a romantic beat at its heart.

As we walk along it gets busier as the volume of people walking in the same direction is funnelled into the narrower pedestrian thoroughfare. With the contrast of the brilliant blue of the sky against the pale yellow and terracotta hues of the buildings, offset against beautiful old stonework, there is a richness to the scene. It's bustling and vibrant, full of life. The general hubbub of chatter and everyday background noise seems to fill my ears as a steady stream of people start to turn into more of a crowd.

Suddenly Arran turns to me, laughter in his eyes. 'You have reached your Mecca.'

A tall archway on our left, with oversized metal gates pinned open, heralds the entrance. The first thing I notice is what appears to be graffiti and on closer inspection the stonework is covered with handwritten messages. A sea of colour: black, white, red, blue – from a distance it looks like there's been a paint explosion. The walls of the entire entrance tunnel – to just beyond a reachable height – are covered and some people have attached notes written on small pieces of paper. It's tightly packed with sightseers and the acoustics are such that the volume of chatter is very loud indeed. We thread our way through with difficulty. Arran clasps my hand quite tightly as he leads us into an inner courtyard, which thankfully widens out.

The building is beautiful and the balcony is in the far right hand corner. The façade is a mix of brick, stonework and cement but the balcony itself isn't large and is made up of carved, creamy white stonework. The wall adjacent to it is covered in a rampant climber and a large castor oil plant at the base is the backdrop for a statue of Juliet herself. She stands with her head turned towards the house and her left hand clutched to her breast, covering her heart.

Arran leans in to me as I take it all in. 'The gift shop is just here.' He steers my elbow in the direction of the other side of the courtyard.

Hmm. He's right. It's jam-packed with people, small children diving around in all directions and a couple of crying babies – it's bedlam. Somehow, I need to tune out from the noise and bustle going on around me. Shaking my head in dismay, I spin back around and direct my gaze upwards.

For one single moment I imagine the courtyard empty, as Juliet glances down at her lover, knowing in her heart all hope is dashed. I can feel Arran's eyes upon me and he moves even closer, making sure I don't get jostled. Suddenly his arm snakes around my waist and he gives it a gentle squeeze. An action that's not prompted in any way but I feel… special. And Arran doesn't think he's the romantic sort. Well, maybe that isn't strictly true.

'I'm done. I've had my moment, thank you for indulging me. Now let's get away from the madness.'

21

Facing Facts

In the minibus on the way back Arran asks everyone to share the highlight of their excursion.

The responses are enthusiastic, from Silvia, holding up a very smart designer carrier bag containing some extortionately priced shoes, to Rick, who is an architectural buff. He spent most of his time at Castelvecchio. It has seven towers and a castle keep, with four main buildings inside it which now form a museum housing art, as well as artefacts, he informs us. Arran declares the Romanesque style Basilica di San Zeno Maggiore with its huge bronze doorway as being his highlight, then he turns to me as I'm last in line.

'Um, let me see.' Having fallen in love with Verona, its Renaissance buildings and the people, so larger than life that it felt consuming, I'm at a loss. How can I pick one solitary thing? 'It has to be that simply wonderful meal. The Italian style pork steaks with butter and sage was beautifully simple: exquisitely cooked and presented. The perfect end to a perfect trip.'

Arran looks surprised, lowering his voice and leaning in to me. 'Oh, not *the* balcony, then. Now that's a surprise.'

I shake my head. 'Sometimes expectations run high and you were right. What spoilt it for me was the crowd and the noise. I had my moment, though.'

'You didn't believe me, did you, when I said it was over rated.'

'I thought you simply failed to appreciate how powerful, emotive and romantic a setting it was going to be. I mean, it was all of those things, but hard to enjoy given the throng of people and the noise. So, you were right in one way. But when I switched off for a moment it was everything I wanted it to be and that's something I'll always treasure.'

Arran shrugs his shoulders, his face reflecting the fact that he still doesn't get it. 'Oh well, glad you're happy. I'm going to head up to my room as soon as we get back and start looking at that manuscript. Is that alright with you?'

Reluctantly, I say yes as I need to encourage him to get on with it. But a part of me hates to think of slipping into bed alone when Arran is going to be just one floor below me.

'It's fine. I'll be working, too. I need to get words on that screen as quickly as I can now. But first I must re-acquaint myself with the characters. I find the trail goes cold if I don't commit to writing daily.'

As the minibus pulls into the parking area behind the villa, Arran squeezes my hand. 'I'm grateful for what you've done. I'll be honest – I will miss you tonight. The bed will feel empty without you next to me.' His voice is soft and low as he whispers the words into my hair. Perhaps I was wrong thinking Arran had no idea at all about romance. I mean, that was *sensitive*.

Glancing at my watch I see it's nearly midnight, but I don't feel at all tired. Several of the group head off in the direction of the terrace to sit and have a night cap. I say goodnight and head up to my room, purposely avoiding Arran.

Settling myself out on the balcony, I send an email to Carrie to tell her Arran is about to start work on making those changes to his manuscript.

Then I spend half an hour doing a list of bullet points for the session I'm going to be running in the morning. It's all basically quite standard stuff – book blurb, synopsis and pitching – but it covers key areas where people often make big mistakes. It will be fun though, and I'm looking forward to it.

Then it's time to think about Jed Jackman and Bella Hart. It isn't long before they are tumbling into bed and Bella runs her finger tips lightly over Jed's bruised ribs, following it up with a string of kisses. As Jed starts to get in on the action my body begins to ache for Arran's touch and it's easy to write the scene. I'm more awake than ever now.

To my dismay I find myself constantly having to push to the back of my mind a question that is battling to muscle through and grab my attention. Namely, what on earth am I doing letting this attraction to Arran develop as if it could be something? I need to put it into perspective. We've been thrown together under the strangest set of circumstances, outside which our lives don't touch, at all. I've even offered to lend him my life's savings as if he's some long-standing acquaintance and trusted friend. And it's an offer I would still honour because… well, just because.

Just after three in the morning I decide to at least try to get some sleep. Surprisingly, the next thing I'm conscious of is the early morning sunlight creeping into the room and I flick my eyes open to see it's half past six. Something woke me, and I think it must have been a ping, so I grab my phone.

Are you awake?

It's Mel and this is early for her.

Almost, I think. It was a late night. What are you doing up at this time of the morning?

I've known her to sleep through her alarm and no one would ever call her a morning person.

Can't sleep. Thinking about Ross. Is it too early to call?

I immediately dial her number.

'Morning. Can't quite believe you are awake, let alone texting. So how is Ross? I take it that things are still going well?'

She gives a low chuckle.

'We went back to his place last night and he cooked me a romantic dinner for two. Prosecco and candles, even. I met his fur babies, Bowie and Hendrix. After the meal we snuggled up on the sofa and watched the golf.'

Golf? Golf? Ye Gods, it must be love!

'And?'

'And nothing. Afterward he drove me home. We're going to the cinema tonight and I can't wait.'

She isn't saying much but her voice is different somehow, as if she's trying to contain her joy.

'He's such a compassionate and tender hearted man, Brie. I was wrong to be suspicious. Ross says he's never met anyone until now who made him feel ready to commit. I could hardly believe it when he said that! But we're taking our time to really get to know each other, which is precisely what you advised me to do. We have so much in common, it's unbelievable, and I just want to keep hugging myself when he's not with me, out of sheer happiness.'

That touches my heart.

'Aww, Mel, you have no idea how wonderful that is to hear! But what if… hmm… I mean…' Words fail me.

'I have no doubts at all that when we get to the point of falling into bed neither of us will be disappointed. It's wonderful to be courted in the old way. It's a bit like unwrapping a chocolate bar and savouring how it looks, how it feels and how it smells before taking a first bite.'

I burst out laughing and Mel isn't far behind me.

'You are one crazy lady and I'm so blessed to have you as a friend.'

'How is life at Lake Garda?'

I lay my head back against the headboard, not sure what to say. After the little lecture I gave Mel last time we spoke I'm going to sound like someone who can give good advice, but can't take it. What's weird is that we're in the same (love) boat, at the same time, but our roles seem bizarrely reversed. By nature, I'm the cautious one and Mel has always been a little more adventurous. Or do I mean optimistic? Trusting?

'Arran is a fascinating guy. He's not at all what I expected! He sounds rather like Ross without the flowers. I mean, he's not really a romantic because he isn't wired that way. But I can't get enough of him. I want to be glued to his side, constantly. How stupid does that sound?'

There's a second or two of awkward silence.

'You *slept* with him?' She sounds horrified. 'You hardly know him! And aren't you in danger of giving out the wrong impression? You've been there what, five days?'

I can see why she sounds scandalised because I'm well aware this isn't my style and I'm acting a little out of character. Well, maybe more like one of my characters, quite frankly! I don't know quite what to say to explain myself.

'Seriously, Brie, what were you thinking? You get annoyed when people meet you expecting some sort of worldly, party girl then you meet Mr Academic and more or less confirm the stereotype. I'd be speechless if I wasn't so shocked!'

Mel hasn't met him, and she has no idea how intensive this experience has been. I've been drawn into Arran's life and I already feel like I've known him for a long time. I wish she could understand that I'm literally living with Arran full time and this isn't some momentary madness. If our time together had been spun out over a series of dates, the timeline would be a long one in terms of what we've discovered about each other already.

'You think I've turned into one of my headstrong, grab-what-you-want heroines but it's not like that. This is a mutual attraction and we couldn't help ourselves. It wasn't planned, it just happened. And then it happened again—' I trail off, embarrassed.

'Un-be-lieveable! That's even worse. Don't either of you have any self-control? You are stuck there together for the next three plus weeks. I mean, a little flirting and romance… okay, I could understand that if there's an attraction between the two of you. But to full on get down to business knowing you can't just up and leave if it becomes awkward: that's really not such a great idea, Brie. After everything you went through with Paul, I'm really scared you are going to get hurt again. It's too much, too soon, and I'm worried you're dropping your guard for the wrong reasons. It's wonderful to think of you being on a high at the moment. And no one deserves it more than you, but following on so soon after a… profound low, alarm bells are ringing in my head.'

Her concern is palpable.

'I'll be fine, I promise. I'm over the blip, let's say. I don't need Arran to be romantic because he's perfect as he is… really. And this isn't just about the sex.' I hesitate for a moment over that statement but let it go. 'But if we spent the entire rest of my trip in bed I wouldn't be complaining.' Argh. I shouldn't have added that last remark; it's the truth but I didn't mean to say the words out loud. 'When I leave here, who knows what will happen?'

What I hear back is a cross between a raucous laugh and a choking splutter.

'Oh, Brie. You're the hopeless romantic here, remember, the one born on Valentine's Day? You're always bemoaning that sex sells more books than a poignant tale of the pursuit of true love. That overwhelmingly sensual fizz will wane and then what will you be left with? It's like a holiday romance – exciting for a brief while. Closeted together in such a wonderful environment and away from reality, the adventure of it all has sucked you in. But I know you, lady; when it comes to *forever after* you don't want a sizzling sex god, you want a romantic hero and what if you're left wanting… more? It has disappointment stamped all over it and I wish I was there to drill some sense into you to slow it down a little!'

'Maybe this is my summer of simply getting things back into perspective – that's a win-win situation. Which is just what the doctor ordered. Every single moment we're together makes my confidence soar even higher. Arran thinks I'm beautiful just the way I am and I know it's silly, but I did need to hear a man say that. My pride hadn't simply been dented, it had been pulverised.'

It's true. But does she have a point? Arran's face flashes before my eyes and my body instantly starts to heat up. The impact of her words has made me stop and think though.

'Are you falling in love with him?' She sounds aghast.

'I don't know. Probably not.'

'Has he indicated that he's falling in love with you?'

I pause, chewing my lip. 'No. He said he could get used to having me around…'

'Were you just about to have sex when he said that?'

'Yes, but—'

She's relentless and that's why she's the *best* best friend in the whole world. She is also the person who put me back together after I fell apart, so I know why she wants me to exert caution. But this is different.

'I don't want to burst your bubble, lovely lady, but you've just clawed your way back up from a truly nightmarish situation. I'm glad you are out of the way of the trolls and taking a break from social media, but it sounds like you're glossing over all of that. I'm so happy this trip to Italy has revitalised you but you're in *lust* and it's too early to say if it's going to turn into *love*. You aren't equipped for the overload of emotions you're feeling now that you're living life again. That's understandable after Paul, because that episode spiralled way out of control. So far, that it sent you into recluse mode and now... this, whatever it is, smacks of trying to prove something to yourself. Remember those warnings you gave *me*? You need to listen to your own advice and step back a little, or you are going to be the one getting hurt.'

The sadness in her tone is a wake up call. She's panicking on my behalf and yet I'm so elated and happy! We have each other's backs and only Mel could give it to me straight like that. And I'd expect no less.

'I hear what you are saying, and I know there are no guarantees, but I have never felt like this before. Arran's been through a lot and it might be a while before he's ready to commit to anyone again, but I can wait if things between us do progress. But either way, we're having fun together, against all the odds. Anyway, I can't help myself, even if this goes awry.' Nervous anxiety has made me a little breathless and I stop talking.

'Well, I'm here for you whatever happens. Maybe I'm wrong and a few weeks of wanton behaviour is exactly what you need. But if this was suddenly splashed all over the tabloids, I'm worried about how it would look; and how you would react. But what if you are falling in love with him, Brie? You're the romantic one and that's what your heart ultimately craves. I'm not saying that great sex isn't important, it is, but once things settle down it's only the icing on the cake. It's important to choose the right cake though, and not one you'll tire of quickly.'

At that point, we both burst out laughing. Ooh, I really do want to have my cake and eat it. *Brie, stop*, I tell myself. Mel is making a valid point.

Plus, I freely admit Arran's background is wildly different to mine as, no doubt, are our friends. And our families. Oh dear. What if the only two things we have in common are writing and sexual compatibility?

'I've been getting ahead of myself,' I admit, suddenly. 'Arran is just as surprised and caught up in this little… thing, as I am. To be honest, he has so many problems I think he's just overwhelmed right now. You're right, Mel, and maybe I'm thinking with my heart and not my head.'

'Heart?' And with that she starts laughing again. 'That's not how it sounds to me!'

When the call ends, I lie here for a while considering the points our conversation threw up. I'm not a jet setter and my roots are firmly in the UK. Arran travels as a natural consequence of his diverse range of work activities. But he regards this as home. Maybe after four weeks this will be a wonderful memory to look back on and we will both be able to walk away with no regrets. But what if that's not the case?

As for my reputation, well, I know what Mel meant. However, we're consenting adults and it takes two, as they say, so we're even on that score whether or not it's alien to our respective natures. But for me there's an enormous amount of churning emotion attached to this little… diversion. What if that's not the case for Arran? Is this simply a little interlude to help get his mind off the heavy financial worries he has at this particular point in his life? How devastated will I be if we part with a kiss on the cheek and a *see you around sometime, maybe*?

I listen to the little voice inside my head. *Come on Brie, you're a big girl now. You have enjoyed every second in his company and you don't want it to stop. Since when did having a little fun become a sin? You are both single and free to do whatever you want.*

That makes me feel better until another little voice creeps in.

Oh, yeah? Who are you kidding? You know you're falling in love with him and it's probably already too late. The real question is what are you going to do about it?

A quick glance at the clock tells me nothing at all at this moment in time. The session starts in ninety minutes and I need to get my act together, quickly.

22

A Defining Moment

It feels like today is never going to end. The morning session goes extremely well. Afterwards Rick, Kris, and Will ask for one-to-one sessions as all three intend pitching their current work in progress to a publisher. Having been enthused they naturally want to go away and work on their synopses and cover letters, then have me cast an eye over them. In the end I suggest a mini critiquing session late in the afternoon, where we all get together and they each read through what they've produced. I figured four heads were going to be better than one, especially as I was beginning to wane a little. I didn't want to risk missing anything and it worked well.

I've texted Arran twice asking how it's going and received the one response saying *good*. Carrie has texted several times asking how he is doing and saying he isn't responding to her. I just keep telling her he's hard at work and that's a good sign. The reality is that I have no idea whether he's sitting in a depressed funk, feeling I've tried to steer him in the wrong direction, or if his keyboard is on fire.

It isn't until I pack the group off to La Pergola at seven thirty that I realise how wired I am. It's been an intense day and I can fully understand why Arran can't do this on his own. In fact, having to cope without my help while I was working on his revisions put an extra strain on him on top of everything else he's battling with.

I asked Elisabetta to take Arran up a breakfast and a lunch tray, but he really does need to take a break now. Heading upstairs, it's weird when the villa is so quiet but as my foot hits the top stair I can hear his voice. He's on the phone and while I can't distinguish any words, the tone is enough to tell me he's angry. I hover, not quite sure what to do. I decide to creep back downstairs and hang around in the kitchen for a while.

Opening the fridge door, I pull out a bottle of white wine and cast around for something suitable for dinner. Then I have an idea. I ring Antonio at La Pergola and ask if he can deliver a meal for two. I order the special for Arran and something light for me, grateful that Antonio will get someone to bring it down in the next forty-five minutes.

Grabbing two glasses I take the wine out onto the terrace and sit in one of the reclining chairs next to the pool. With the lights reflecting off the water it's very relaxing, although I'm tense thinking about Arran's phone call. It's unlikely to be good news given his tone and I'm not sure how much more he can take. Looking up, he isn't on the balcony, but the light is on in his room. Suddenly it flicks off and I know he's making his way downstairs.

I lie back trying to look calm and composed but my heart is racing. I haven't been in his arms since the early hours of this morning and it feels like forever.

'I'm glad you waited for me.' He sidles up alongside me, placing a hand on my shoulder. 'I hate to think of anyone drinking alone. How was today? I bet you're shattered. People don't realise how exhausting it is because you can't simply switch off when a session ends.'

He pours out two glasses of wine, passing one to me and we chink.

'To the end of a very productive day.'

As he settles back in the chair next to me, I don't take my eyes off him. He doesn't seem down, but he does seem depleted – he's probably tired.

I can't mention I overheard him on the phone so all I can do is give him an opportunity to talk. 'Tell me all about it.'

'One of the hardest days I've ever had, I think. You did a good job, though, and it was mainly a case of accepting the proposed changes. I worked on that extra chapter, taking your brief outline and expanding it. I had quite a bit of background research about Rose's time while Arthur was away, and you were right, there was a gaping hole in the story.'

'Have you spoken to Carrie at all?' I don't want to tell him about the texts this morning, but he does need to get in touch with her.

'Yes. I sent the manuscript off to her about an hour ago. It's done. Finished. Let's hope the two publishers get into a bidding war over it.'

I don't know whether to feel anxious that he took on board everything I said, or flattered. I know Carrie will go through the changes in detail to satisfy herself it's been taken in the right direction and I think that's important. But I also know she'll drop everything to do that, knowing how critical Arran's situation is at this precise moment.

'I'm starving,' he admits, reaching out to put his glass on the small side table nestled between our chairs.

Before he can lever himself out of his chair, I put out my hand and rest it on his arm.

'Don't move a muscle. Dinner is on the way, courtesy of Antonio. I thought it would be nice if we could both sit and chill for a couple of hours. The group have had a great day. I ran an afternoon session for Rick, Kris and Will so they could perfect their first pitch. The others headed down to town for a couple of hours. So you can relax knowing that they all went off to dinner in high spirits, having had yet another good day.'

He places his hand over mine, running his thumb gently over my skin.

'You know you've spoilt me forever, now? How can I run another course without you by my side? We're a team.'

I look at him and he isn't joking or being playful, he means it. The doorbell chimes, breaking the moment and I jump up and head inside. By the time I've plated the delicious smelling ravioli for Arran and my chicken and lemon zucchini, Arran has already set a table for two on the terrace.

'Here, let me take those. Can you grab a large bottle of water?'

I follow him outside, thinking it would be nice if we had some candles. Not for additional lighting but just because the flicker of a flaming candle adds to the ambience. Arran pulls out my chair for me while I sit and then passes me a paper napkin with a flourish.

'Now, tell me, is this a romantic or a gentlemanly gesture?'

I can't suppress a giggle and he gives me a look of disappointment before sauntering around the table to sit opposite me.

'Gentlemanly.'

'What would you consider to be a romantic gesture?'

I toy with the lettuce leaves in the small salad bowl next to my plate.

'Doing something unexpected; something thoughtful and personal that makes someone feel special. It's hard to put into words. Why?'

He switches off for a moment and I watch him eating. He attacks his food with relish, never talks with his mouth full and you can tell when he's really enjoying something.

As if to prove my point he nods his head vigorously, pointing his fork at the plate until his mouth is empty. 'Now that's good ravioli. How is your chicken?'

'Delicious. I need the recipe for this,' I enthuse.

'Good, Antonio will be delighted to hear that,' Arran replies, in between devouring a forkful of pasta. 'There were a couple of small changes you made in the book, so minor I felt they were trivial, but it made me stop and think. You just seem to look at some things very differently to me. It made me feel guilty, actually.'

I put down my fork, lifting my glass to take a swallow of wine simply to have something to partly obscure my face with. Where is this leading? If it's bad news, then I might not be able to control my reaction.

'Guilty?'

'I… um… wouldn't want you to think that I was using my personal problems to get the sympathy vote. I mean, I shouldn't really have exposed you to all that because it was unfair of me.'

Oh no, he thinks I've been comforting him because I feel sorry for the mess he's in. He's certainly misread my moral code of conduct.

'I've only ever slept with someone when it meant something, Arran. That might not be what you want to hear but it's the truth. I wouldn't jump into bed with anyone merely because I felt sorry for them.' There's a sharp edge to my tone and this time I take a large gulp of wine, feeling disappointed in him.

'That's not what I meant, really, Brie. I don't quite know what we have going on between us, but I didn't want you to feel I was taking advantage of you in any way. I don't make a habit of this—'

'Oh, and you think I do?'

He drops his fork and it clatters against the plate.

'Sorry, sorry. I'm not doing a good job of explaining myself here. It's not your fault, it's mine. You're a genuinely kind and caring person, Brie, and I'm not used to being around someone who cares that much about anyone besides themselves.'

Why would he feel guilty, unless—

'What did Carrie say to you?'

My suspicions are correct because his expression changes immediately and he presses his lips together as if he's afraid of talking.

'She said something, didn't she?'

He shakes his head but it's an unconvincing gesture.

'Arran, tell me exactly what she told you.'

He can tell from my tone I won't be messed around. He swallows hard and the index finger of his left hand begins to drum on the table.

'I'm not good at this sensitivity stuff. She asked how you were coping and I said you were the perfect stand-in. When I explained that you've been working away quietly in your room quite a bit, fixing my manuscript, she sounded concerned. She asked me if you were avoiding mixing with the group. Of course, I said no. But then I started questioning her because her concern seemed rather odd. I wondered if there was something I should know.' He reaches forward to pick up his glass, taking a small sip and clearing his throat before continuing.

'She told me you'd been through a rough patch shortly before you arrived and that you'd been avoiding people. When you mentioned the backlash from Paul's fans I didn't realise it had affected you quite as much as it obviously did.'

I groan inwardly, not even sure if a sound did, in fact, escape from my lips.

'She was simply checking you were fine, Brie. I felt bad afterwards as I forced it out of her. I don't know the details, but I sort of got the impression she thought a change of scenery would do you good. Afterwards I realised that not only had I encumbered you with my life story and the mountain of problems that need to be resolved, but that knowledge put you under additional pressure. Turning that manuscript around so quickly was intense and if you haven't been well—'

I owe him an explanation.

'Look, let's not spoil dinner. Let's eat first and talk afterwards.'

The eye contact is a little awkward, but we manage to continue eating and I change the subject. I figure that getting him to talk about his favourite music is bound to lighten the atmosphere and I'm right.

After clearing away we're both conscious that the others could arrive back at any time. So, we saunter down to the library, figuring we're unlikely to be disturbed. I owe Arran an explanation for Carrie's unnecessary concern and for the fact that it has now made him feel awkward around me. That's the last thing I want him to feel and I need to clear the air.

Although we are walking inches apart, he doesn't reach for my hand.

'I know Carrie meant well and I will admit I needed to spend some time on my own away from everyone. I felt

I'd lost my way and then I realised I was married to my work and going through the seven year itch.'

We step over the threshold and Arran closes the door behind us, indicating for me to take one of the cosy winged chairs. He takes the seat opposite me, drawing it a little closer.

'Seven year itch?'

'An old wives' tale relating to marriage. It's when the newness is long gone and there's a real danger that things will become boring and predictable. In terms of relationships the honeymoon period is effectively over. For me, in terms of my work, that was how long I'd been writing about hot, sexy men and feisty females, having left my contemporary fiction days behind me. I'm earning a good living because of the switch, but something is missing. When I began writing it was all about the romance; about finding one's soul mate. Lives that hadn't been easy and lessons learnt that had scarred the heart. But above all there was hope that somewhere out there would be that one, true love, just waiting to be discovered. I wrote about the lessons life teaches us all along the way.'

Arran's face is quite blank.

'I thought that was what you were doing anyway; you said you were working on two stories. Why did you feel you had to hide away?'

I frown, and a sigh escapes my lips; it seems to echo sadly around the room.

'For a while I couldn't write a word. Well, I wrote thousands and ended up deleting them all. I will write both stories but it's not quite as cathartic as I thought it was going to be. Maybe I've always been a little delusional when it comes to my rosy view of the perfect love affair. The one that will last forever. Or perhaps I've simply watched too many romantic films over the years. I mean, anything can happen on screen but in real life? I blame the fact that I was born on Valentine's Day. It messes with your head until you get to understand why it's a day when the world is full of ostentatious outpourings of love. Then you wake up to the cold reality that it's a big earner for anyone selling hearts and flowers. And a lot of people give gifts because it's the done thing. So what's the point of it?'

Now he looks worried.

'It definitely wasn't because you were in love with Paul Turner when it went wrong?'

I'm chewing on my lip and I make myself stop.

'No. I never really wanted Paul, but I needed something exciting to happen to make me feel alive again. I thought I could step outside myself for a while and that it would be fun; something was missing and I'd become jaded. That had nothing to do with what happened afterwards, except that I chose to comfort eat and it got out of control. But what triggered it was writer's block. So, yes, I did go through several tough months and I sure as hell wasn't going to act that out in public.'

Arran clears his throat. 'Or with the support of family or friends.'

He's listening to my every word and I know my expression is one of acceptance.

'I didn't want to have to worry about being an author, a daughter, a friend or anything to anyone. I wanted to wallow. Facing up to reality is tough. Now I'm over it because I'm not the sort of person to give up. I've lost my pride so many times over the years, it's no longer something I worry about. But I do value the people I love and there was no way I was going to inflict my misery on them. Yes, I'll write both stories and whichever has the highest sales will determine what I write in future. If Carrie is right, then that's my fate.'

Now he looks confused. 'But isn't that giving up?'

I shake my head vehemently. 'No, it's called being practical and earning a living. I've decided to stop being a dreamer.'

The silence between us is heavy but I don't regret telling Arran everything. I know Carrie was checking I really am over my little episode and she meant well, but it's a message I need to take on board. I can't live my life as a dreamer, wanting the impossible and feeling constantly let down.

'While I'm being totally honest with you, can I ask why Carrie's questioning made you feel guilty?' I don't believe this is just about sharing his problems, this is about the fact that we're sleeping together.

'Look, I didn't know you were fragile and let's face it, I'm a walking disaster right now. Maybe I always have been when it comes to women. My focus has always been my work and in hindsight I allowed Harriet to manipulate me. But it's easy to see that now, after the fact. She sort of inserted herself into my life and made me believe I couldn't live without her. Harriet can be very charismatic when she wants something and I see that now. I was a sucker; she pandered to my ego and I was dazzled by her. I think the only people I've ever truly loved are my grandparents and Nanny Hope. It's only since I met you that I've actually realised that.'

Now it's my turn to be shocked.

'Why?'

'Oh, because you put your own problems to one side and took time out to listen to me going on and on. I care about losing the villa because it's the last tie I have to my grandparents and the memories we made here. And when I knew that Carrie was worried about you, I started to worry too. Now, caring might not be love. I don't know. But I care. I don't want you thinking I'm using you to bolster my flagging ego, or to vent sexual frustration. Or just because you happen to be here. This thing we have going on means something to me but that's all I know. You deserve more; someone who can give you everything you dream about because they are connected to their emotions. I'm a reject in that department, I'm afraid. I simply don't want to disappoint you.'

Flowers are boring and predictable; hearing a speech like that, spoken from the heart with sincerity, is without doubt the most romantic moment of my entire life.

Seconds later we're in each other's arms and rolling around on the two inch thick fur rug. I'm sure the contents of the Jane Austen shelf above us will be swooning, while the tomes of the Cambridge Union debating society will be prostrate with shock.

Me? I've never been happier. And Arran? Well, he's lying next to me now with a big enough smile on his face to convince me we're doing something right.

23

A Glimmer of Hope

Last night we headed back to my room again and Arran crept out early this morning, shooting me a huge grin as he quietly closed the door behind him. We need each other, and it feels right, for now at least. Will I be able to walk away from him in three weeks time, just like that? I don't know. But then he doesn't know either.

All I do know is that the moment he closed that door behind him the room felt empty and my heart felt heavy. Then a flashback of waking up in the early hours of the morning to find Arran propped up on one elbow, watching me sleeping, pops into my head. It makes me smile and the look in his eyes filled me with joy.

'Let's always be honest with each other, Brie. I won't keep any secrets from you, I promise. I'm not a complicated guy and I don't do lying or cheating. I know that's not a lot to offer, but I hope it's a start.'

Once he'd said his piece he lay back down and immediately closed his eyes. It wasn't long before he was softly snoring, and I fell back into a deep and dreamless sleep, feeling content. Now, as I swing my legs over the side of the bed, I know I can't ask for more than that.

As I'm getting ready I find myself humming the chorus from Nick Jonas' 'Find You' and I feel… happy. I stare at myself in the mirror in surprise, then give my hair one last sweep with the brush. It's another sunny day and the group's last one at the villa. Tomorrow morning, they all fly back home and by late afternoon a new group will be settling in. Before Arran left, he asked if I'd join him for this morning's session covering social media and advertising. I know that this afternoon he's running a special workshop focusing on setting up a website and I think at least four of the group are involved. Unfortunately, I have my interview with Jordan at three o'clock, but it should only take an hour and I can make myself available for the remainder of the group afterwards.

Checking the time, I decide it's probably best to skip breakfast as I have a couple of phone calls to make. The first one is to Carrie and I'm not at all surprised when she answers on the third ring.

'Well, what do you think?' I jump straight in.

'How did you know I've been up all night reading Arran's manuscript?'

'You're predictable. You like helping people and your bark is always worse than your bite. I gather he accepted most of the suggestions I made but did I go too far?'

'Nope. Pretty much nailed it, I think. I made a couple of minor amendments to one scene as there was a little repetition, but I think I'm ready to draft the email now and send it off to the publishers without further delay.'

I offer up a silent *whoop*.

'Let's hope you get a quick response because the situation is growing even more urgent by the day. There's a real chance he could lose the villa. And that reminds me, you worried Arran by checking up on me. What was that all about? We've had enough contact for you to know my little episode is well and truly over. You have some explaining to do because it made things awkward at this end.'

'Ah.' Pregnant pause. 'Well.' Another pause.

'I'm waiting.' And I deserve an explanation.

'Mel rang me and asked if I knew you were sleeping with Arran.'

'I don't believe it! You both need to relax a little. I know what I'm doing, and Arran is no bad guy, believe me.'

'Okay. Sorry. I was just… making sure everything was good. After all, I sort of talked you into this in the first place. I didn't mean to interfere, but Mel sounded concerned.' She does at least sound apologetic.

'Well, I'll forgive you just this once. But from here on in you ask me first if you want an update. I'm off to ring Mum and I can only hope Mel hasn't spoken to her, too.'

In fact, Mel hasn't phoned Mum and it's an easy conversation. I explain that I couldn't call yesterday because I ended up taking Arran's session and that seemed to please her. I guess I'm lucky to have so many people worrying about how I'm doing and wanting me to get back into my stride. What I'm beginning to realise is that

I'm going through a time of personal growth, changing in ways I never thought I would. Perhaps it wasn't so much about going through a seven year itch, as it was simply a need to stand back and review my life. Coming to Italy has made me do just that and suddenly I'm seeing a lot of things in a very different light.

Tonight, everyone is in high spirits and Arran is the most relaxed I've seen him all week. There's a lot of banter around the table and each member of the group has expressed their thanks for what they all agree has been a very informative week. I can almost see the relief etched on Arran's face but tomorrow he has the pressure of having to do this all over again.

As we stroll back to the villa I end up walking with Yvonne and she raises the topic of how isolated she sometimes feels.

'Living in a village and not really knowing any other writers, there isn't anyone who understands how darn right frustrating it can be at times. I mean, we all go through the same processes and anxieties, I suppose. This week has made me realise how motivating it is to just have those conversations with people who really understand. I'm going to miss that.'

'You're right, Yvonne, and it's understandable to feel that way. It's a labour of love filled with a lot of daunting lows before you get to experience any high points. Have you thought about joining the Romantic Novelists' Association? I'll send you the link.' I explain that they hold local chapter meetings, as well as meet ups in London several times a year. She hurries off to catch up with Kris and Silvia, no doubt to see if they are members. I'm really glad we talked, because it will open up a network of like minded friends and professionals for her.

Looking around I see that Arran is bringing up the rear and he appears to be deep in thought, so I slow my pace a little.

'It was a great last supper, wasn't it?' My attempt at a little humour doesn't register and it's easy to see that his mind is elsewhere.

'Yes. Everyone seems to have enjoyed their stay. It will be interesting to see what the feedback forms say, though. I do ask people to be honest as that's the only way I can ensure I'm meeting expectations.' He looks tired and that's understandable. 'How did the interview go?'

'Good. Jordan Lewis is an interesting man. I assumed, like any athlete, he had to be highly disciplined to achieve the optimum level of fitness and stamina. But I don't think I fully realised how it dominates every aspect of his life. He monitors everything he eats and often takes his meals separately from his family as they rarely eat at the same time, or the same food.

'When he was talking about his daily nutrition, he could have been a trained dietician; food didn't excite him at all, it was simply a means to an end. Lots of protein shakes and supplements; choosing foods for their nutritional content and not for their taste or as an indulgence. Then there is his daily workout programme which changes constantly and his general cardiovascular work. Cage fighting is a brutal sport and when Jordan fights, he's like a machine. Relentless. His manager was there, and he played a YouTube video of one of Jordan's shortest fights, so that he could talk me through it. It was hard to watch, if I'm honest. One man beating another one until the referee stopped the fight.

'But when I asked Jordan about his wife and family, this man turned into a gentle giant in front of my eyes. He pulled out his phone to show me some photos and suddenly he wasn't that professional fighting machine but a family man, like any other. He does what he has to do to provide for them and set things up for the future.'

I look across at Arran and he's shaking his head. 'It's not an easy way to earn a living, that's for sure. It must be hard on his wife and kids.'

'Jordan told me his wife has never watched him fight but she has watched him train. He said he's been lucky and listed his injuries, saying they were all minor, but it didn't sound that way to me. I think what he meant was that it was rare for him to have to delay a fight because of injury time. Jordan said that pain was managed first in here,' I tap my head with my finger, repeating his own action earlier on, 'and that's the key to being a winner.'

'It sounds like an extremely interesting insight into his life. Did you get all the information you needed?'

'I did. The guy has a sharp brain and when it comes to retiring, he has already lined up a number of options. But he isn't ready just yet and he intends to go out on top. I could feel the real issues though; he skirted around his wife's concerns about the toll it takes on him and how long he can sustain that. In the story, Jed Jackman must decide between the fight of his life and his love for Bella. He can't have both. I can appreciate the enormity of having to make that choice, now I fully understand the life of a cage fighter. It was probably one of the most emotive interviews I've ever conducted.'

We filter into single file as we take the path down towards the back of the villa. Once inside everyone congregates in the kitchen, grabbing glasses and an array of drinks to take out onto the terrace.

Arran disappears to turn on the garden lighting and set up some music. There's a buzz going on tonight and a part of that is because everyone has had a good time, but home and loved ones beckon tomorrow. As with any holiday, it's an enjoyable experience but there comes a point when you long for the familiar.

Sitting and chatting aimlessly about a vast range of topics, we while away the rest of the evening until eventually it's just Arran and me sitting alongside the pool.

'Wild thought. How about we take a dip? Everyone's in bed so we won't be interrupted,' Arran flashes me a cheeky smile. He's expecting me to say no.

'Last one in is a chicken,' I say as I strip down to my underwear. Heck, it will look like I'm wearing a bikini, anyway. Arran is still struggling to get his trousers off, hopping on one leg as I slip into the deliciously cool water. I feel goosebumps run up and down my arms as my skin adjusts to the temperature but it's bliss.

Arran slips in next to me, looking very attractive in his navy boxers.

'Jordan impressed you then?'

Arran's comment takes me by surprise. I wonder what made him think of it now.

'It was only research, I wasn't evaluating him in any way; only trying to understand his line of work. He was very genuine and open. But, yes, I suppose I was somewhat impressed. I'm not just talking about all that solid muscle.' I steal a look at Arran, a meaningful grin on my face. 'The arrangement made between my publishers and his manager is that Jordan will get a mention when Heidi officially *leaks* the teasers about the new book. It's just a publicity angle to grab people's attention in the run up to publication. Readers love all the detail behind how an author gleans information to flesh out their characters. And, of course, Jordan has a very loyal fan base, many of whom are women who buy romance novels. It's quid pro quo.'

'It never occurred to me that romance novels required such a detailed level of research. I simply assumed it was all about relationships. Guy meets girl and falls in love, isn't that the common preconception?'

I peer at Arran, rather disappointedly.

'That's where making assumptions can get you into a lot of trouble. Of course, real life issues come into every story I write. I've tackled death, divorce, cancer, redundancy, addiction – you name it. Just because it's a romance doesn't mean the author doesn't have to get their facts right, or that it's all pure fluff. In the same way that your new manuscript is factually correct but at the heart of it, it's a love story, too. You had to do justice to both halves to make it work.'

'Touché and well put. I'm totally ignorant here, but do many men read romance novels?'

I burst out laughing. 'Clearly a lot more than you think, by the sound of it. Everything from historical to chick lit and all of the categories in between.'

'I'm not a good example of a modern guy, am I? Guess I spent too much time studying and not enough living in the moment.' Judging by the expression on his face, he is taking this seriously. I don't think he's ever really given it any thought; why would he?

'The hole you are digging yourself into is getting bigger by the moment. No offence taken but your education is sadly lacking in that respect. If you read one of my novels I guarantee it will bring you up to speed.'

He starts laughing and, in fairness, I've witnessed how he's tried his best to be light hearted tonight and not to dwell on his own problems. I only wish his questioning wasn't quite so annoying at times. It is good to hear this laughter, though, as it's real and now I can see he's just the teensiest bit embarrassed.

We lapse into silence and it's pleasant to float around and enjoy the balmy evening. The sounds and the smells carried on the night air wrap themselves around us and the gentle lapping of the water is comforting. Already the house is in darkness and now only the lights on the terrace emit a soft glow. I can see something is troubling him and he turns his head unexpectedly, catching me staring at his profile.

'I wish you'd share it with me,' I mutter softly, as our eyes connect.

He sighs, rubbing his index fingers in circles around the sides of his temple as if to alleviate pain.

'This villa is what keeps me grounded, like the roots of a tree. This is the only place I ever experienced emotion, as a child. When I was here I could admit I was afraid, or that some things didn't come naturally to me. I could be that boy growing into manhood and struggling to discover who I was, acknowledging my strengths and my weaknesses, without apology, or shame. I know it's fairly common, but for a while I was convinced I'd been adopted. I was nothing at all like my sister, my mother, or my father. My grandfather said I reminded him of his own mother. When I asked him why, he said she didn't always take the easiest route. It's only now that I think I understand what he meant. But if I lose the villa, I lose the only memories that mean anything to me.'

I reach out, placing my hand on his arm and giving it a gentle rub. Arran drifts closer.

'If you can just make the next payment then I'm sure that advance will help with the one after that. Carrie has already submitted the manuscript. Let me lend you the money. It's earning hardly anything at all sitting in the bank. It would give me a good feeling to think of it at least doing some good. You could repay it at your leisure, really.'

His head is slumped down now, his chin almost touching his chest as it dips just below the water line. He replies without altering his gaze.

'I can't, Brie. That's not the sort of man I am. But it is very generous of you; too generous, in fact. I know that temporary solutions are just storing up problems for the future and I can't risk not being able to repay my debts. What I need to do now is get a grip on my financial affairs and only an accountant can help on that front. Actually, there is a favour you can do me that would take one worry away.'

I search his eyes and my heart misses a beat. This man hasn't even begun to tap into the emotions he's holding back. Being brought up in an environment where achievement was everything, he wavers every time his emotions get in the way. Like refusing to let his mother help him; he looks at the situation with his head and not his heart. But the emotion is there, I'm sure of it, and I want to be the one to coax him into recognising that fact. It's just going to be a slow process.

'Ask away.'

'I've managed to line up several projects for my next trip back to the UK in mid August. One of them is doing the voiceover for a series of tutorials on Ancient Greek civilisation. It's for a small production company and their offices are in Wales, about half an hour from Cardiff. Apparently, the CEO has a purpose built recording studio in the grounds of his obscenely large country house. That's reasonably close to the Forest of Dean, isn't it?'

My heart begins to skip in my chest.

'Yes, probably less than an hour's drive away. Of course you can come and stay with me. I can pay you back for your hospitality while I've been here.'

He chuckles. 'This isn't exactly a holiday, Brie, and I really owe you a lot considering everything you've done for me. But I would love to take you up on that offer. It's one thing less to worry about but only if you are sure I wouldn't be putting you out.'

I run my hand up and down his forearm, tiny droplets of water flicking up in the air reflect the pool lights like little prisms. 'I told you, I have a guest room doing nothing at all and you are very welcome to use it at any time. If any of your other work happens to be within easy driving distance, then feel free to come and stay for as long as you want.'

Arran pushes against the side of the pool, does a couple of strokes and swims back to face me, treading water. He rubs his hands over his face before replying.

'I can't ever recall asking anyone to do me a favour before. It's hard enough for me to acknowledge I'm in a hole, let alone turn to someone for help. It feels wrong, if I'm being honest, but with you it's different. I don't feel you're judging me, or even pitying me. You are the definition of a Good Samaritan, Brie, do you know that?'

He leans in to brush his lips against my cheek and the sudden movement sends a few splashes up into the air, several landing on my face. I laugh, wiping them away as he tries to kiss me a second time.

'You're special, Brie. And just knowing we'll be seeing each other again after this…' He stops to look around for a moment and I realise he's battling with feelings that are alien to him. 'Well, it would have been a terrible shame to just say goodbye, have a nice life, wouldn't it?'

I think that's probably about as romantic as he's going to get for now but it's a start.

'I don't think I could have done that, anyway,' I answer with total honesty.

Suddenly I'm kissing him with a fierceness that leaves him in no doubt at all that I don't intend to sleep alone tonight.

24

My Keyboard is Smoking Hot

It's just after four in the morning when I creep out onto the balcony and begin typing. With the image of Jordan in my mind, Bella begins to infiltrate Jed's head and his heart in a way that no other woman has ever done before. Physically she dominates him, knowing he's powerless to resist her and mentally he can't handle that loss of control.

His life is about routine, rising above the pain and being fearless – conquering every problem that stands in the way of victory. As he begins to let her in, he can see the dread she feels before each match. It becomes increasingly difficult to cope with the growing sense of confusion within him. His life centres around the space within the four walls of that cage and the triumph of leaving it as a winner. Without that, what is he?

'Hey, how long have you been out here?' Arran saunters out, rubbing his eyes and stretching his arms before he looks down and realises he's naked. 'Oh, erm… is it too early to fetch you a cup of coffee?' He looks back at the bedside clock, which shows it's just coming up to six.

'Coffee would be great. I'm on a roll at the moment, and I don't want to stop until I run out of words.'

Arran looks convincingly apologetic. 'Of course. Don't let me disturb you.'

I have no idea how long he's gone but he very quietly creeps up to place the coffee next to me and backs away with me hardly noticing. He does lean in to give me a kiss on the cheek, but it takes a mere second before he's gone again. It feels so good to have the words pouring out of me so fast that my fingers can barely keep up. This really is the old me and I find myself laughing, then sighing as the scene develops on the screen in front of me.

I'm so grateful to Jordan because he helped me to understand the dilemma and in a way, I can compare him to Arran. Both are men who, albeit for different reasons, find it easy to rationalise everything they do on a professional level. Every decision made has a consequence and that's acceptable because they weigh up the gain versus the cost. But suddenly when things become personal they venture onto unfamiliar territory. Emotions complicate matters. Even more so, because these are feelings they've been trained, or brought up, to perceive as a weakness.

This morning it's been difficult making myself stop to pace around when my tracker warns me I've been inactive for too long. Three hours fly by and eventually I have to drag myself away to shower and get dressed. It's the group's last breakfast together and it would be wrong of me to miss it. I do feel a little sad to be saying goodbye and, admittedly, a little anxious at the thought of the six strangers who will be arriving late this afternoon. But the euphoria of being back in my writing zone has left me on a high, safe in the knowledge that the story is speeding along, and nothing can stop me now.

It's a pity it takes a week for everyone to feel the ease, comfort and level of friendship that abounds over our last breakfast together. I half wonder if the writing retreats would benefit from an extended stay of maybe ten, or fourteen, days. Imagine how much more interactive the sessions might be, but it's down to cost in terms of time and money, I suppose.

Waving everyone off and then walking back into the villa hand in hand with Arran, I feel full of optimism. Just the knowledge that we will be seeing each other again after spending this time together in his villa, adds to the growing sense of excitement. Okay, the reason behind it is work orientated, but he wanted me to know that he isn't used to relying on other people. And yet he already feels comfortable enough to reach out to me. A warm glow begins to work its way from the pit of my stomach into my chest.

I realise Arran has drawn me towards the bottom of the staircase. We stand facing each other and he catches my hands, looking at me with a serious expression on his face.

'You have almost seven hours until our new guests arrive. Go write.'

I open my mouth to stop him going any further, but he shakes his head.

'I'm not going to be a distraction. I'll be in the study and Elisabetta will be here soon with a friend to give the house a good blitz between them. So we both need to keep out of their way.'

I let the sides of my mouth droop, sulkily.

'I'll organise a picnic lunch in the garden if you're good.' He grins at me and I find myself giggling.

'Okay, that's a deal.'

It's hard to turn and walk away from him but once Elisabetta arrives we would have to be on our guard, anyway. Arran is right, and I climb the stairs slowly and with a real sense of reluctance. Before I reach the top step though, Bella's voice is already inside my head. She thinks she can change Jed Jackman and grab that elusive happy ever after, but it's never that simple, is it? The layers of conflict are beginning to build.

I snuggle closer to Arran, my body still tingling as if every nerve ending is alive and on fire. I know it's going to be a while before sleep will allow my brain to shut down.

He groans softly as he shifts position to wrap himself around me and it's the sound of a man who is still coming down from a high. We're both a little breathless as our skin touches once more.

'I'm shattered.' His softly spoken words are diffused by my hair, but I heard what he said.

'I'm not surprised.' My words are full of innuendo. 'What you need is a good night's sleep for a change.'

He groans again but this time it's edged with tiredness.

'Do you think the new group will gel?' I can't believe he's worrying about that now.

'Yes, of course they will. Frank will be the joker of the group and he's harmless enough. I think the two ladies will mix, rather than sticking together because they are two very different characters. So, this isn't going to end up being a four-two split, which is a good thing.'

I pull myself up, digging my elbow into the bed and letting my cheek rest on my hand as I gaze down at Arran.

'Did you realise you touched my arm several times during the introductions? It threw me a little. I think it's best we keep things strictly professional in front of the guests, don't you? Or are you bored of creeping around in the early hours of the morning?'

Even in the semi-gloom I can see he's thinking about it. Instinctively he runs his tongue over his bottom lip, which makes my own mouth twitch.

'Oh. I didn't realise. Sorry, I don't want to make you feel uncomfortable. But you're right, it's probably best we watch what we do and say, so I will try my best to be more careful in future. I had a difficult situation the year before last when two of the guests had a bit too much to drink and slept together. Unfortunately, the lady concerned was married and had come along with her best friend. It was an absolute nightmare situation. The next day he claimed he was drunk and made an open apology to everyone because the atmosphere was so dire. So I guess keeping up appearances is the right thing to do but it's going to be hard. See how you've snuck up on me and tied me in knots! I can't even control my actions any more.'

It's weird hearing him joking about how close we've become. But when I think back just one week to welcoming the first group, I was well outside my comfort zone. Arran had simply introduced me before getting the group to introduce themselves. I felt like a guest and the odd one out, someone lurking in the middle. Last night Arran and I were a team, often dipping in and out of each other's conversations to share our expertise with the newcomers.

'I hope everyone will assume we've worked together quite a bit and that we're just good friends. It shouldn't be a problem. I know I'm doing the Tuesday morning session but I'm happy to join in on any of the others if you'd like some company.'

Arran begins to trail his fingers up and down my forearm.

'You're quite something, Brie. Normally I find the first evening quite stressful but tonight, for the first time I can remember, I felt quite relaxed. Just knowing you have my back means a lot.'

There's a question I've been meaning to ask him and now seems as good a time as any.

'I can imagine you would work very well alongside Kathy Porter. There isn't anything that would flummox her, and she has a wealth of experience. Did Kathy help out with any of the other sessions?'

Arran's eyes are closed now but he's only resting them because his voice, whilst low, is fully alert.

'Not really but she loves to organise group discussions. Kathy is quite formal in her approach and her preparation. But in the evenings, she often kicks off an ad hoc session by throwing out a question and getting people to talk about their experiences. I think last week's group were a lot more relaxed together and I've come to see that even informal sessions can curtail the general social side of the week. It's something I'll take note of from now on. It will be interesting to see if the same approach works this time around.

'I put this group together because one of their main objectives for the week was obtaining feedback, as they are all writing their first manuscripts. I would like to fit in at least two extra sessions to achieve this and maybe we could split the group into two for those?'

'Sounds good to me. I know I was tied up a lot last week, for good reason as we both know, but this coming week will be different. Until people settle in, it's hard for one person to make sure everyone is included in the conversation. At least with two of us it will be easier to manage and the quicker they bond the more productive it will be.'

Arran's eyes flick open.

'I can't even begin to think of next year without you here. Maybe I'm having too much fun with you around.'

I give him a gentle punch on his arm.

'Oh, so I'm fun, am I?'

'I keep doing it, don't I? Putting my foot in it. You are fun to be around, but you've been a great listener and I value your professional advice, too. You also make a great tutor and I'd like to think that's something you will want to pursue in the future. And besides, I love having you here.'

His eyes are closing, involuntarily this time. His breathing begins to deepen, so I lie down, snuggling into him once more. It feels so good to be here, like this, with Arran. Obviously, he feels the same way but what if when we meet up back in the UK things feel different? Could this be a result of the stunning scenery, the charm of the Italian sunshine and one of the most beautiful lakes in the world?

And as for next year... Kathy will be expecting to pick back up where she left off and I won't be needed. There's nothing I can do about that, other than to be grateful that I'm here now.

I watch Arran's face as he sinks deeper and deeper into sleep, a peaceful expression taking over. Falling asleep in your lover's arms makes you feel safe and... wanted. It's a wonderful feeling, like none other. Have I finally found my Jude Law?

This evening I saw an alternative side to Arran, maybe because the new group have a different dynamic going on; it was a little daunting to begin with. Four of the guests know each other very well and are part of the same critiquing group, so meet up regularly. That leaves the other two having to integrate and at first it looked like it was going to be quite a barrier. But as the evening went on Arran managed to find areas of common ground to draw everyone together.

I forgot that Arran has personal contact with each of the attendees well in advance of their arrival. It's clear he spends a great deal of time trying to get the mix right. I will admit I'm impressed. Finding two people to make up the numbers can't have been easy but, cleverly, he chose two individuals whose personalities are strong enough that they can hold their own.

Both will bring their own experiences to the group as a whole, giving an insight into specific areas of the publishing process. One is a full time copyeditor and the other designs book covers and marketing materials. Immediately after the introductions were made a myriad of questions were directed their way and I could see Arran settling back in his seat. There was a measure of satisfaction displayed in his body language and I reflected upon the fact that he is such a complex character. There's so much going on inside that head of his and I've only scratched the surface when it comes to getting to know him.

And now Arran's breathing has turned into a gentle snore, his eyelids moving as he's drawn into some dream or other. I wish I could switch off my brain and I wonder if I should get up and write. I love lying here next to him though, and it is with reluctance I roll away from him to ease my legs gently over the side of the bed.

I pull on a strappy cotton top with matching shorts, then grab my phone and tip toe out onto the balcony. As soon as I open the laptop I see there's a DM on Facebook and it's from Mel. It was sent just twenty minutes ago.

Only me! Another fabulous evening out with Ross. We went to visit Mum and Dad. He's the first boyfriend of mine that they've ever taken to immediately. How ironic is that? Perhaps I should listen to them more often! But then there is nothing at all about this guy to dislike. Oh, Brie – I can't wait until you are back, and I can introduce him to you. If he gets your seal of approval too, then it's a done deal as far as I'm concerned!

How are the new group shaping up?

It's funny but I'm thinking the same thing. I can't imagine Mel wouldn't like Arran, but it will be nice when we can all get together. And that could be sometime next month.

I'm sure I'll be as impressed by Ross as you are. It's good to hear that things are going so well. Arran is coming over to the UK mid August and will be staying with me for a while. Perhaps we can all go out as a foursome? Won't that be something? I'm wondering what my parents will think of Arran – Dad can be a bit of a challenge at times. He took an instant dislike to Paul, which puzzled me at the time. I think maybe he'd checked him out online but hadn't the heart to warn me off. Do we ever listen anyway?

The new group are going to be demanding, I think. They are very enthused and have already asked what felt like a million questions tonight. Arran was buzzing, so it's all good here. And I'm writing. And liking the way the words are coming together ha ha! Speak soon.

She's probably in bed now and won't pick this up until the morning. I miss spending time with Mel. I can tell her anything and she instantly seems to sense what I'm thinking by just looking at me. I know she's a little uneasy about my situation here with Arran, but no more so than I am about Ross – at least until I meet him. He'd better be the real deal because if he isn't he'll have me to answer to; Mel and I are as close as sisters and I'm no pushover.

25

Life is Full of Unexpected Highs… and Lows

By Wednesday morning Arran is beginning to look a little edgy. It's been an intense couple of days as everyone was keen to begin the extra critiquing sessions on Sunday morning. After a very productive few hours, it was going so well that, after breaking for a leisurely lunch, we split back up into two groups again to work through the afternoon. I was a little worried about Arran, as there really was no break for him.

However, Sunday evening was a real surprise as when this lot let their hair down, they really know how to do it in style. By two in the morning Arran and I were both shattered and we left them to it, wondering whether anybody would have the energy to turn up at 9 a.m. for the first of the official workshops. But they did, Arran confirmed. Although he did say there was a constant flow of trips to the kitchen for coffee.

Meal times are very jolly, anyway, and when Arran doesn't need me I spend the time out on my balcony writing. But after breakfast today my first job is to ring Carrie, as it's obvious Arran is stressing because she hasn't been in touch yet. I did tell him it was too soon. These things take time. Obviously, she can't tell me anything, but she promises to get an update and phone him sometime today. She asks how the writing is going and I'm delighted to confirm I'm now way ahead of target and Carrie sounds not just happy, but delighted.

Probably no more than an hour later my phone rings and I pick it up without checking the caller ID, surprised when I don't instantly recognise the voice.

'Brie?'

'Yes?'

'It's Auntie Olive. Oh, my darling, I'm afraid I have some bad news and there's no easy way to say this without worrying you. Your mum asked me to call. We're at the hospital. George has had a heart attack. She said to tell you he's responding to the drugs they've given him, but they want to get your dad into surgery as quickly as they can.'

I'm in total shock. Dad? Surgery?

'I… Oh God! Have you seen him, Auntie Olive?'

'No, Brie. Your mum was able to spend a little time with him just now, but we'd been here for over three hours waiting for news. Wendy is understandably very upset and in shock. I made Uncle Henry take her off for a cup of tea. We don't really know too much at the moment, I will admit, as I don't think she's taking any of this in. When she's a little calmer I thought we'd ask the doctor to go over what's happening, as when she came back out after seeing him, she was in a daze. I'm so sorry, my darling. It's a horrible thing to have happened and you are so far away.'

My head is spinning, and I feel faint.

'I'm coming home. Tell Mum I'll be there as soon as I can.' The words are little more than a croak and I end the call, barely aware of what I'm doing.

I need to get home. That's all I can focus on, but I can't seem to think about what I need to do next. I hit the list of recent calls and stab my finger at the first one on the list. The next voice I hear is Carrie's again. But now the tears have come, and I blurt out the words whilst in full flow.

'Carrie, I need to get home. Dad's had a heart attack and is going into surgery. I'll pack my things; can you find me a flight? I… everything is just… I don't know what—'

'Oh, Brie! That's awful! Listen, just focus on getting your things packed. I'll sort something out and text you the details. Does Arran know?'

'No. He's taking a session. Oh, Carrie – what if something terrible happens and I'm not there?' Just the thought of that turns the gentle tears into full on sobs.

'Listen, concentrate on getting ready to leave. I'll jump online and see how we can get you home. Once you're on the plane I'll head to Heathrow and we'll get you to the hospital as quickly as possible. Be strong, Brie, and try to hold it together. The doctors know what they're doing, and your mum will ensure your dad is in good hands.'

Everything happens so quickly, and it's hard to take it all in because the thought of losing my dad is so overwhelming. Elisabetta calls me a taxi and I write a quick note to Arran, leaving it with her. The session is in full flow and I don't know what else to do.

When I arrive at the airport I'm already feeling overwhelmed, but following Carrie's instructions, I head for the Alitalia sign. The woman at the airline bookings desk recognises my name and is expecting me. She explains that I have a confirmed same-day change ticket, which means I'm guaranteed a flight today but at the moment I don't have a reserved seat on a particular flight. I say a silent *thank you* to Carrie. I'm instructed to take a seat and now it's a waiting game.

I've been sitting here, adjacent to the ticket desk, for just over an hour and a half so far. At least I feel a little more in control of myself now. I try my best to remain calm while I wait and the customer services advisor at the desk has promised I will get the first available seat. The next flight out is in less than an hour but it's too early to tell if there are going to be any no shows or cancellations. I couldn't believe it when she explained that people don't always give them advance warning, even if they have no intention at all of showing up. I suppose it depends on their situation. If, like mine, it's due to a family emergency who cares about the cost of a ticket?

I sit back, resting my head against the wall behind me, trying not to think about what's going on at the hospital. Out of the corner of my eye I see a blur as someone comes hurrying along to the desk. As I turn my head, momentarily distracted, I'm shocked to see it's Arran. He rushes up to me and I stand. He wraps his arms around me, cradling my body against his chest and hugging me as if he has no intention of ever letting me go.

'I came as soon as Elisabetta passed me your note. Is there any news?'

He leans back a little and our eyes lock. I shake my head. 'Nothing. But I doubt Auntie Olive knows how to text and Mum won't be in a fit state to talk to me. I can only assume that no news is good news. Oh, Arran, I can't bear this, not knowing what's going on.'

Arran leans his head up against mine and I'm touched to see how much he's affected by this on my behalf.

'Is there any chance you can get on the next flight?'

'I have to wait until my name is called. There are only two of us waiting and the other lady simply missed her original flight because of a traffic accident on the road. She arrived here ahead of me but has kindly asked them to give the next available seat to me.'

He doesn't loosen his grip and we stand for several minutes taking in the enormity of what's happening.

'I want to come with you,' he whispers into my hair. 'You shouldn't have to go through this on your own.'

It's heart-breaking because I know he means what he says. 'There's nothing at all you can do, Arran, and now it's going to be tough on you, too. Oh, why did this have to happen? What if my Dad isn't going to be okay?'

He tips his head back and stares into my eyes as they begin to fill with tears.

'You can't think that way, Brie. Stay positive, do you hear me?'

We're oblivious to what's going on around us and suddenly someone touches my arm.

'Sorry to interrupt but we have a seat for you. Come this way.'

My knees almost buckle from under me and Arran swiftly moves an arm around to circle my waist. As my legs take my weight once more, we follow the woman across to the check in desk. I drag out my credit card and passport, while Arran fetches across my two suitcases.

Arran and I glance at each other, unable to believe what's happening. There's hardly time for a goodbye and we simply hug each other for a few seconds, exchanging a quick kiss. And then I head off in the direction of the security checkpoint to begin the next leg of my journey back home.

I knew saying goodbye to Arran was going to be hard, but I never, ever envisioned it being like this. I'm going home, and I have no idea what I'm going to find when I get there. My world has suddenly been turned upside down, without warning. I feel heartbroken and alone.

Dad had heart bypass surgery three weeks ago. A part of one of the blood vessels in his left leg was grafted onto the coronary artery above and below two sections that had become blocked. He was only in hospital for a week but had post-op problems with an irregular heartbeat. Finally, things seem to have settled down but both Mum and Dad were exhausted, given the strain they'd been under.

I spent the first week ferrying Mum around and making sure she at least ate a little something in between hospital visits. I'd never seen her look so lost, or so frightened and I know she was fearful we were going to lose him. It didn't matter what the doctor said, she was living from minute to minute. The day he was discharged she said it was too soon and I could see how scared she was to be home alone with him. So, I slept over there for five nights and on the sixth day she hugged me, then made me go back to my cottage.

I've been here now for eight days, sinking myself into work and constantly checking my phone for text updates from Mum. I pop over late afternoon every day and we sit over a cup of tea for an hour or so. Often one of their friends, neighbours or a family member will join us, and it helps. You run out of things to say and Dad gets a little cross if you ask him more than once a day how he's feeling.

'I'm not a bloody invalid. I'm getting over an operation, that's all.' Mum and I had exchanged a grimace the day he'd had his little meltdown. The last thing we wanted to do was to upset him because he's a proud man. He hated the fuss and the fact that I'd had to come back from Italy early.

It's been hard getting my head around work and trying to blot everything else out. But I've had no choice because if I'm not actively doing something then my mind simply churns. I haven't resorted to comfort eating though, and at times of peak stress I now stop what I'm doing and go for a walk. Even in the rain I find it revitalising and it clears my mind. The phone rings and I see it's Mel, checking in.

'How is everything today?' She has been an angel. In those difficult early days, she fussed over me as I was fussing over Mum.

Ross, too, has been great and I can't wait to meet him in person. When I eventually arrived back at the cottage they'd worked as a team to get everything ready for me. Mel got the cleaners in to spruce everything up and the two of them tidied the garden. I expected to feel glad to be home again, knowing Dad was on the mend and that the tension was lifting for Mum. But I felt hollow inside.

I realise I haven't replied to Mel's question, my mind going off at a tangent. 'Sorry, brain ache today from all the words I wrote yesterday. I'm on the home stretch with the manuscript now and usually this is the fun part. Everything suddenly comes together, well, I hope it does, but I'm not getting the glow of satisfaction I normally get.'

Mel tuts. 'After what you've been through that's hardly surprising, but you're nearly there. I bet Carrie is pleased. How's the other story going?'

It's the other story that is keeping *me* going, but I can't say that. Well, that and Arran's daily phone calls. You see, the love story I'm writing suddenly turned into *our* story. But now I'm stuck because I have no idea how it's going to end. Only time will tell, so it's sitting in a folder, waiting. Waiting. Just like me.

'Good. I'm rushing to do this final read through, so I can get this off to Carrie, even though I'm way ahead of the new deadline. It will be nice to write the last part of Ethan and Izzie's story with nothing else clouding my mind.' And if it doesn't work out then I will have to grit my teeth and give it the fairy tale ending of my dreams. But it would break my heart to have to settle for that.

Real life has even seeped into my other story. The sexual tension between Bella Hart and Jed Jackman became an extension of my physical longing for Arran. As Bella's anxious pleas for him to give up fighting after suffering a serious concussion were brushed off, it marred the passion between them. The story seemed to be mirroring my life. As distant as I was beginning to feel from Arran, so Bella began to feel the same way with Jed. But when it comes to fiction anything is possible and everything came together again in the end. Carrie and my readers will be expecting that heart-rending, happy ever after, and I wanted it, too.

Somehow, I need to keep believing that true love can survive anything, and this is one hopeless romantic who has suddenly woken up. If the man of your dreams is hot and sexy and intellectual, then who cares about the sentimental stuff? I thought I wanted a man who arrived at my door with his arms full of flowers and violins playing in the background. Well, that was the fantasy for so many years. As it turns out that isn't necessary. All I want is to have Arran standing on my doorstep with a suitcase in his hand. It's not that I'm settling, it's simply that he has captured my heart and sex sells books for a good reason.

'I'm pleased for you, Brie. It hasn't been an easy time, but you kept going. When does Arran arrive?'

I glance up at the calendar pinned on the wall above my desk with the days ticked off in red pen.

'A little over twenty-three hours. Not that I'm counting.'

'Oh, less than a day, then,' she replies, laughing at me.

'The last group flew back home at the weekend. He sounds tired, but he says little. I can't even begin to imagine how he coped because he avoided talking about it. During his calls he simply wanted to support me, and I admit that without the two of you I think I might have gone to pieces.'

It's the truth and both Mel and I know that.

'Are you planning a romantic dinner for two when he arrives?'

I spend a long time each night lying in bed in the dark trying to imagine what it will be like when Arran and I meet up again. On the phone it's been easy, but then he's simply asked me questions to get me talking. I've shared every little detail of what's been happening with Dad and it helped, it really did. But there was no sense of *us* in the phone calls, other than just before we hung up. Exchanging a fleeting 'I miss you' followed by well meaning words of encouragement, felt detached and unreal.

'Yes. A quiet dinner here.' I won't know if it's going to be alright until I'm in his arms again. Will the passion between us have cooled? The mere thought sends an icy chill through me.

'Once you've caught up it will be fine, Brie. I know you are worried that things will be different between you. But you are still both the same people.'

'Yes, but he's coming over for work, not simply to see me.' Doubt begins to gnaw away inside me, once more. I've spent most of the day trying to push it away but it's like having a shadow that never disappears.

'I know but you originally said he wasn't flying over until the middle of the month, so that tells you something, doesn't it?'

It tells me he has something to say that he feels he can't deliver over the phone. Arran is first and foremost a gentleman. I dismiss my anxiety, making an effort to smile, and give a lift to my voice.

'I'm sure it will all be fine. When I know what's happening I'll give you a call and we'll all go out for a meal.'

There's a slight pause.

'Brie, you won't push him away, will you? If you'd been in Italy for the entire four weeks you would have come back on a high. It's understandable that you are on a low but it's no one's fault. Just don't let that negativity rub off onto what happened between you both. You didn't choose to part ways, it was forced upon you. Remember that.'

26

Making the Best of a Bad Situation

When the doorbell finally rings my heart begins to thud. I've been too nervous to even look out of the window, knowing that Arran could arrive at any moment. I'm anxious about how I'm going to feel when I look into his eyes for the first time. It's the fear of losing something I'm not even sure I had. What if… my hand is on the door as the shrill sound of the bell rings for the second time. I compose myself, plastering on a pleasant smile as I swing it open.

We stand looking at each other for several moments. It feels strange. Arran here, standing on my doorstep and about to step into the reality of my world. This is where he gets an insight into the real me, as I've had an insight into his world. Arran's world is cosmopolitan, glamorous even, in a way. Here, my life isn't like that at all. I spend most of my time alone, writing, and could count on two hands the number of times each year I rub shoulders with sophisticated people.

I step back, and he hesitates. 'My bags are in the car. Shall I get them now?'

I nod; my smile has slipped and the awkwardness we are both feeling gives me that now all too familiar cold feeling in the pit of my stomach.

'Tea or coffee?' My voice wavers at the effort of trying to sound upbeat.

'Coffee, please,' he throws over his shoulder, before disappearing back up the path.

As I walk into the kitchen, leaving the door ajar, I want to kick myself. My hesitation stopped us greeting properly and he was thrown, unsure of what to do next. I have no idea if he intended to kiss me on the cheek, or catch me up in his arms, but I desperately need to know which.

As the water boils I clatter about with mugs and spoons for a minute or two before I realise he's standing behind me.

'Brie, put that down and turn around.'

I swivel, looking beyond him to see his suitcases standing in the hallway and the door firmly shut. This is it. The moment of truth.

When I drag my eyes back to his face I can see it's full of emotion. One step and we are in each other's arms.

He begins by planting swift little kisses along the curve of my cheek, working his way with increasing impatience down to my mouth. It's like we've never been apart, and the fire is still there between us, that longing that instantly disengages the brain. Nothing else matters because nothing else appears to exist.

Then Arran's phone pings and a second later, pings again. He groans as he pulls away, reluctantly yanking it out of his pocket. I take a deep breath, turning back to my original task but this time with my heart bouncing around crazily in my chest.

When I turn back around with a mug in each hand, his head is still bent over his phone and he's texting. He glances up at me, apologetically.

'Sorry, almost done.'

'No problem. When you're ready follow me out to the garden room.'

Seconds later he's by my side and joins me, sinking down onto the ochre coloured couch.

'This is some cottage you have here. I was expecting small rooms and floral curtains. And the thatched roof is a real surprise. This is the quintessentially British chocolate box cottage but with a contemporary twist. Did you do the renovation work?'

I nod. 'Yes. I got it for a song because it was a wreck and employed a building company who took it from the architect's plans to completion in only nine months.'

He's studying my face intently, and the smile on his face is so broad it almost looks unreal.

'Your smile is freaking me out,' I state, laughing at him.

'It's just so good to be here with you.'

It's my turn to study him now and I see there are dark circles beneath his eyes and when he isn't smiling he looks a little drawn.

We both kick off our shoes and lie at opposite ends of the sofa, our legs entwined. Arran wants an update on Dad and there isn't really anything further to report since we spoke on the phone yesterday. Now it's all about the healing process, but the shock of what has happened has taken a toll on us all. I'm eager for his news but sense he isn't ready to start talking yet. That means it's not going to be good news.

So instead we talk about the garden and then I take him on a tour around the cottage. It is too big for me and I do rattle around, but it's an investment. If my books stop selling overnight, then it's a comfort to know I could get a nice sum for this place and move into something more modest. When you are on your own there is no safety net other than the one you provide for yourself.

We while away the afternoon, heading out for a walk along the country lanes and up through onto the common at the top of the nearby hill. The sky is grey and particularly uninspiring today; together with the chilly breeze it feels more like autumn than summer. Arran keeps commenting on how chilly it is and even though we're wearing jackets, we've had to keep up a brisk pace to avoid feeling cold. Longingly, I remember the heat of the Italian sunshine and I can appreciate it must take Arran a little while to adjust every time he comes back to the UK. We have had some beautiful days, it's true, but we've also had torrential rain that seems to last for long periods. Sometimes it's hard to believe the sun will put in an appearance again.

When we get back I lead him into the sitting room and I notice he makes no attempt to relinquish his jacket. I slip mine off but then I am wearing a thick jumper.

'I'll just put the heating on.' I turn on my heels, but he immediately starts speaking.

'It's a long time since I've warmed myself by the heat of a fire. Does this thing work?'

He points to the log burner, a wistful smile sweeping over his face.

'Of course it does! I use it a lot actually. Summer evenings can be quite chilly.'

He gives a chuckle. 'Some of the days, too, I have on good authority.'

Arran settles himself on the sofa, watching as I perform the ritual of making fire. He's clearly delighted, although I know that turning on the central heating would have warmed things up more quickly. Sitting with my back to him, I lay out a row of kindling, then add the firelighters. Next, I begin stacking the logs.

'Are you going to tell me what happened?' I break the silence, knowing that I can't rest until I know.

I don't have to turn around and look at Arran's face because I can tell by his drawn out sigh that he's had a rough time.

'It's hard. I don't even want to hear myself putting it into words, to be honest with you.'

I place one last log on the top of the pile and light a screw of paper, nestling it next to a firelighter. Then I join Arran on the sofa and we both focus intently on the little flame as it slowly spreads and turns from a silvery blue to a yellowy red.

'When I arrived back from saying goodbye to you at the airport I didn't know what to do. All I could think about was that I wanted to be by your side, not going back to pretend everything was alright. It wasn't alright because you weren't there. I wanted to help because I was worried about you and instead I had to try to push my anxiety away and carry on.'

I reach out and he wraps his hand around mine, pulling me into him. We lie back as he begins to tell me what has happened while we've been apart.

'I'm not a big drinker, well, aside from the night you got me drunk.' I think if I could see his face now he'd be trying to raise a smile, albeit a half-hearted one, because his tone is strained.

Arran squeezes my hand lightly, his other arm sliding around my shoulder to pull me even closer. The warmth of his body next to mine makes me tingle all over and it's a truly wonderful feeling.

'I let the group go off to dinner and then took a bottle of vodka up to my room. I spent, I don't know how long, trying to clear my mind enough to work out what I was going to do. I rang Carrie, in case she knew of any writers who were holidaying in Italy and might have been able to step in at short notice. I even contacted a writer I know who retired a couple of years ago and lives about a two hour drive away. When we both drew a blank I had to face the fact that at the very least I needed someone who could act as a host. If I only had the sessions to cope with, then I could probably get through it.'

I half turn to look at him, fearing that he's going to tell me something I'm not going to want to hear.

'Inviting Harriet back to Villa Monteverdi was the hardest thing I've ever done in my life. It's been two and a half weeks of hell, but...' He pauses, letting out a deep breath. 'But she was the perfect hostess. She chaperoned the groups on the two organised trips and took my place at every evening meal. I couldn't shake off this overwhelming sense of loss without you there and I sure as hell couldn't make small talk. Without her help I don't know how I could have gotten through it and that hurt so badly. But there's always a price to pay because Harriet doosn't do favours.'

I swallow hard to disperse the lump in my throat, as I take in the hollow look in Arran's eyes. After a few seconds he begins speaking again.

'The villa is hers now for the next two months.'

I know that must be hard for Arran to accept, as when she left I'm sure he vowed that she would never return. It's his home and sitting here, knowing she's living at the villa again as if she belongs there, must be galling.

'It's just two months, Arran and for most of that you will be in the UK. It could have been worse, and you had no choice. It's no one's fault and there was no alternative. She could have refused you.'

Arran nods, shifting uneasily in his seat.

'I reorganised all of my commitments to be with you as quickly as I could. And yes, I didn't have any other options but getting her out once the two months are up might not be so easy. Because I still owe her a lot of money, in her eyes she believes she has a right to be there. I think I can manage to scrape the next payment together. I negotiated an advance on one of the voiceover jobs and together with one of my six monthly royalty cheques and what I have put aside, I can cover it. But that's it and there won't be enough coming in to make the one after that unless a miracle happens. Harriet has been aware for a while now that my disposable funds have virtually run out and I believe she's been talking to my mother. She made me an offer I'm supposed to be considering.'

He pauses for a moment, assembling his thoughts. I'm horrified because this is my fault, isn't it? I mean, not the money side but the fact that she's back in his life, and this makes it personal again, rather than arm's length contact via solicitors. My problems have created a nightmare situation for Arran and yet he's not blaming me in any way, or angry at the turn his life has taken through no fault of his own. My head is full of 'if only' and having to accept that fate dictates the timing of events leaves me feeling frustrated and a tad bitter.

'I wish I wasn't the reason why she is back in your life, now.' I find myself struggling to choke back the tears, hating the fact that this has unwittingly opened the way for Harriet to complicate Arran's life again. 'What is it that she really wants?'

We both sit for a moment watching as the logs on the fire begin to spit and hiss. I wonder if it's only the villa, or whether it's Arran, too, that she's after. Has he the stamina to continue fighting with her, or is he at the point where he admits defeat?

'Whether I like it or not, the choice is between putting up with Harriet in my life, because she made it clear she wants us to try again, or losing the villa.'

My heart sinks faster than a stone thrown into a deep body of water, but I say nothing.

'My father doesn't care what happens. My mother, well, she asked about you, but she's on Harriet's side and feels I'm being unreasonable. She thinks I'm having a little moment of insanity turning my back on Harriet because she is, after all, my ex-wife. Beautiful, intelligent and well connected. What more could any reasonable man want? But she's as cold as an ice house.'

He doesn't add that in his mother's eyes I'm just a little interlude as, clearly, to her I wouldn't be suitable daughter-in-law material.

'The day after Harriet moved back in, my mother rang and withdrew her offer of the loan. She said it put her in a difficult position with my father, but I know the truth. Harriet spoke to her, no doubt putting her professional spin on everything, and now she has a revised agenda.'

'I'm horrified, Arran. If Kathy hadn't broken her foot at least you would have been spared this.'

He draws his arm even tighter around me.

'Don't say that, because then I wouldn't have met you, Brie.'

It's an impossible situation but his words are spoken with sincerity.

As the flames begin to lick up and around the logs on the top of the pile, my brain is working overtime.

'Is there any news about your manuscript?'

I pull away, desperate to see his expression and search for clues about where this is going.

'I wasn't sure if Carrie had spoken to you. It's looking promising; she now has three publishers interested.'

I slip my hand over his and give him a smile.

'It's confidential information, so she would never divulge any details to me directly. But that's great news! There could be an auction.'

He shakes his head, looking slightly amused.

'Well, yes and no. Two are only interested if I write the sequel, which is the story of what happened after Arthur returned. Only one publisher will consider taking it as a stand alone and the advance on offer is only twenty thousand pounds. They admit that most people will want to read the conclusion to the story.'

But that's not even half of the money he needs to meet one payment, including interest.

'With ten payments still outstanding to Harriet, it's something, but the likelihood of my defaulting becomes increasingly more likely as each month passes. The money isn't coming in at that sort of rate. I'd run back to back writing retreats if I could, but it takes five months to set everything up and most people want to come in the summer months.'

We sit in silence for a few minutes, staring at the fire as a distraction. Harriet's hold over Arran puts her in a position of power and she sounds like the sort of woman who knows exactly how to use it.

'You don't have a choice, do you?' My voice sounds small, the only other sound in the room being the crackle from the logs as they begin to blacken amongst the hungry flames. The room is finally beginning to warm and Arran leans forward, slipping off his coat. He turns to look at me.

'I feel like a failure; I've let my grandfather down. He left me the villa because he felt I would cherish it for generations to come. But it's been a battle since day one. Initially it caused a problem between my sister and me, aside from the fallout with my father. She hasn't spoken to me since the day the will was read. But I knew for her it was about the monetary value and that's why my grandfather chose me to inherit it. Everything else was split between my father and her. And they sold it all, as if there was no sentimental attachment to anything he left behind. His beloved old cars and the penthouse flat overlooking Hyde Park.

'We often stayed there as children, and yet it seems I'm the only one for whom it held special memories. My grandmother loved it there. And now it's looking increasing likely that it will be down to Harriet as to whether the villa is sold or stays under my control. All of this because I was a fool and didn't even consider protecting my inheritance against any future financial claims made by a spouse. Ironically, Harriet insisted on keeping her assets very separate from the start. The fact that she had moved everything she had into a savings account in her own name was enough to exclude it from the equation when it came down to working out the settlement. I was a trusting fool, but then I thought she was a very different woman to the one I've seen as time has moved on. She can be quite ruthless when it suits her.'

The fire is now throwing out a generous amount of heat and Arran leans further forward, soaking up the blast of warmth.

When he relaxes back into the sofa I can see that tiredness is taking over. I lie back next to him and we clasp hands, sitting in silence.

Sometimes the answers don't come easily. And sometimes they come in a dream.

It's a gentle awakening; Arran's lips on mine and then, before we know it, we are rolling around on the soft white rug in front of the fire. No longer roaring, the logs half eaten by the flames, the heat is marvellously bearable against our naked skin. The passion is all consuming and the only escape from the nagging worries hanging over us.

Afterwards, I roll over onto my stomach, raising my head to look up into Arran's eyes.

'What happens next with us?'

He tilts his head to look at me, amusement flickering over his face.

'All I know is that I could live the rest of my life quite happily with you on this rug, in front of the fire and never have a regret. No matter what happened in the world outside the front door. I love you, Brie, but I wish I could offer you more than I have right now. I can understand if you decide to walk away.'

Oh. My. God. This is the moment when I wave goodbye to Jude. You are simply my fantasy, but Arran is my reality. The big surprise is that I don't think Jude could have answered that question as beautifully as Arran did.

'Come on, don't leave me hanging,' Arran asks, anxiously. 'I'm putting my feelings on the line here, and I'm speaking straight from my heart for the first time ever.'

'I'm not just in love with you, but I'm in lust with you, too. In my world a love story doesn't get any better. I couldn't have written it more perfectly. But what does it mean given the current situation? I only want you, nothing else, but I also can't be the reason you lose everything, Arran.'

We lie with our heads touching as our bodies relax, trying to get our brains around what comes next.

'Arran, do you trust me enough to do me a favour? Can you just say yes to make me happy?'

'Yes, but it depends on the favour. Why do I think I'm not going to like this?'

I roll onto my side to look directly at him.

'Because your pride gets in the way, that's why. Grab whatever advance you can get and I'll be by your side when you need me to help with Rose's story. I will make up the shortfall so that means you will have the next two payments sorted.' He starts to object but I put up my hand to stop him. 'That will give you, what, almost three months grace to decide how you are going to come up with the rest of the money. You can't creak by as you are doing now. It's too stressful to be worrying about money every hour of the day.'

'Thank you, but no. And you are right, I know I have no choice as I need to make some tough and unpalatable decisions. As it stands, Harriet's claim on the property amounts to a quarter share, which reduces a little after each payment. I can't afford to take up a loan to repay her in one go, because together with the running costs, financially it would be too big a burden. Aside from selling it, the only other option is that she forgoes the money and we formalise her part ownership. I spend between three and five months a year in the UK anyway. I know that not being able to entertain her friends at the villa was a big loss to her and although she'd no doubt want the summer months, it's a potential way out, I suppose. I'd just have to grin and bear it, but it would hurt.'

'But what about the income you'd lose from running the courses?'

'I'd have to make that up in another way but if that's the only pressure, then it's do-able. I want us to be together, Brie, and I don't plan on letting Harriet prevent that.'

He looks accepting of this as a solution, but I can see how wounded he feels, deep inside. And the fact he'd do that for us tells me more than a string of flowery words.

I reach out and touch his cheek, letting my fingers trail down to the curve of his chin. He doesn't even realise he's clenching his jaw and the lightness of my touch is enough to make him stop.

'I don't want you to regret any decision you make, Arran. Let me help you out and at least it will gain you some thinking time. If you really do love me, you will do this to prove it. I would hate you to end up living with regrets. As for Arthur and Rose's story, the sequel makes perfect sense. I also think you should do it for them. A love like theirs deserves to be remembered forever.'

Arran rolls onto his side and our faces are inches apart as we stare at each other.

'It's not an easy thing that you are asking, you know that? As for the sequel, think about it – the war is over, and that's where my interest begins to wane.'

I frown. 'Now I know that's not quite true. You were the one who decided to write Arthur and Rose's story and, yes, while war is the main topic throughout the first book, what inspired you about them was the people they became because of what they had been through; and their daughter, Hope, who was destined to play a significant part in your life. She was a second mother to you.'

Now it's Arran's turn to frown. 'I can't deny the truth but telling that part of the story isn't one of my strengths, you know that. You could write it, though.'

I shake my head. 'No, I can't, because I didn't know any of them, so it wouldn't be me telling their story at all. It would be me writing fiction. That's not quite the same thing.'

He can deal with facts, no matter how harsh and brutal, but he can't cope with emotional trauma. Or maybe the hurt of a little boy who clung onto the woman paid to look after him, who gave her love freely when his own mother couldn't, lies just below the surface still.

Arran sits up, opening the door to the log burner and using the poker to redistribute the glowing red embers, then he adds another log. The flickering of the flames in the darkening room light up his skin as he bends to tend to the fire. He's really here, in my life and it seems almost too good to be true. I'm going to fight to stop anything that threatens to get in our way.

'What if we wrote it together?' I'm almost wondering out loud, the idea suddenly popping into my head.

Arran turns around, the look on his face one of surprise. 'Would that work?' He lowers himself back down beside me and I let the fingertips of my left hand trail down his back.

'Yes, we'd make it work. I should imagine it was a tough time for Arthur, adjusting to his injury and faced with rehabilitation. Didn't most of them come back with battle fatigue? I wouldn't have a clue about that side of things, but if I could access what you have about Rose, and with a little additional research, I'd love to collaborate with you.'

Arran looks pensive. 'For so many of the soldiers who made it back it left a permanent mark. We recognise it now as post-traumatic stress disorder, but you're right and it encompassed such symptoms as hypervigilance, paranoia, depression and even loss of memory. It was central to what happened after Arthur's return. Having lived under the duress of life threatening events and experiencing severe trauma on an almost daily basis, the new norm seemed anything but normal. Arthur found himself constantly on edge, emotionally numb and disconnected. Rose had a tough time trying to drag him out of his growing sense of isolation, depression and guilt, for being a survivor. With a baby suddenly on the way it was tough for her, but then it was tough for him, too.

'Okay. You win. It doesn't sit well with me taking money from you, Brie, but maybe there is a way out of this. And I'll tell Carrie that there will be a sequel and it's going to be a joint venture. I can't imagine what her reaction is going to be. You're the only person who understands what the villa represents, and it means more than I can put into words. But if, in the end, I lose it, then at least I'll have you.'

He leans in and his lips are soft on mine. It's a moment that challenges anything I've watched on the big TV screen behind us.

'It's only money, Arran,' I whisper as I draw back. 'Look at my dad. If you asked him now what the most important thing is he'd say good health, not money.'

It's a sobering thought as we begin searching around for our clothes.

'Well, I don't know about you but I'm starving,' I admit. Arran starts laughing.

'I love you, Brie. More than anything else in the entire world. And I never, ever thought I'd hear myself saying that to anyone and knowing for sure it was real.'

27

Taking Control

I've had my epiphany – that defining moment in my life when suddenly I know what I'm going to do. I always thought that would arrive with a firm plan to map out my future. But I've discovered that isn't the case, at all.

'Good morning, you're through to Allen, Able and Cole. How can I help you?'

'Hello. My name is Brie Middleton and I want to make an appointment for someone to call around to give me a valuation on my property. I'd like to put it on the market as soon as possible, please.'

Arran left just after 7 a.m. as I warned him the traffic builds up quickly on the M4 heading towards Cardiff. Luckily, the lavish Brockleigh House, which has its own recording studio in the grounds, is a few miles away from the outskirts of the city itself. It will be his daily commute for the next two weeks and while he's not around I want to get things moving on selling the cottage. I don't plan on breaking the news until I have a buyer because I have no idea how long it takes to sell a property these days.

As soon as I press *end call* my phone instantly lights up and it's Carrie.

'What on earth is going on?' Her voice seems to boom at me from out of the speaker.

'Um… give me a clue.'

'I've just had a long conversation with Arran. When he said I could sign him up for a sequel and that you would be co-writing it, I nearly fell off my chair. Do you have the time to commit to that?'

Admittedly, it isn't going to be easy. I don't usually write without a break in between books, because every new release brings a hefty marketing workload. But being exceptionally busy for a while is a small price to pay.

'Of course! I'm almost done on my read through of *Taming a Man's Heart* and I hope to get that over to you by the end of the day. My love story is going well and as soon as it's finished, I'll press on with the one scheduled for the second half of next year. Arran and I are going to sit down and draft out a sequence of chapters and who is writing what. That way it will be easier to slot it into our schedules. Piece of cake!'

Well, that's the plan of action Arran and I came up with after two glasses of red wine and a scrumptious meal. Maybe, in the cold light of day, we were a little too relaxed and a tad optimistic given the wonderful feeling of well-being surrounding the evening. But we will make it work. I have no doubt about that, at all.

'So, is he staying with you for his entire trip? He did a poor job of trying to convince me it was just a convenience thing while he's over here working. I was too shocked to ask any questions as he sounded so different!'

I can hear a cautionary note in Carrie's tone of voice. She isn't just my literary agent, but my business manager, my publicist and a trusted friend. I mean, she cared enough to mount an intervention and rally everyone around me. So I'm not surprised she's a little concerned, as we haven't really had a chance to talk since I arrived back; well, except for updates about my dad's health.

'He's a gentleman and he doesn't realise you *know*. But of course, he's living at mine. Look, there is nothing at all to worry about. People meet and fall in love every hour of every day. Once Arran has sorted out his current financial problems we can then start making plans for the future.'

The sound of a sudden, sharp intake of breath travels down the line.

'Well, I really hope you can find a way around his complex circumstances.'

Silence reigns for a few seconds and, to be honest, I don't know quite what more I can say at this point.

'It's just that you two are such an unlikely combination, but I'd hoped you could help each other on a professional level. I sincerely hope nothing goes wrong because if it does I'll never forgive myself.'

Ooh, that's not really the reaction I was hoping to hear.

'Well, we are very different in lots of ways but that's what makes it so interesting between us.'

'Interesting?' Cassie's response is just a tad too high pitched for my liking.

'Look. He's Mr Conservative in some ways, I will admit. And I'm fully aware of the fact that our backgrounds are very different. But he's an intelligent and gentle man; and a gentleman. All that counts is that when we're together the world feels like a much happier and brighter place to be. We are both going into this fully aware of the potential problems. So stop fretting. After the scare I've been through with Dad it's made me realise that we all take it for granted that there will always be a tomorrow. It's time to start living and enjoying life, rather than worrying about every little detail.'

I hear a soft 'hmm' before Carrie replies.

'I'd hate to see either of you get hurt, Brie. You are both good people who don't normally make rash decisions and that's what's worrying me. I seriously doubt you'll take my advice about easing yourselves into this new relationship slowly, so there's nothing more I can usefully say on the matter. Anyway, changing the subject rather diplomatically, I can't wait to have a first read of Jed and Bella's story. I'll look forward to receiving that.'

When Carrie is in work mode her tone instantly changes. I know her parents are very affluent, and she attended boarding school. Ironically, I'm sure a dating agency would be more likely to match Carrie with Arran, than me. I'm not saying Carrie isn't an emotional person because she is very caring, but she isn't a hopeless romantic. Her heart doesn't rule her head. I think Arran thought he was the same but overnight he's come to realise that when it comes to love, everything can change in an instant. The look on his face when he's watching me tells me everything I need to know. I make him feel as happy and complete as he makes me feel. And that's the one little factor a computer can't replicate. I can't wait until Carrie bumps into Mr Right. She's in for a big shock!

Next on my action list this morning is a call to Mel. Before I can get back to work I need some advice. With quite a workload ahead of me I'm going to be chained to my keyboard, so I'm going to have to hire in some help.

Mel picks up on the second ring.

'What's this? Why aren't you working? Is that a good or bad sign? Is he there now?'

She hits me with a volley of questions. I glance at my Vivofit to see it's coming up to 10 a.m. Usually I wake early, jump on social media for an hour and then begin writing. That makes me very unsociable until lunch time.

'I have a few things to sort out. Arran left early this morning. I'm phoning to ask your advice. I know you use agency staff all the time and I want to hire a personal assistant for a short period. Hopefully, no more than a couple of months. But they have to be discreet. I wondered if there was a particularly good agency you could recommend.'

I can hear a hollow sound in the background and suddenly it stops. When Mel starts speaking, I can tell she's walking.

'I'm just heading back to my desk to get you a contact name and number. It's unusual for you to delegate. What's going on?'

'Okay, this is just between the two of us, right? I'm going to put the house on the market and sell up as quickly as I can. I don't have the time to liaise with estate agents about viewings because you know what I'm like when I'm working. It's pure concentration. So, I need someone to be the main contact managing it all and then updating my electronic diary so I know when I have to make myself scarce. I'll pop into town and work from the coffee shop when the estate agent is showing the cottage. I doubt a viewing takes more than an hour max.'

'You're *what*?' She sounds stunned and then I realise without knowing everything that's happening this must come as a total shock to her.

'Eek! Sorry, Mel. Yesterday when Arran arrived we both knew, instantly, that no matter what happens we're going to be together. It wasn't about *if*, but about *when*. At the moment any plans he has are being hampered by his ex and when I dropped everything and flew home I unwittingly brought her back into his life. It's a long story, but where I live isn't a big concern to me at the moment. The funds it would release would solve the biggest of the problems. But I can't let Arran know what I'm doing until it's done because he'll stop me.'

I hear an ominous gasp.

'You're doing this without his knowledge? And based on being back together for one day? Brie, have you totally lost your mind? I know I was encouraging you to pick up where you left off once he arrived, but I'm astounded.'

The clock is ticking, and work is calling. Besides, this isn't something I can explain over the phone.

'Probably, but I don't care. I just need that contact if you have it. And when we all meet up you'll be very careful what you say, won't you?'

I can hear her tapping on a keyboard and she gives me a name and a number.

'Of course, I won't say anything. But I really want to meet Arran very soon, Brie.'

Why do the people around me feel I need protecting? Almost as if I'd voiced that out loud, Mel answers.

'When someone whose usual style is to think everything through in great detail then sleep on it before moving forward, making a snap decision is a red flag. This is a major change that will throw everything up in the air. You've been very happy there, Brie, and the cottage is so close to your family and friends. Besides, it's your security for the future.'

Inwardly I groan. It wasn't my intention to send Mel into a panic. 'And I've also been very unhappy here, Mel. All the angst over Paul wasn't about him at all. It was about feeling that something was missing from my life. I wasn't really living, just getting through each day. Now, suddenly and, admittedly unexpectedly, I've found that special someone who makes me feel complete. It puts everything else into perspective.'

'You'd fly back to Italy and leave us all behind?'

'No, Mel. You couldn't be more wrong. This is my nest egg and now I want to free up the cash, that's all. I could buy something for half the price of this and still have a very comfortable home. But it does signal the start of some pretty major changes, as Arran and I move our relationship forward; I can't deny that fact. He lives in

Italy for a large part of the year but some of his work is over here. But all of that is in the future and I would never simply up and leave everyone at a moment's notice. I thought you'd be happy for me.'

The rustle of tissue paper makes me wonder if she's shedding a tear and my heart sinks.

'I am happy for you, of course I am. It's a lot to take in though, and I wasn't expecting things to start happening quite so soon. I can't believe you're doing this for a guy I haven't even met. We're like sisters and I'm not sure…' Her voice wavers and I feel like the worst BFF in the world.

'Nothing is going to change imminently, other than Arran is going to be staying here. Besides, you don't think I'd go off and leave Mum alone with the worry of Dad, after what happened, do you? And I have a frenetic workload ahead of me, so I really will be chained to my desk. That's why I need that personal assistant.'

I'm trying to cheer her up, but a little niggle of guilt is telling me that my future with Arran is a big unknown. The only thing I do know for sure, is that we'll be together and somehow, we need a solution that is workable.

I end the call by arranging for us all to meet up for a meal at the local pub, The Farrier's Arms, on Friday evening. It seems to brighten her mood but if this is how Mel takes the news, how on earth are Mum and Dad going to react?

Mid-afternoon, my phone begins to ring, and I jump on it. Usually, when I'm working I don't answer and pick up my messages later in the day, but I hope it will be Arran.

'Hey, how's it going?' Even though he hasn't said a word yet, just the fact that I know he's on the other end of the line and less than an hour away, makes me break out in a big smile.

'Good. It's been a productive day. We're finishing at four and I wondered if you had any plans for tonight because I thought I'd cook for you.'

'You *cook*?' I didn't mean to sound so taken aback.

'Of course I cook – doesn't everybody? Admittedly, some people do it better than others. I think I'm quite a good cook, actually.'

I should have realised that because his kitchen at the villa was well equipped, as was his larder. He's only been here a day and already I'm discovering new things about him and this is a real bonus, as I hate cooking.

'That would be great.'

'Are you allergic to anything other than gluten?' Hmm, a thoughtful chef, too.

'No. Unfortunately I have this tendency to eat everything that is put in front of me except squid. So make the portions small,' I reinforce.

He chuckles. 'I didn't want to spoil tonight in any way at all.'

Having experienced the effects of my gurgling stomach he's wise to be wary.

'Oh, you won't. Just get yourself back here because I'm missing you like crazy.'

'Yes, boss. And shouldn't you be finishing off that final read through?'

I groan out loud.

'I was until you interrupted me. I have five pages to go and it's looking good.'

A little groan travels down the line but it's an entirely different sound to mine.

'I'll be there as soon as I can. Nothing beats a solid day's work and then heading home to cook dinner for your woman.'

I burst out laughing. Well, that counts as a romantic moment. With renewed determination I tackle those last few pages and finally press the send key. It's going to be the usual anxious wait until I get Carrie's initial feedback, but I feel I've done the story justice. Then I head upstairs to make myself presentable for our cosy little dinner for two.

28

Emotions Run High

Arran arrives back bearing two loaded carrier bags of groceries.

'How many people do you intend to feed? I thought it was just going to be the two of us?'

'Well, I don't actually know anyone else round here so I'm afraid you're stuck with me. But I wasn't sure what you keep in your larder, so I bought everything I need and a few impulse buys. Never shop when you're hungry.'

I follow him out to the kitchen, a weird smile flitting across my face that could well be described as the teensiest bit smug. Arran deposits the bags on the floor and turns around, catching the tail end of it.

'Were you laughing at me there for a moment?'

I step forward, circling my arms around his waist and gazing up into his eyes. He peers back at me questioningly, one eyebrow slightly hitched.

'No. I was thinking how surreal this is and how lucky I am.'

He shakes his head. 'Lucky to be involved with a guy who has zero in the bank, owes a fair bit of money to his ex and owns a property that's probably way beyond his means? But, ah, I forget. This particular woman is a romance writer, for which I'm very grateful.'

He stoops to plant a kiss on the tip of my nose.

'The implication being that I'm steered by my heart and not my head? Is that such a bad thing?'

Arran tilts his head back, a small frown creasing his brow as he considers my question. 'I feel a little guilty, if I'm being honest with you. The life you have here is so settled and you aren't simply welcoming me into it, but all the chaos that is around me at the moment. It's more than many women would entertain. Huh! When I think of Harriet, she made everything about her. You don't ask for much, Brie.'

Standing so close to him is making my pulse race and I force myself to concentrate and listen to what he's saying. 'I don't ask for much because there's nothing to ask for. Happiness is a state of mind and you make me exceedingly happy. I don't care about the problems, but I did have an awkward phone call with Mel this afternoon. I think I'd better pour us both a glass of wine before I tell you all about it.'

Arran homes in for a kiss and we're both loath to break the moment. Then the sound of his rumbling stomach makes me pull away, laughing.

'Okay, I need food,' he admits. 'You pour the wine and I'll get things underway.'

As I scuttle around getting glasses and opening the bottle, it gives me a little thrill to watch as he slips off his jacket and hangs it in the hallway cupboard. Then he rolls back the sleeves of his shirt to just below the elbow and walks over to the sink to wash his hands.

I slip up onto one of the bar stools in front of the island and begin pouring. It's hard to take my eyes off him for even a second, as this is like living a scene from one of my favourite films. When he turns around we toast, and Arran says, 'To a romantic dinner for two.' His eyes are filled with a mix of happiness and desire when he looks back at me. Something at my core begins to glow, rather pleasantly.

'Umm…' I halt, looking around as if I've lost something.

'What?'

'You said romantic. Where are the flowers and the chocolates?'

'Really? That's a bit over the top, isn't it? I did buy organic, free range, corn fed chicken. Nothing but the best as I wanted to impress you.'

Hmm. I'm not complaining but maybe I need to introduce Arran in person to a few of my favourite films. If he's never seen *Love Actually* or *Notting Hill*, it might be quite enlightening and provide him with a few clues about romantic etiquette.

'So, what happened with Mel?'

I stop daydreaming and focus.

'Chopping board and knives?' he enquiries, shrugging his shoulders.

'Top drawer beneath the island and the knives are in the wooden block just inside the larder unit. Mel had a bit of a wobble. She thinks I'm going to up and leave for Italy again.'

Arran stops to fiddle with the oven settings then, after selecting a knife, walks back to the island. He peers across at me.

'I can understand her concerns. Knowing we want to be together is one thing, but how on earth we're going to sort everything out, I don't know. My accountant is on the case now looking at the cost of taking a mortgage out on the villa. He said another option is to let it out for the peak holiday season every year to cover the cost of the repayments. Obviously, that's a great idea but it means I wouldn't be able to run the courses and I'd have to rent something myself if I didn't have work here in the UK. Well, at least, that was my gut reaction. Then I remembered about you. Sorry, us. It changes everything.'

I swallow a sip of wine and replace my glass on the counter top. I'm torn over whether or not to tell him my little plan, but I'm pretty sure he'd try to talk me out of it. I have no idea how long it might take to find a buyer anyway, so I opt to say nothing.

'Well, you'll stay with me, of course. If that's a workable solution and you don't mind having strangers in the villa when you aren't around.'

I can see by his face even the thought of it is painful. It means it would no longer be his permanent home. I think about that wonderful vinyl collection and the library. It's not really a place set up to use as a rental property. He's probably equally as anxious knowing Harriet is there now, pretending she's the lady of the house.

'Interesting. You're doing the same thing I did. Being a couple will take some adjustment. Whatever we do has to work for both of us,' Arran replies.

I watch as he chops up two shallots and then begins peeling a few cloves of garlic.

'Oh, I see what you mean. Maybe we've both been on our own for too long.' We exchange an awkward half grimace.

'Well, I for one never thought I'd get married again,' he adds.

My wine glass is about an inch away from my mouth and suddenly my hand is frozen.

'Married?' I gulp.

Arran shoots me a glance, his head tipping back in surprise.

'I just assumed… I mean, we are on the same page, aren't we?' He stops chopping to stare unwaveringly at me, as I lower my glass back down with a slightly shaky hand.

Now, when you've written a shelf full of romantic novels, one of the highlights is the proposal scene. I don't know whether to feel deliciously excited or cheated of a moment that should rate as one of the most memorable in a woman's life.

Where were you when he proposed?

Oh, sitting opposite him in the kitchen watching him chopping garlic.

Did he get down on one knee?

No, but he did stop chopping for a moment.

I can see he's a little worried by my silence. I swallow hard to disperse the knot of emotion that is now sitting in my chest and give him a heartfelt smile. The man I love wants to marry me and that's all I need to know.

'You bet. But how we're going to accommodate your life in Italy, our work in the UK and managing two homes – it's a lot to think about. And then although Dad is recovering well, it's been a reminder neither of them are getting any younger.'

I casually leave out the fact that I have major concerns over whether I could simply slot into his world. Our backgrounds are so very different and my fear is that he'll tire of me because I'm too provincial. My world has been quite insular in many ways, whereas he was brought up in a refined, academic environment full of culture and privilege.

Arran continues chopping again, seemingly satisfied with my answer. I'm still reeling a little if I'm honest and a tiny voice inside my head keeps repeating, *Arran just asked you to marry him.*

But then it turns out to be a night of surprises, as the meal demonstrates that Arran isn't merely a cook, but a chef. Fried scallops and a salad drizzled with aged balsamic dressing, followed by chicken in red wine with roasted root vegetables, and ice cream with baked peaches. All beautifully presented and in small enough portions that I could happily enjoy every morsel. As delicious as it was though, nothing could top that moment when Arran uttered those words and took me totally by surprise.

My heart squished up once it had sunk in, but my initial reaction was that it took my breath away and I was almost rendered speechless.

Was it any the less magical given that he spoke the words over a board covered in chopped shallots and garlic? Or that it was in my kitchen at home and not under some beautiful, starlit sky – like the terrace at the villa?

And do you know what? I decide it was perfect exactly as it panned out. Perfect because in the short time we've been together and despite his first, traumatic experience of married life, Arran wants to marry *me*. It hadn't even entered my mind, I just assumed because of what he'd been through that he wouldn't want to risk formalising a relationship again. So maybe it wasn't the big rocket going off in the sky and exploding with a loud bang, attracting everyone's attention. It was more like a sparkler; something that wasn't for the benefit of the crowd but much more personal and without ceremony.

This Valentine's Day baby, who has spent her entire life enchanted by the trappings of romantic gestures, learnt the biggest lesson of all tonight. When the person you love, loves you back in equal measure with no reservations, then you know it will all be fine because they have a good heart. You don't need to dress up that kind of love; it's a very beautiful thing. Maybe background and breeding don't matter that much in the grand scheme of things. The point of life is opening one's mind and expanding that horizon. We can teach each other and in doing so grow together.

But… but… I'll never be that slim, privately educated social climber whose graceful elegance can command a room. I'm just me. What if it's not enough and Paul was right to see through me? Underneath it all I'm someone who is happier staying in than going out.

As Arran follows me upstairs, I stop halfway and turn around. If I let my insecurities eat away at me now, I'll lose the only thing that I've ever truly wanted. He stifles a yawn but gazes up at me with a silly grin on his face.

'Have I told you just how much I love you, Arran Jamieson? You grabbed my heart before I even knew what was happening. You turned out to be the biggest surprise ever.'

I gaze back at him and his silly little grin grows in size.

'I'd much rather you showed me, than told me. But you'll have to be fairly quick because I'm so tired after all that cooking.'

I burst out laughing.

'I won't hang around then. It would be a shame to spoil the most perfect evening of my life so far.'

'Glad you said so far. Because I have plans.'

It turns out that he wasn't quite as tired as he thought.

'Arran, this is my mum, Wendy, and my dad, George.'

'I'm delighted to meet you both.' Arran's smile is warm but behind that I can see how nervous he is; he steps forward to give Mum a hug and then steps back to shake Dad's outstretched hand.

Dad still looks rather pale and as he half turns to lower himself back down into his chair, Arran hesitates and reaches out once more to offer Dad his arm.

'Are you okay there, Sir?'

'Please, call me George. Thanks, just a little unsteady from time to time. I have low blood pressure, which is a good thing but if I get up too quickly my head starts to swim. But as for the heart, I'm on the mend. So how long will you be in the UK, Arran?'

Mum and I are watching nervously, knowing that first impressions carry a lot of weight.

Arran takes the seat at the end of the sofa next to Dad's chair and I sit next to him. Mum takes the chair opposite Dad. Obviously I've told them a bit about Arran and my trip, but with everything that's happened, I've avoided the subject completely the last few weeks. I didn't want to unsettle them in any way.

'I have about six weeks of work but hope to extend my stay a little beyond that. Today was my second session in the studio doing a voice over for a series of tutorials about Ancient Greek civilisation. It's for a small production company and it will probably be picked up by the Open University.'

'It sounds like you're going to be busy. Do you have family in the UK?'

I glance at Arran, but his face is turned in Dad's direction and I can't see his expression.

'I do, but we aren't close, I'm afraid. I am hoping to have some productive meetings about a couple of new projects coming up early next year.'

I feel myself cringing. This isn't what Dad wants to hear as he won't understand why Arran isn't close to his family, or that it really isn't his fault. Mum glances across at me anxiously, and I jump in to steer the conversation a little.

'Arran was close to his grandparents. He inherited their lovely villa in Italy. You guys would love it.'

Arran takes my lead. 'It was a little neglected when they bought it but my grandfather was a modernist and worked with an architect to turn it into something very special. I had the back wall of the kitchen and dining area taken out and glass doors installed, but aside from that nothing else has changed.'

'Italy is your permanent home then, and you'd never consider moving back to the UK?' Dad enquires and I look across at Mum, whose eyes are glued to Arran's face.

Arran looks a little uncomfortable. 'Well, I do spend quite a bit of time in the UK every year. I used to have a home here, too, but that ended up being sold as a part of the divorce settlement with my ex-wife.'

I jump in, horrified, because this isn't going in the right direction at all. Arran's honesty is a drawback at times; it's a wonderful trait but there is a time and a place for everything and this isn't it.

'You remember Arran from the TV series, don't you, Dad?'

There's a small frown on Dad's face and then suddenly it lifts.

'Of course! A fascinating series. I wondered why it was never repeated. Very interesting, indeed.'

They settle into an easier conversation as Arran talks about what he does and how his career began. Mum and I escape to the kitchen.

'What's really going on, Brie? I've never seen you so on edge and judging by the look on your face every time you catch sight of Arran, there's more to this than you are telling us. There's nothing wrong, is there?'

Remembering Mel's reaction acts as a warning but I can't lie.

'No, of course not, Mum; in fact it's quite the reverse. The truth is that even before I flew back, we both knew that we wanted to be together. It just happened, out of the blue. But there are obstacles.'

'He's told you he has no intention of getting married again?' Mum looks at me anxiously.

'No, and that wouldn't make a difference to me, anyway. But it's a long story as he still owes his ex a share in the villa. It's something that needs to be resolved before we can plan our future together. Arran doesn't come from a loving family background and I know that you and Dad will find that hard to understand. But Arran is a very sincere person and he has a good heart; he wouldn't lie to save his life and we both know this was meant to be. It's only that it will take a bit of sorting out to make it all work.'

Mum lets out a little sigh, moving closer so we can hug.

'I can see that you're besotted with each other, Brie. I'm sure Dad isn't missing the signals either and that's why he's edgy. He's not comfortable with this and that's understandable. How much of that is down to not really knowing Arran and the fact that he's so protective of you, I don't know. Or whether it's because he's still recuperating.'

'And how do you feel about it?'

'Well, it does sound complicated and let's be honest, that's not a helpful start to a new relationship. Obviously, first and foremost both Dad and I want you to be happy, so let's focus on getting to know each other as a starting point. Now grab that tray and we'd better check that the guys are playing fair. Dad isn't in the best of moods today and no one is ever going to be good enough in his eyes, so Arran has a bit of a task ahead of him.'

As we walk back into the sitting room Arran looks up at me and I can see he's struggling. It sounds like Dad is grilling him.

'… so none of the work that comes your way is guaranteed? It must be very difficult not having a regular source of income.'

Oh dear, now Dad thinks Arran doesn't even have a proper job. As an academic, just one of the projects he takes on could be worth a year's income in lots of other professions.

'Next time we get together I'll show you some of Arran's textbooks and novels, Dad. He's just written one about a young soldier who lost an arm in the Second World War. It looks like there's going to be a bidding war between three publishers, imagine that!'

Arran is so outside his comfort zone that I instinctively look away, feeling dejected. At least Dad is now looking mildly impressed and he nods his head.

'Well, that's good news. You've done alright out of this writing lark, haven't you, Brie?'

I smile good naturedly, hoping it doesn't come out as a grimace.

'Of course, she won't let me read any of her books,' he informs Arran.

Mum passes Arran a cup of tea and I catch her giving him a nervous, almost apologetic smile. In fairness, Dad doesn't really know anything about Arran and Arran isn't the sort to sing his own praises. Dad probably assumes he's staying with me to save on the cost of a hotel. I'm going to have to sit Mum and Dad down and go through everything in detail with them, but for now we need to drink our tea and get out of here before any more damage can be done.

My phone starts ringing and as I go to turn it off, I see it's Carrie.

'Sorry, I'd better take this.' I head out of the sitting room and into the hallway.

'Hi Carrie, there isn't a problem with the manuscript, is there?'

'No, but are you sitting down?'

My legs turn to jelly. I'm not sure my nerves can stand to hear bad news after such a disastrous evening. I turn towards the staircase and lower myself down onto one of the steps.

'Yes, I'm sitting.'

'Heidi Hoffman just phoned to ask whether I was aware of the article about you that went live two hours ago on *Gossip Queen*'s website. She sent me the link and I'm just forwarding it to you now. I don't know what to say, Brie, other than I'll do my best to get it taken down and I'm on it. Speak later.'

Article?

When the line falls silent I stare at my phone for a second, my mind whirling. Opening up the browser, I type in the website name. It's generally known for starting rumours based on misleading information or dodgy photographs, and it's not a site I visit. I can't see anything on the home page, which is a list of the most popular articles. Even the titles are enough to make you doubt the content before you read it! I can't see anything about me though, so I open the message from Carrie and click on the link.

Arran appears in the hallway.

'I said we had to get back, Brie, I hope that's… what's wrong?'

My face has fallen, and I can't believe what I'm seeing. I hold up the screen to show Arran.

'What the—'

It's obviously taken from the balcony of Arran's room, probably on a phone. We're both naked, Arran is reclining on the bed and I'm on top of him. It's a tiny bit blurred, thankfully, but still identifiable and it's obvious what we're doing. I bet whoever took it was annoyed that they didn't have a steadier hand.

'Are you two alright out here?' Mum's voice calls over Arran's shoulder and as he spins around she clasps her hand over her mouth.

'Oh, my word! Is that on the Internet?'

Oh. This is bad. This is very bad.

'There,' Arran says, quite calmly. 'I told you that you looked beautiful and you do.'

29

Creating Our Own Little Bubble

I've had some embarrassing moments in my life, but this beats even the day of the intervention. As I shut the door and pressed up against it, trembling and with no intention of letting them in, I sort of thought I'd hit rock bottom. Little did I know…

'Well, I think this rates as a day neither of us will forget in a hurry.' I know I'm stating the obvious but the horror of it all keeps coming over me in relentless waves.

Lying in the dark with the covers pulled over our heads, I know that the exact same words are probably on the tip of Arran's tongue, too. What a disastrous evening all round!

'The look on your mum's face. It's etched into my skull. I have never felt like such a rogue in all my life.'

The whole evening has traumatised us both and we've been lying here sporadically talking about not a lot for the last hour.

'It's down now, isn't it? I mean, definitely?'

I squeeze my eyes together, wincing as an image of the photo flashes across in front of me.

'Yes, yes, it's gone,' I assure him. Carrie's final call is still ringing in my ears.

'And how long was it up for?'

'Two hours and forty-eight minutes.' I didn't add that Carrie had to threaten legal action.

'I don't believe it, I really don't. Who do you think took the shot?'

We continue in silence, trying to think of possible motives and opportunities, and decide which of the attendees would be capable of doing this. It's hard to believe it of any one of them.

'It's a big thing to accuse someone of, isn't it? We might have to accept that we will never know for sure,' Arran eventually concludes. 'I don't like to think any of them would have been capable of doing it, knowing how much embarrassment it was going to cause. Tell me what Carrie said, I think I'm calm enough now to hear it.'

I pull the sheet down a little to draw in some air, starting to feel the teensiest bit claustrophobic. Suddenly, Arran starts laughing and the bed begins to shake. Moments later I'm laughing, too.

'This is awful, isn't it?' I ask, shaking my head in disbelief.

'Well, Mel hasn't even met me, and she's already upset because she thinks I'm going to take you away. Your parents think I'm some sort of penniless philanderer who ditches women when he tires of them. But after a copious amount of gratifying sex, of course, as per the photographic evidence. And when this gets out, who is going to want to employ an academic whose cavorting went viral, courtesy of an online scandal magazine? It doesn't get much worse.'

Unfortunately, he's right.

'Carrie said not to panic. It will be a day or two until we know what the fallout is likely to be. It all depends on whether it was picked up anywhere else before the original article was taken down. She has a techie guy who has set up a little programme to scan all of the social media outlets and the internet for the next twenty-four hours and he'll keep her updated.'

Arran's head appears above the covers.

'I mean, it's not as if we're A-list celebrities, is it?'

Being a man, Arran can't quite grasp how I suffered at the hands of the trolls on social media. Ridiculing me affected my mental health, but I didn't lose weight because of the comments about my body size or shape. I was using food as a coping mechanism and I instinctively knew that was wrong and unhealthy. But it was a phase I had to go through to come out the other side more motivated and with a clear picture of the person I wanted to be.

The question is, if they latch on to this and start trolling me all over again, will I spiral out of control? What if my self-esteem is still rather fragile? Maybe I won't have the inner strength to shake it off. I really can't bear to dwell on that now, but I have to let him know it's concerning. And hope this doesn't turn into an absolutely worst case scenario.

'No, but we need to be careful.' It's a juicy piece of gossip. *Writer of hot, sexy novels caught in bed with TV presenter and historian for a night of passion.* Well, that wasn't the *exact* title, but it's close enough.

'You're not still dwelling on the past, are you?' He looks surprised.

'Dwelling, no. But the memory hasn't totally faded yet. What I do realise is that some habits become addictive and I reached a point where I wasn't happy because I wasn't making good choices. That was entirely down to me.'

He looks relieved. 'Good. People will always judge you when you're in the public eye, but you don't have to take it to heart, Brie.'

A phone pings, then pings and pings again in quick succession and we both jump up, reaching out to see whose it is and it's Arran's.

'Grr.' The noise slips out between his gritted teeth and he looks livid.

'What is it?'

'It's from Harriet; all three of them.'

Reluctantly, he hands his phone over to me and I utter a loud exclamation as my hand instinctively flies up to my mouth.

You bastard! You've made me look like a fool!

Forget peaceful negotiations and goodwill, I want the money you owe me and I hope you lose everything.

And, by the way, I've sent the link to your parents.

'She didn't!'

Arran leans back against the headboard. 'Oh, I bet she did! That's Harriet's style of payback. We're screwed, Brie. I have no idea what we're going to do.'

'Let's wait and see what Carrie has to say tomorrow.'

I reach out and Arran takes my hand in his.

'I'm gutted because I don't ever want to think of anything hurting you. I will admit I didn't take this too seriously when I first saw it. But I'm beginning to understand the implications for you. If it was only me in the photograph I wouldn't have cared that much. We're consenting adults and what we do behind closed doors is our business, no one else's. If I ever find out who sold that photo I will be called up on an assault charge and, yes, I know that will be yet another thing to add to the list of my failings. Sometimes, though, you have to fight back, literally.'

Last night we were so happy and now it feels like everyone and everything is conspiring against us. *That's not fair, universe. It's not right.*

'Look, let's assume the worst. It's the talk of the internet for a short while. Ironically, Carrie did say I might be in for a big spike in sales. How it will affect you, we don't know, but let's assume you do lose some of your income. Are we going to live under a cloud, or make an action plan?' I sound determined and maybe that's the only way to cope with this: refuse to let it pull me down.

Arran looks at me in earnest. 'Isn't this about firefighting, though? It's too late to take any preventative measures.'

'It's even simpler than that. I love my friends and family, and I love my work, but you and I have a real chance of happiness together. This leak isn't our fault and we've done nothing wrong. I'm putting the cottage on the market because I'm sitting on well over half a million pounds of house and at the end of the day it's just an asset.'

'Whoa. Hold up. You're not selling this place because of me?'

He tugs my hand and I slide across, to get closer to him.

'No, I'm selling it because of *us*. Just listen to me, please.'

I fix him with a stare as he shakes his head in total disbelief.

'We'll buy something smaller, a cosy little two bed cottage will suffice as a home for us in the UK. The benefit is that the running costs will be modest, so from an investment point of view it's the right thing to do. Tomorrow morning an estate agent is going to start the process and confirm the marketing price. But my guess is that it would leave us with at least a hundred thousand pounds in the bank after paying off Harriet.

'Any potential damage to our income streams is going to be a dent. As a couple pooling our resources it means we should still be able to afford to take out a mortgage to add to that little nest egg and buy a small place over here.'

Arran looks stunned. 'And you'll marry me?'

I kneel next to him, throwing my arms around his shoulders.

'Yes, I'll marry you. We'll do a quick, cheap and cheerful registry office affair. No guests, just drag in a couple of strangers to act as witnesses. We won't tell anyone until we've shown them all that what we're doing is the right thing. Once we're happily settled with no financial worries, and managing to flit seamlessly between the UK and Italy, then I'm sure they'll all come around to the idea.'

Arran rests his head against mine. 'But isn't it supposed to be the most romantic day of your life? No parents, no Mel, or Carrie… it doesn't seem right. And how can I expect you to give up *this* for a villa that will take you miles away from everyone you care about?'

'I've been to enough weddings to know even the most perfectly planned day can go wrong. And then, even when everything does go right, some of the marriages don't last very long. Perhaps that's because if you aren't careful, all of the energy goes into the planning of the event, rather than into the relationship. All I want is to be with you, Arran. I don't care about the rest of it. But I want us to be financially secure and feel equally at home in both places. Once Mum and Dad see how happy we make each other, they will welcome you into the family, I know it.'

Arran picks up my hand and kisses my fingertips.

'You're not just a surprise, you're a breath of fresh air, Brie. Earlier on this evening I wondered if you would walk away from me because I seem to have become this disaster zone. If this is what you want, and it makes you happy, then we'll do it. I don't have an alternative plan I can offer, although I wish I did. Nothing would please me more than the ability to solve all the problems standing in our way, like some fictional hero. But I'm only a man and clearly I skipped out on attaining anything that remotely resembles a super power.'

We hug each other and before long we're recreating the scene from the infamous photo. I have to say it was even better this time around. There's something very sensual about saying to the world at large 'enough, we're doing this so get over it'; it feels empowering.

It's nearly 1 a.m. before we're ready for sleep and Arran brushes a tendril of hair away from my cheek as he leans in for one last kiss.

'Goodnight, my soon-to-be wife. One day I'll make it up to you, I promise.'

I'm about to reply when I hear his breathing instantly deepen and I settle instead, for watching my man sleeping peacefully until my eyes refuse to stay open any longer. We'll address the problems together, one at a time, and eventually everyone around me will come to love Arran just as much as I do. There isn't one single thing *not* to love!

Arran is demolishing his scrambled eggs like a man who hasn't eaten for a week. He must leave for work in the next ten minutes or he will catch a lot of traffic and I need to update him after my phone call with Carrie. She rang while he was in the shower and she wasn't in the best of moods. Her tone was rather blunt but then we have caused her a major headache and she sounded tired.

'The clock is ticking. What did Carrie say?'

'She says it might rumble on for a while, but no one seems to have the actual photo. There have been a few mentions popping up here and there on some of the online celebrity chat forums. But unless the photo reappears, there's nothing we can do.'

Arran nods, his mouth full and his expression one of acceptance.

'The sting is that Heidi Hoffman from *Cosy Living* wants an exclusive interview to go out on the front page of their website. As she was the one who alerted Carrie the moment she spotted the post online, we don't have a choice. Carrie says that the quicker the official version is up, the better. Leaks only work when information isn't already in the public domain.'

Arran swallows the last mouthful of food and lays down his fork, pushing the plate away as he wipes his mouth with a napkin.

'Agreed, but how on earth are we going to do this? I'm about to leave and once I'm at the studio I can't be interrupted. Aside from two short breaks for coffee and doughnuts yesterday, we worked straight through.'

I had explained to Carrie the situation Arran is in.

'We came up with a plan. Heidi is going to Skype me shortly after nine this morning to get the full story from my perspective. Heidi has been told that your schedule is tight, but that Carrie will provide her with a quote. Expect a call on your way to Cardiff sometime in the next half an hour. The two of you can agree on something suitable.'

He nods, seemingly happy to go along with it.

'And the story is?'

I let out a deep breath, visibly sagging. 'What people want to hear, basically. We met in your beautiful villa in

Lake Garda and under the romantic spell of the Italian lakes we fell in love. Heidi is on the ball and I'm sure she's gleaning as much backstory about you as she can right now. She will probably raise the topic of your divorce. Obviously, I won't get pulled into that, although she might refer to it in the article. I will ask her not to mention Harriet by name but there are no guarantees. I'll focus on the whirlwind effect and how happy we are to be together, but I'll say we're both so busy that our plans for the future are still up in the air.'

Arran eases himself up from the bar stool, then carries his plate across to the sink. When he turns to head back in my direction I can see he's anxious.

'Look, it's not that I'm making light of this, but I really do have to go or I'm going to be late. However, it is ironic that I suggested creating a bit of publicity to deflect from the Paul Turner thing. I wish now we'd pursued that as it would have given this leaked photo incident less impact. You are sure this is the right thing to do, given that it's after the fact?' He leans in to kiss my neck as he throws his arms around me.

'I am.'

'Okay. Do whatever you think is best. I feel bad leaving you to deal with this today as I know you are equally as busy and you have the estate agent coming in this morning. I will give you a call as soon as I get a chance, but it might not be until early afternoon. Jeez, you smell so good.'

He buries his head in my hair and inhales several times; obviously this shampoo does deliver on its promise.

'Extract of jasmine and honeysuckle,' I laugh.

His arms wrap around me even tighter.

'It reminded me of the villa there for a moment. That waft in the air late at night when the breeze is coming off the lake. It made me feel a little homesick for a second, I will admit.'

And suddenly I feel the same way. The villa is calling out to me, too.

As I wave him off I can't help wondering how we're both going to adjust to a life split between two very different locations. The love I feel for Arran is filling me with unfettered optimism that we can overcome anything and everything, but the world is full of unknowns. And the downright unexpected.

I wonder if I should ring Mum, but I tell myself I need to focus on preparing for the interview. It's rather like telling a story and yes, it will be based on fact, but no one wants to read about the problems, only the fairy tale.

30

The Farrier's Arms

'Ah, so this is your local pub. Very quaint. I haven't been in a country establishment like this for a long time. I'm looking forward to downing a good pint of local ale.'

Arran follows on behind me and I point to one of the massive oak beams in front of us.

'Mind your head on this one, it's a bit low. Mel must be in the snug.'

The corridor off the main bar still has the original flagstone floor and it's not exactly level. I glance behind to see that every time we walk under a beam Arran has to stoop a little so he doesn't bang his head. My stomach feels distinctly unsettled as nerves start to kick in. I have no idea if Mel knows about what happened yesterday, or whether I should mention it if she doesn't.

We step up into the snug, which is one of the smaller restaurant areas. There are only five tables in here and three of them are already occupied. I glance across at Mel and Ross, who are seated in the far corner, as she waves out to attract our attention.

'Take my lead.' I half whisper the words over my shoulder, not even sure Arran heard me, but I don't want a repeat of last night.

'Sorry we're a bit late, it's been a crazy day.' My voice is light and enthusiastic as I give Ross a warm smile, then wait while Mel walks around the table so we can hug.

'You look nice,' she says but her eyes immediately travel across to Arran.

'Arran, this is my best friend, Mel, and we're both meeting Ross for the first time. Hi Ross, lovely to meet you.' He's wedged into the corner but rises and I lean across to shake his hand.

'There's not a lot of space, I'm afraid. Lovely to meet you too, Brie.'

He's another tall one and I wonder who will be the first to forget to duck next time they pass one of those low beams. I stand back so Arran can lean in to shake the hand Ross has extended in his direction.

'It's a pleasure, Ross.'

I can see that Mel and Arran aren't quite sure how to greet each other but Arran only hesitates for a split second before stepping in front of me to give her a hug.

'Hey, Mel, lovely to meet you at last. Sorry about all the madness of the last few weeks. We're hoping to slow things down a little, now.'

Well, it's a better introduction than I was expecting and as we settle into our seats, I give Arran a reassuring smile.

Ross is rather reserved but as he begins to feel more comfortable in our company he warms up. As soon as Arran finds out Ross is a graphic designer and into all things technical, they strike up quite a conversation. Mel and I don't want to talk over them, so we listen in and there's a lot of head nodding. But I can see that she's finding it harder and harder to contain a myriad of questions.

'How long have you two been together?' Arran asks, maybe feeling it's time to draw Mel into the discussion. Now I'm fearful she'll turn this around and make him feel uncomfortable.

'A little over a month but we chatted online for a couple of weeks before we actually met up for the first time.' The merest hint of a pink hue washes over Mel's face as she talks. She's making direct eye contact with Arran, which is a relief.

'We met through an online dating agency. When they get it right, they really get it right,' Ross chimes in, turning to gaze at Mel.

The pink hue deepens a couple of shades as she gazes back at him. These two need to get a room and really get the party started!

'Mel said you guys met in Italy?' Ross looks directly across at Arran. I half consider jumping in to answer him but I'm a second too slow.

'We did. What was supposed to be a working trip ended up turning our lives upside down. When you meet the right one you instantly know it and that came as a huge shock to me. I'm still getting over it.' He starts laughing and looks in my direction. Before I have a chance to open my mouth, Mel has taken up the conversation.

'I can imagine Lake Garda is a beautiful place and the perfect setting in which to fall in love. I bet it has inspired a lot of holiday romances. But how on earth are you going to cope, given the distance between the two of you?'

Arran reaches across to grab my left hand, which is resting in my lap. He gives it a squeeze and turns to face Mel.

'We're hoping that friends and family will help us sort out how to make it work. It's going to mean some adjustments all round and we don't want anyone to feel left out. I'm not close with my family, unfortunately, so for me it will be a case of introducing Brie to my circle of friends and neighbours; people I've known for a long time as Italy has been a part of my life since I was a child. Over here, it's mainly work colleagues, some of whom have become friends because we've known each other for a while. But my network isn't as tight as Brie's and I'm keen to get to know everyone who plays a significant part in her life.'

Ah, my heart skips a beat.

'How did it go when you met Brie's mum and dad, last night?' Mel's question results in an awkward silence. I have no choice but to step in.

'They're both keen to get to know Arran but Dad isn't up to long visits as he still tires so easily. I thought he looked vastly improved in the few days since I'd last seen him but he's still very pale. Mum says his consultant has recommended they ease into a daily walking regime and

I'm sure the fresh air will bring back some of the colour to his face.'

Mel realises it wasn't really an answer, but she lets it go. As we peruse the menu, ready to place our orders, the general chatter becomes a little more relaxed.

It's an enjoyable meal, both of the guys enjoying the hearty, pub grub portions but I only toy with my meal and Mel leaves quite a bit of hers.

I spend a fair bit of time watching Ross and taking in every little word he says. That shy persona of his means he is really making an effort. Mel instinctively helps him out and many of his conversations end up with a back and forth going on between them.

It's a great relief to see this mutual reliance going on because Mel needs to be needed. They only have eyes for each other and several times their furtive glances cause me to smile. By comparison, my interaction with Arran is overtly obvious. He's touchy-feely all the time and doesn't even realise he's doing it so I practise a few avoidance techniques.

At the end of a very pleasant evening we bid our goodbyes and as I tell Ross how thrilled I am to see my best friend so happy, Arran and Mel are having their own little conversation. It doesn't appear to be awkward in any way and that's something, I suppose. When I hug her, I whisper into her ear, 'You're right, Ross is a great guy and I'm thrilled for you, Mel.'

We pull away and she gives me her usual smile. Tonight has gone well – well, better than last night – and it's a good start. But we haven't totally won her over yet.

★

Arran kicks the engine into life to start the drive home.

'I'm sorry I was late back, and it was such a rush to get here. They seem like a well matched couple. Do you think Mel approved of me?'

I think she's taking her time to form an opinion.

'Well, she wasn't her usual self but then we've never been out on a double date before. I suspect she was nervous about my reaction to Ross. It's easy to forget that our line of work exposes us to situations where we're often meeting new people. More so you, than me, because I do treasure my reclusive writing zone and when it's time to switch into marketing mode I find it tough at first. It's the same with getting out there and meeting new people.'

'Ross did well. Did you notice that after the introductions he avoided talking directly to you all night? I think maybe you have a fan there.'

I pause for a moment. Hmm.

'Well, according to Mel, he's one for very romantic gestures and that's part of the attraction. Her ex, Justin, wasn't like that at all. After living, unknowingly, with a cheater, she needs a guy who can give her that sort of reassurance. His shyness isn't a problem, because Mel is so protective of him. I thought that was rather touching. But I doubt he'd be one of my readers. More likely one of yours; something a little more macho.'

'Is that a sexist dig? Macho men can't be romantic? I'm sure I can rise to that challenge, but it might need a bit of forethought. Anyway, did Carrie tell you the not quite so good news?'

I turn my head in Arran's direction. He doesn't look too disappointed, so it can't be that bad.

'One of the publishers has dropped out. It's a two horse race, now.'

'Did they say why?'

He grimaces. 'She said, reading between the lines, they'd heard about yesterday's little fiasco and felt that not all publicity is good. Which is fair enough. She said the interest of the other two remains strong and it's a numbers game now. The fact that your name is now a part of the deal has proved to be a bit of an incentive and she hopes to be able to go through the two respective best offers in the next day or so.'

Well, I will be relieved when the negotiations are over.

'Harriet is being particularly unpleasant and bending my parents' ears. I had an email from my father requesting that I have no further contact with him after my appalling behaviour. He informed me that I was an embarrassment to both him and my mother, who would be supporting Harriet through this difficult time.'

'No! Really? I know the divorce was messy, but it wasn't your fault. Will Harriet cause a lot of trouble for you back in Lake Garda?'

Arran shrugs his shoulders as he weighs up the implications.

'There might be one or two who might fall for her "poor me" story. But they are the sort who would find a revelation like this shocking and distasteful, so would distance themselves anyway. Most, I feel, will wonder why she's making a fuss now we're divorced. She doesn't seem willing to bow out of my life gracefully, even though we haven't lived together for several years.

'There will probably be some sterling support on my behalf but even her closest friends won't be too surprised by her behaviour. She seems to live her life veering between emotional highs and lows. I'm not the sort of guy people would associate with this sort of scandal, to be honest. In a way we are victims and that fact will annoy some people, who will be incensed by the intrusion and want to show solidarity.'

'I'll feel better once you've been back and it would be great if I could accompany you, just for a short visit. What do you think?'

Arran's eyes are firmly on the road ahead, but I can see the smile as the contours of his profile change.

'I'm glad you said that. I know this might sound like I'm rushing you but what if we see if it's possible to tie the knot before this trip comes to an end? We can both fly back and maybe take a week as a sort of honeymoon.'

'But where would we stay? You aren't in a position to kick Harriet out of the villa.'

Even sideways on, I can see a big smile creeping over his face.

'I have just the perfect little place in mind. A friend of mine has a holiday apartment in Salò, overlooking the lake. We can have a little house party and see which friends turn up and which don't. At least we'll know for sure and it will get everything out in the open. It would be wonderful to be able to introduce you as my wife.'

'That doesn't give us a lot of time but then there's not really a lot to plan, is there? Okay. I'm up for it!'

'Oh…' He hesitates for a moment. 'I didn't mean to spring it on you like that. I was sort of thinking out loud. Look, I know you're busy bringing your new personal assistant up to speed regarding the cottage and everything, so what if I make the arrangements? I'll check with you before I book anything, I promise, but it will make me feel useful. I'm sure there's going to be a fair bit of form filling to be done, so I can suss that out. I might have to extend my stay a little, but it will be worthwhile.'

I relax back in my seat. It's kind of nice that Arran wants to do this, and I love the idea of flying back to Italy as his wife. Keeping this a secret over here will be difficult but I think it will take time to smooth things out and there's little point in pretending otherwise. At some point in the future we can have a big party to celebrate our new status with the people closest to us. But by then Arran will be an accepted part of my life and hopefully everyone will be happy on our behalf.

I'll gloss over the fact that this is beginning to read more like a storyline from a work of fiction. Being in love, I've found, changes the way you look at everything. Arran and I will make this happen because failure is not an option!

31

A New Reality

Well, Italy this isn't. The rain continues to pour for the next six days and the sun seems to have totally given up. But I hardly notice as I spend long hours sitting in front of the screen, knowing that I have no choice other than to be as productive as possible when Arran isn't here. Then, when he is – well, we are otherwise occupied.

The interview with Heidi went as well as it could, I suppose, but it made us both uncomfortable to see our names, and details of our relationship, splashed all over a website. After which, to my abject horror, his father sent me an email via my website – something I haven't shared with Arran yet. He said that because of me he would never speak to his son again and that the family wanted nothing to do with Arran, or us. What really hurt was that he said that my sudden appearance in Arran's life had prevented a reconciliation between him and Harriet. The way it was penned made it very clear that he felt his son deserved better and that I would live to regret ensnaring Arran. At some point, he warned, Arran would wake up and realise the mistake he was making but by then it would be too late.

I'd read the email, recoiling at the bitterness and the tone that the words on the screen in front of me exuded. For a moment I began to doubt myself. Was I robbing Arran of the chance to start over and find happiness with Harriet? Had he been angry post break-up and getting everything out of perspective? But suddenly this new inner strength welled up inside me and I responded, knowing it was the wrong thing to do but I couldn't help myself.

Dear Mr Jamieson

As we've never met and, after reading your email it's unlikely we ever will, I felt the need to respond. Arran is your son and you deserve to know what's really happening as opposed to what you might read in the press.

If things were going to work out between Arran and Harriet, then it would have already happened. I think you know that only too well and that's why you sent the email in the hope that it would put doubts in my mind.

The truth is that I love your son with all my heart and there is nothing I wouldn't do for him. If I genuinely believed there was any feeling left in his heart for Harriet then I would have walked away, believe me, no matter how painful that would have been. Because I, too, want him to have no regrets.

Loving someone isn't conditional. It's selfless. It means you put them first in everything you do because you want to make them happy. I want to make Arran happy and I'll do whatever it takes to achieve that.

If I'm ever lucky enough to have children, then I hope I will have the good grace and the unconditional love to let them live their own lives – and make their own decisions. I will love and support them no matter where life's path takes them. And I'll be there to pick up the pieces if they get hurt and things go wrong, because I've lived safe in the knowledge that my parents are there for me no matter what. Always and forever.

As each day passes and my family and friends can see how happy Arran and I are together, their love for him grows. But you can't learn to accept someone if you don't give them a chance. It saddens me that you aren't prepared to extend me that courtesy. All I do know is that Arran is an amazing man and together we are going to build a wonderful future. Our door will always be open to both you and your wife, if you ever want to reach out.

Best regards,

Brie Middleton

Somehow, I felt better after I'd pressed send and, at some point, I will show Arran the content of our email exchange. But for now, he's happy, and after a hard day's work he arrives back here, content to relax and feeling completely at home. He's online a lot every evening planning our wedding and I keep telling him I want no fuss. The last thing we need is to have another photo disaster if we are going to succeed in keeping this a secret for a while afterwards. Arran asked me last night why I was so intent on doing it this way and it took me a few minutes to find the right words.

'If this was happening to Mel, then I'd be very concerned. The speed at which things have happened and the problems we need to overcome... well, I'd be trying to talk her out of it. I'd warn her that when a relationship is new nothing is guaranteed, and the wisest course of action is to wait and see how things develop.'

Arran's face reflected the fact that it was sound advice.

'But that isn't us, is it?' He'd beamed at me, unable to hide his enthusiasm.

'No. Once the deed is done then no one can talk either of us out of it.'

His head tipped back a little then and his expression changed.

'You feel that could happen?' I felt his frown was tinged with disappointment.

'No, of course not, silly! But I don't want guilt spoiling my joy; which it would do because I would feel awful ignoring good advice from people who are only trying to protect me, well, *us*. You know you have wormed your way into my mum's affections and Dad is looking very proud when he sees us together. But it's still a little *soon* for all of them. Let them get used to the idea of us living together first, because there's still so much to sort out. Sometimes you have to go with your heart and I've waited all my life to say that in such a meaningful way.'

He'd picked me up in his arms then and span me around, his eyes lit up with love and happiness.

'You had me worried there for a moment. I just don't want you to feel robbed of anything. But when things have settled down, and we can finally tell everyone we're officially man and wife, we will have the biggest celebration, I promise you! Well, the biggest we can afford, that is.'

I half wondered if it was an opportunity to talk to him about his father's email but I didn't want to put a damper on the rest of our evening. Besides, I had good news to share. My new assistant, Vivian, had phoned mid-morning to say there were two viewings booked for Saturday afternoon. Arran and I chinked wine glasses and peered at each other over the top of them, like two excited kids.

Admittedly, I initially thought the valuation was rather high, but I went with the estate agent's suggestion and I guess he was right, because it's only being advertised online at the moment. The brochures haven't even been printed yet! It seems when it comes to investing in property I chose a winner, but Arran isn't aware we might have more money in the pot than expected. I don't want to jinx it, so that's another little secret I'm keeping to myself. Well, until an offer comes in – and I have everything crossed that will be a lot sooner than we'd both expected!

★

With the last part of my love story still to be written, this morning I'm locked away in my study. Vivian is here overseeing the cleaners, who are going to make the cottage sparkle, ready for tomorrow's viewings. Arran and I will make ourselves absent between the hours of two and four in the afternoon. His reaction was that it wouldn't be a problem because he had a little trip in mind.

I've decided that it's silly of me to feel finishing off this story could jinx what's going on in real life. The readers, and the characters, deserve an ending worthy of the silver screen. The sort of ending that leaves you feeling elated and punching the air because life when it's good can be amazing!

Ethan Turner is a worthy hero, but he has lost his way. Izzie Martin is the woman who turns him around and rescues his heart and his soul. I have poured all the emotional highs and lows running through me since I met Arran into the telling of this story. And now it's time for Ethan to show Izzie she chose the right man. He is about to step up to prove he can be that strong, dependable partner who will be her rock, no matter what life throws at them in the future.

I chuckle to myself as I begin to write about the plans for their lavish wedding. It's so totally opposite to what's happening now in real life for Arran and me. My phone rings and I'm still smiling to myself as I answer it.

'Hi, Mel.'

'Am I disturbing anything? You sound happy.'

'Laughing to myself, actually. You know how I enjoy it when I'm at the point in a story where it's the beginning of the end. All that power over my characters and what happens. It's heady stuff and it satisfies my soul to have a hefty dose of unbridled romance.'

She sighs. 'Shouldn't that be unbridled passion?'

Now it's my turn to sigh. 'What's up?'

'Well, you know how romantic Ross is, which is totally great, but...'

There's an awkward pause.

'Oh, so, you're beginning to get a little bit impatient for some action?'

She groans out loud.

'Brie! Not *impatient*, exactly, more anxious. I mean, what if it happens and it's a disaster?'

The same thing has been running through my head because I know Mel, and this isn't a conversation she could have with Ross. Reading between the lines, which is something I'm an expert at, they've been about to tumble into bed for the first time for several weeks now. But it sounds like they've been thwarted at every turn by circumstances and it's time to engineer a night away together. It's the last unknown between them.

'I know it's been a while for you, but how about Ross? Maybe he's nervous and that's why something always seems to get in the way of you two—'

'Nervous? Do guys get nervous about sex?'

You see, that's precisely why I worry. People's expectations can be unreal if they believe everything they hear or read. Of course guys get nervous! Admittedly, not all of them, but the longer you wait, the more the pressure builds.

'If it's been a while for him too, then maybe he needs a little encouragement. Create an environment where there will be no interruptions, so he feels relaxed and see what happens. Maybe consider a night away together. There's no point in worrying about something that will come quite naturally when the circumstances are right. You're overthinking this and that's a bad thing – without realising it you may be a part of the problem. Stressing about it is going to make you appear nervous, too. He won't want to disappoint you, Mel, you know that. The guy is clearly very much in love with you.'

'So get away, or ask him over, wine and dine him and put on the soft music?'

'Precisely. I'm sure I've written this scene before, in great detail, many times. Maybe I'll look it up and send over the best example I can find.' I start laughing and Mel joins in.

'All tips gratefully received. Just pick one that wasn't too wild as I like my underwear to be more than a teeny bit of lace which doesn't cover anything. I never thought I'd be the one pushing for sex because I love the fact he isn't pressurising me in any way, but now I need to know it's not going to be a… problem.'

I think I'm right and her unspoken concerns are probably being communicated to Ross loud and clear without Mel knowing that.

'It's like we've swapped places, Brie. I mean, you've spent a long time looking for your romantic hero and holding back because you wanted it to be perfect. I know that you've been disappointed before, so that's why I'm surprised at how abandoned you've been. Suddenly, along comes Arran, and all of that goes out of the window because you two are like proverbial rabbits. Where did I go wrong? I mean, every woman needs to think they inspire passion in their partner.'

I shake my head in dismay.

'Stop looking for problems that aren't there. If you relax about it, then so will he.'

When I put down the phone I realise that the conversation has steered my thought processes in a slightly different direction for finishing this story. Instantly my head had gone into 'sex sells' mode and I realise, after chatting with Mel, that sometimes less is more. When Ethan and Izzie discover each other's bodies, they don't need anything other than to surrender to each other. Completely. Irrevocably. And forever.

And Mel is very astute. I have no idea why I felt everything was so right with Arran from virtually the very beginning. Despite my real reservations about him, my gut instincts were pushing all of that aside for good reason. He isn't a flowery, poetic sort of person but he's very honest, practical and easy to please. Maybe I've spent a large part of my life being a dreamer and my career sort of depends on that quality, I suppose. Arran has taught me what's important in life and that's the love of a good man who doesn't dress it up because that's not in his nature. And do I care? No. Because I'm ecstatically happy.

The glow that Arran inspires within me begins to work its way into the words on the screen in front of me. I'm so caught up in what's happening that it's a surprise when Vivian pops her head around the door to say goodbye.

'The cleaning is all done. It looks gorgeous. I'll be back tomorrow afternoon to greet the agent.'

'Do you have your key?'

She nods. 'Yep. Enjoy your afternoon out. Are you going anywhere nice?'

I shrug my shoulders. 'I have no idea. Arran says it's a surprise.'

'Well, fingers crossed the couple from the first viewing stay a long time and the second couple arrive before they leave. Nothing sharpens the mind more than a little competition and who wouldn't love to live in this beautiful place?'

Vivian is so young and vibrant, she reminds me of me when I was in my early twenties, too.

As soon as she leaves I begin typing again and before I know it Arran's voice carries up the stairs.

'I have takeaway,' he calls out, no doubt heading into the kitchen.

Rather reluctantly, I finish the sentence and back up the file before heading downstairs. I say reluctantly, because that first bedroom scene is behind closed doors and the following chapter skips to the next morning. Now I'm going to be in suspense all night until early tomorrow. I'll steal away to my computer before Arran wakes up. I can think about it all I want but it isn't until my fingers are flying over the keys that all will be revealed. Until it is there's an anxious void within me – it's always the same when I get to this point in the story. I worry I won't do it justice and this one is so important to me. This is for the true romantics out there.

'Relax, Brie,' I say to myself out loud. 'It will be fine.'

'What will be fine?' Arran appears, no doubt wondering what's taking me so long. 'Oh, I found out the source of our leaked photograph. It seems Rick Preston, week one attendee at the course, has managed to get some *free* publicity for his first book. I knew eventually it would get back to me. Nothing we can do about it now, and we survived.'

'We did.' I gaze across at Arran, a slight frown on my face. 'Rick had to get pretty close to get that shot and I find that thought very disturbing. I wonder how long he'd been watching us?'

Arran shakes his head sadly. 'Well, he was in the next room to mine so it was easy enough to hop over the divide between the two balconies. Most of the time we spent in your room though, so let's hope it was a one-off. He must have realised I'd have thrown him out if either of us had spotted him.'

He saunters over as I stand, and leans in to kiss me. His hands cup my face as he takes in every little feature.

'I missed you today. I mean, really missed you. Thank goodness it's Saturday tomorrow and we have our little outing.' He sounds pleased with himself

'Hmm… is this something I'm going to enjoy?'

He stands back a little, frowning.

'Well, I'm going to show you the proposed venue for our little ceremony. Then we're going shopping. You get to choose my outfit and I get to choose yours.'

I burst out laughing, raising my hand to slap it against my forehead.

'What have I done?'

I said no fuss, but I had hoped it would at least have a little romance to it. But do you know what, if Arran takes us to a costume place and we end up as Beauty and the Beast, I really don't care.

'Trust me, it won't be that bad. Oh, and I've been listening to the audio version of your book, *The Man Who Can*, on my journeys to and from work. A few surprises there, actually.'

The sparkle in his eye is full of suppressed laughter. I'm glad he threw that in because it suddenly occurs to me why he's so keen to get the wedding over and done with. I bet his marriage to Harriet was an elegant, extravagant affair. No doubt costing thousands of pounds and in which his voice might not have been heard over and above the demanding bride and her entourage. But perfect as it might have been, it still failed.

From humble beginnings… and in that respect, we are both on the same page.

32

The Big Day is Here

What a whirlwind this last month has been. Accepting a cash offer on the cottage was exhilarating, but the reality of moving out so quickly soon pushed everything else to the back of our minds. Arran, Vivian, Mel and I have worked non-stop every spare moment to get it all organised.

With everything packed up and in storage, as I turn the key in the lock for the last time it's a curious moment. I thought I'd feel sad but instead I'm excited about what's to come. I'm also ecstatic that in the next hour or so I'll have enough money sitting in my account to transfer the funds to Arran, so he can pay off Harriet once and for all. The big surprise, though, is that there's enough left over for us to go house hunting. Okay, it will be a much more modest abode, but at least we'll have a base in the UK. And that is going to make Mum, Dad and Mel a lot happier, I think, once they find out what's really going on.

The phone vibrates in my pocket and I pull it out, smiling when I see it's Mum calling.

'How's it going, Brie? Are you nearly finished at the cottage?'

'I've literally just locked the door.'

There's a momentary pause.

'The start of a new life together, my darling. How marvellous and well deserved. Dad and I were wondering if we could take you both out to lunch, you know, to mark the start of this new phase in your lives.'

My stomach does a dive as Mum has no idea how true that is. Today is the day Arran and I are tying the knot but it's a secret still. Ironically, it needn't have been because in the few weeks he's been over here he has grown close to everyone around me. All of their concerns have melted away because we are the perfect fit and it's obvious to them all.

But accepting that Arran and I wanted to be together and that it would take a lot of juggling financially to make that happen, is a big deal; to throw in a quick wedding on top of the upheaval is quite another. We're both exhausted at the moment and doing it this way makes life easier. I do hope they will appreciate that when we eventually break the news. But that will be after everything has settled down and the concerns about having homes in two different countries have melted away. Together we will make this work and keep everyone happy. Well, that's the general idea.

Arran is putting the final bits in the car and we're heading off to a Holiday Inn to get ready. I glance down at my watch and see that time is running away from us and we can't be late.

'It's a wonderful idea, thank you both so much, but maybe we can do that tomorrow. Today's a bit… chaotic. Love you and we'll speak later.'

Arran saunters towards me, a hesitant look on his face.

'Everything alright?'

'Yep. Just Mum, checking in. I'm all set.'

Arran reaches out to grab my hand and we turn to take one last look at the cottage.

'I feel absolutely gutted that you're giving this up for me – for us. It shouldn't be necessary because it isn't fair on you. If you'd fallen in love with anyone else—'

'I wouldn't be marrying the man of my dreams then, would I? Don't be an idiot. You're everything to me and this is simply bricks and mortar. It was only ever an investment. Besides, I have a little surprise. Do you fancy house hunting? We might just be able to find a cosy little place tucked away in a quiet village location with what's left over.'

'After you write that cheque to settle my debts, you mean.' The look on his face reflects his mixed feelings. He really isn't comfortable about this and I know I've forced his hand.

'If it wasn't for the fact that she played to my ego, I wouldn't have fallen for Harriet's manipulative behaviour. My stupidity allowed that to happen and I feel so badly about what I'm putting you through. You're paying for my mistake and that's an awful thing to inflict on anyone.'

I shush him, throwing my arms around his shoulders and hugging him tightly.

'Do I look like I'm concerned about it?'

He tips my chin back, staring into my eyes.

'No. And that's why you're such a special lady. You ask for nothing. But, in precisely two hours and thirty-seven minutes' time you will be the joint owner of Villa Monteverdi.'

I gasp. When I'd hurriedly signed the papers Arran's solicitor had drawn up I assumed it was a pre-nuptial agreement to safeguard his ownership of the villa. After what Harriet has put him through, I thought it was understandable and there's no way I would want him to feel vulnerable like that again.

'But I wouldn't have signed if I'd known that. I never meant there to be a trade off, Arran. I sold the cottage because I love you and between us we'll always have somewhere to live. But I wanted you to feel that at last your grandfather's inheritance was safely back in your hands. That means a lot to me, because I hate to see you feeling powerless over something so meaningful in your life. And that was my gift to you.'

I can't deny the feeling of disappointment that wells up within me.

'Love is a two way thing, Brie. This is my gift to you too, and I knew if I spelt it out you'd tear up those papers. What I want to say is that I know my grandfather would have understood if I had walked away from the villa, so that I could have you in my life. But I also know it's meant to be our home and he would rejoice in that thought.'

We hug in silence, interrupted only when my phone kicks into life.

'You'd better get that. I suspect it's the solicitor to confirm completion. Besides, we have a wedding to attend. And it just happens to be ours!'

As registry offices go, this one is at least in an old building and carries with it a sense of history. Births, deaths and marriages… life in a nutshell.

Arran is nervously pacing back and forth. I reach out and grasp his arm so he'll stop, and he turns to face me.

'Is my tie straight?' he enquires, that quirky, left eyebrow lift of his making me smile.

I put up my hand to adjust it a little, but he looks amazing in his navy suit, with a crisp, white shirt and that blue tie with a perfect Windsor knot. We decided to replicate the outfits Rose and Arthur wore in the photograph Arran has of them – well, as close as we could get. My knee length dress is in silver grey lace, with a shimmery silk layer beneath it. Simple but elegant.

Arran asked the woman on the reception desk to take a quick photo of us after we'd snapped a few selfies. When we stared back at the one she'd taken, we were both overwhelmed. In the original photograph what stood out was the way both Arthur and Rose's eyes sparkled. And staring down at the screen of Arran's phone we knew we'd nailed it, because we saw the exact same thing captured in our own special moment.

'You look so beautiful, Brie, you take my breath away,' Arran whispers into my ear.

I feel my cheeks heating up as the seconds tick by. People come and go, but we're the only ones who are standing on our own together. A large group are congregating quite noisily on the other side of the waiting room and I should imagine they're for the appointment after ours. Every time the door opens yet another person joins the party. I can see Arran looking their way, pensively. As he watches the bride, head back and laughing, it raises a smile on his own face.

He turns towards me, leaning in as if he's going to say something really important, but instead we end up spinning around when we hear his name spoken, out loud. Two women hurry over to us and I half wonder if Arran arranged for witnesses. I'd assumed the registrar would invite two of their admin staff to do the honours.

'Harriet? What on earth—'

The colour drains from Arran's face. He spins back around to look at me wearing a horrified expression that makes my stomach begin to churn. My feet suddenly feel like lead and I'm frozen to the spot.

'Thank God we're not too late.' The other woman directs her glare at me, then turns her head away as if to dismiss me as merely something bothersome. 'If Harriet hadn't had you followed, Arran, we wouldn't have been able to prevent you from making the biggest mistake of your life. Have you totally lost your mind?'

So, this elegant, impossibly slim and rather haughty woman is the former Mrs Arran Jamieson. She's utterly stunning and doesn't have a single hair out of place. I'm guessing the older woman is—

'Mother, this is none of your business. As for you, Harriet, you had me followed?' Arran sounds appalled. His voice is raised a little and eyes begin to turn in our direction.

'Well, after your girlfriend decided to ignore the pleas from your father, it left us with no other option. You can't go ahead with this, Arran, it's insanity. The two of you have nothing in common, at all. Have you read any of her novels? The woman peddles sex; it's almost bordering on pornography. Think of your reputation.'

I'm speechless, standing here watching a scene that doesn't feel real.

Arran's mother is quick to jump in. 'How convenient that photograph of the two of you was leaked to the press. Don't you see how clever she's been in trapping you? And as for this fiasco, here, today… well, clearly, she's in a hurry to tie this up before you have a chance to change your mind. It's indecent on all fronts, Arran. Your father was too embarrassed and appalled by your behaviour to escort us here for fear of the scene he would cause. What on earth would your grandfather think? Have you no sense of propriety?'

I take a step backwards, unwittingly relinquishing Arran's hand in the process but he doesn't seem to notice. In fact, he takes a step forward and I find myself holding my breath. Now everyone is looking in our direction and the silence hangs heavily in the room.

'Have you both no sense of decency turning up like this, uninvited, as if you have a right to meddle in my life? I'm done with toeing the line and being forced down a road of misery.'

Arran's mother's jaw drops and she opens her mouth, but no words escape. The look in her eyes is cold and unforgiving. Harriet, on the other hand, edges closer to Arran, suddenly changing her demeanour from aloof, to sympathetic. She even reaches out to place her arm, rather comfortingly, on the sleeve of his jacket. Woah – Arran wasn't a fool. She's clever, she knows how to get what she wants, and she will do anything to achieve that without reservation. He didn't stand a chance.

'You know this isn't right, Arran, and you're doing this for all the wrong reasons. I'm sorry things went so badly wrong between us and that wasn't my intention, really it wasn't. I had a lot of anger because I felt you weren't putting me first and I took my frustrations out on you. I understand now that your work is important to you and I'm prepared to acknowledge that. I'm sorry and I want us to try again.'

Some of the strangers in the room gasp out loud and my eyes begin to fill with tears. Arran looks devastated and for a few moments I'm fearful of what will happen next. Suddenly, the door opens, and a young woman enters the waiting room holding a clipboard in her hands.

'Mr Jamieson and Miss Middleton?'

All heads spin in her direction but no one says anything. Instead, my eyes are glued to Arran's face. He looks angry and when he begins speaking his words are curt and his tone sharp.

'You're right, Harriet – we're doing this for all the wrong reasons.' To my horror he turns to address the person still waiting to escort us across the hallway. 'I'm sorry, but we won't be getting married today, after all.'

One solitary tear rolls down my cheek and I gulp, forcing myself not to sob. A small smile spreads over Arran's mother's face. Harriet looks at Arran adoringly.

'Thank you, Harriet, for bringing me to my senses. I'm desperately trying to avoid a repeat of what you and I had, because I stupidly agreed to everything you wanted. Brie isn't like that. She isn't Bridezilla – she's the woman who loves me enough not to care about the process and the trappings. In fact, if you check your bank account you will find my debt has been repaid in full, courtesy of a woman who is prepared to give up almost everything she's worked for because she loves me.'

He turns towards me as Harriet looks on, rendered speechless, and the smile is wiped from his mother's face in an instant. Arran drops to one knee and clasps my hand. I glance at Harriet, briefly, and her face is distorted, her mouth partially open like a tear on that perfect, porcelain skin of hers. They are both horrified.

'Brie, it's time we did this properly because that's what you deserve. Can we forget what's gone before? I hope you will forgive me for trying to make you settle because of the baggage I carry around with me. That's all behind us from this moment forwards.

'Brie Middleton, will you do me the great honour of being my wife? And this time around we are going to organise a proper wedding ceremony. Your family and friends have shown me more respect and love than I've ever had from my own parents or my sister. If it wasn't for my grandparents and Nanny Hope, I wouldn't even have a notion what love was. All they ever wanted for me was to be happy and you make me happy in ways I never dreamt existed.'

As he stares up at me, I find myself floundering, my legs no longer firm beneath me. Arran jumps up, throwing his arms around me and I manage to whisper 'yes' before the room begins to fade away, consumed by a grey fog.

33

Toasting Mr and Mrs Arran Jamieson

I knew that everyone would fall in love with Villa Monteverdi the moment they arrived here from the UK for our Italian celebration. With the plans for tonight's big party well in hand, and Elisabetta fussing over the team from La Pergola as they lay out the tables in the marquee, I know that Arran and I can relax.

This is family time, at last. Welcoming Mum, Dad, Mel, Ross and Carrie to our home as a couple is very special indeed. Already, the memories Arran and I have created here prior to our wedding in the UK have made me feel a part of its history. After all, it has been a rollercoaster ride of emotions for us both, given the situation. But coming back here after the wedding did, indeed, feel like coming home for me. And I never dreamt I would be able to say that.

As Arran and I stand on the terrace watching the hive of activity going on around us, our joy doesn't need to be expressed in words.

The fact that Mum and Dad are here for a whole month is really going to kick start Dad's convalescence now he's feeling much more like his old self. Earlier on, Arran announced, rather boldly, that he had been formulating a plan.

'Really?' I had enquired, as I know we have a lot of work to juggle, too. He'd looked at me and waggled his finger.

'I know what you're thinking but all it's going to take is a little careful re-jigging of the deadlines.'

I was impressed and I could see Mum and Dad were, too.

'Well, we don't want to put you out, Arran. We can—'

He'd stopped Mum at that point. 'The arrangements are already coming together.'

That had piqued my interest and I felt excited by his enthusiasm. 'Oh, come on, you have to tell us now, Arran.'

He'd pretended to think about it, but I could see he was dying to share the news.

'First off, we're heading to Venice for an overnight stay at the amazing Aqua Palace, a designer hotel in the Castello Quarter. We return for five days before heading off to the nearby town of Malcesine. We're going to take the cable car up to the ridge of the Monte Baldo mountain range.'

'A cable car?' He could instantly tell from my voice that wouldn't be my first option.

'You'll be fine,' he'd chided me. 'It climbs very slowly because it rotates 360 degrees so you get the full panoramic view.'

Great. It climbs *and* turns. A double whammy of fear for me as my delicate stomach hates sudden movement.

'I've also arranged for a car and driver to do several escorted, half day trips while you and I are working. Oh, and I've planned a special little evening trip because you said I'm not a romantic at heart, Brie.'

He'd shot me a glance and I tried to ignore the fact that Mum and Dad were trying not to laugh. I raised my eyebrows in consternation. We'd gone way beyond that stage.

'We're all going to take the Sunset Cruise around the lake, starting from Sirmione. It's magical at this time of the year and it will take your breath away. As the night air wraps itself around you, the sound of the lapping water will be something you will always remember, I promise you.'

I was touched; we all were. Arran so wanted to embrace my parents and make them feel at home here, that it was moving. And kind. And thoughtful. And I wanted to shower him with kisses, but I managed to restrain myself. For a little while.

And as for Mel and Ross, well, they have that loved-up glow and I know it won't be too long before Mel is buying up those bridal magazines in preparation for their big day.

Then there's Carrie; well, she's been a star. She successfully negotiated a lucrative, two book deal for Arran. It isn't so much about the money, but his sense of achievement, and the fact that we get to collaborate on the sequel is a bonus. It's a story that means so much to him and it deserves to be shared with the world.

But the best news of all is that a film producer has fallen in love with Arthur and Rose's story. Together we will show the world a love so intense that it will rival all other love stories. Casting is about to begin and it's an exciting time, as the sequel will hit the shelves at around the same time as the film airs. Together we're creating something special and we both know that. A story that is symbolic in so many ways and reminds us all that there is nothing stronger than the bond of true love.

When I get back to the UK, I'm doing that extended book signing tour to please Carrie and my publisher, before starting on the first round of edits for my next hot and steamy romance. In between, I wrote a love story; it just happened to be about Arran and me, and it just happened to have sex in it. A lot of sex, as it turns out, because when I read through the first draft I realised I'd written a fictional version of our own love story. It was a bit of a fairy tale; but then I realised the true version was also a fairy tale in its own right. And I wanted to do it justice, not that it was totally biographical, but I've learnt something on this journey that I wanted to share.

Romance comes in all forms. What delighted me was that the story had some of the most heart warming and tenderest of moments that will melt any true romantic's heart. And those poignant scenes weren't mine, but Arran's. The man I did, at one point, accuse of not having one romantic bone in his body.

Sometimes a hero doesn't arrive on a white charger or knock on your door with his arms full of flowers. Often, he makes you laugh when you least expect to – like when you are staring at a photo of you both naked on the internet and your mother comes up behind you. And then he announces, quite boldly, that you are beautiful. Or when you are in a room full of strangers in a registry office. Going down on one knee to ask me to marry him – which he didn't really do the first time around – in front of his ex–wife and his irate mother, came from the heart. He could so easily have sent them away and continued with our no frills, no fuss ceremony.

Antonio waves, attracting Arran's attention.

'I think I'd better offer to lend a hand setting up the drinks table. Why don't you show Carrie the library?'

I glance across and see that she's standing on her own, surveying the view, and is the only one without a drink in her hand.

I gaze up at Arran as his arms circle my waist and he gives me a gentle squeeze. 'I love you, Mrs Jamieson. Thank you.'

I look at him, puzzled. 'For what?'

'For everything. For being you; for caring so much about the things that matter and letting go of the things that don't.'

We both know what he's referring to; I might not be the first Mrs Arran Jamieson, but I'm the last. And as for the other Mrs Jamieson, his mother, well, when he's ready I know he will give her and his father another chance. Whether they will accept his peace offering, who knows, but the important thing is that his heart is full of forgiveness because love and hate don't sit well together.

He raises my hand to kiss my fingertips before heading off in the direction of the elegant marquee. I grab two glasses of wine then saunter across to Carrie.

With my latest novel, *The Story of Us: A journey into love,* shooting straight up the charts, it promises to take my career in a slightly new direction. More fifty shades of happiness than fifty shades of grey. It seems that an increasing number of people are looking for feel good, reaffirming stories with a moral or two woven into the pages. Of course, the press keep saying it's semi-autobiographical, which it is, but I'm not admitting that. The first time I saw those words staring back at me in print I was terrified. Then Arran put it into perspective for me.

'There isn't one thing in that entire novel I'd want you to change. There's no shame in loving someone so completely, both mentally and physically.'

I'd rolled my eyes. 'That's easy for you to say as it isn't your naked rear that keeps popping up on the internet.'

The smile he'd given me was wicked. 'Yes, but you look good, so don't knock it. You worked hard to beat your demons and decide to embrace a healthier lifestyle. Okay, the weight loss was a side effect, but it's still something you achieved. It's tasteful, Brie, and when you're eighty years old I bet you'll get a little thrill when you remember that moment. I know I always will.'

And that's why I love him. But I won't be asking Arran to read my next hot and steamy romance, which is set in an Italian villa on a hillside overlooking a lake. I think he'd be miffed that the hero is Italian and bears a remarkable resemblance to Antonio from La Pergola. Well, people love *love*, but sex still sells books. As I've discovered, I like to have my cake and eat it. In moderation, of course.

34

A New Surprise Around Every Corner

'It's officially wine o'clock, and this glass has your name on it. You're deep in thought. Is everything okay?'

Carrie smiles, gratefully taking the glass from me.

'Perfect. The view is stunning and it's hard to take in that this is now your home. Who could stand here and not be moved by this backdrop? It's beyond beautiful.'

Today there is a gentle breeze and the whole surface of the lake seems to shimmer, like a piece of silk rippling as the wind catches it.

'It's so turquoise against the cornflower blue of the sky,' Carrie exclaims. 'Almost too rich to look real, if you know what I mean. Like a painting where you actually want to muddy the colours a little as water can't be that surreal, or so clear it looks like liquid crystal.'

We stare out over the lake and into the distance. I have to agree with her. Raising my hand, I gesture to our right.

'See the variation in colour as the water sweeps around the south eastern edge of the bowl, over there? Then as it snakes away towards the north the reflection of the mountain range casts a darker shadow, making it look almost shallow along that edge. But it isn't, it's actually very deep at that point, according to Arran.'

Carrie redirects her gaze.

'The depth of the lake varies dramatically and sometimes that accounts for the change in colour. Other times it's the current, apparently. As your eye runs along the entire length of the coast line you can spot some of the coves and beaches in between the mountainous, craggy rock. Then far into the distance all you see is colour and shape, and that slight purple haze at this time of the day. I could stand and stare at this forever and always notice something new,' I admit.

'And Arran spent his childhood holidays here?'

I nod. 'Yes, from his early teens. It was his refuge, albeit a little slice of paradise. When he was here there were no rows going on around him and no pressure. He was allowed to be himself; no one judging him or pushing him to do better. Every child deserves that sort of nurturing and it has nothing at all to do with wealth, or privilege. His grandparents simply loved him for who he was and allowed him to develop naturally. He was an inquisitive young man, he admitted, and I can imagine that.'

It was obvious from the beginning that Carrie has always seemed to understand Arran. She's a tough cookie herself; whether that's just her nature, or it stems from her upbringing, I have no idea. But I wonder if she recognised in Arran that moody, slightly brusque demeanour he sometimes sports as if it's some sort of shield to hide his feelings. She's not one to make excuses for people, but whether she'd admit it or not, she has a soft spot for him.

'Arran suggested I show you the library, it's in a secret part of the garden. Step this way.'

We take our time, frequently stopping to admire the shrubs and different viewpoints out across Lake Garda. Then watching the ferries and smaller boats, mere specks on the surface leaving tell-tale white trails in their wake. That constant little glint as the sun catches on the gleaming paintwork, like some sort of message in Morse code. Dot, dot, dash, dot, dash… and then it changes direction and the eye can hardly make out the tiny shape in such a vast expanse.

As we head past the marquee we pop our heads in to see how things are coming along.

'This is all rather grand,' Carrie says as we stand back surveying the activity. The individual tables look wonderful with their long, crisp white cotton cloths and deep burgundy floral arrangements.

It's a large tent and Antonio has arranged everything, not just the food. Our request was for something simple, but elegant and oh my, well, this isn't simple but it is elegant.

The dessert table is amazing but it's slap bang in the centre and I'm puzzled.

'Come,' Antonio calls out and we saunter across. 'You like?' He wafts his hand in front of the beautiful array of cupcakes and a mountain of cookies set in an icing pyramid.

'Yes,' I declare, in awe.

'Everyone, they dance around the table. Is cookie cake and everyone take, yes?'

'Right, ah, I see. Does it have a name?'

'*Torta di biscotto di nozze*. And these, *confetti crispo* –
a box for each guest.'

He slips the top off one of the small gold coloured
boxes. 'Ah, sugared almonds. Lovely.'

'Is tradition for the *matrimonio cucina*.'

I smile at him, placing a hand on his shoulder gratefully.
'Thank you, Antonio. You have done an amazing job. I
can't wait for everyone to be seated to sample the delights
of traditional Italian cuisine.'

'*Matrimonio cucina*,' he repeats and I chuckle.

'We'll leave you to your preparations. See you in a little
while.'

As we head out of the marquee, we pass Arran carrying
a tray. Both Carrie and I stare at it in surprise.

'Quanti,' Arran explains. 'Dough in the shape of bow
ties, deep fried and sprinkled with icing sugar. I know we
said simple, but there is no such thing—'

'I know… when it comes to *matrimonio cucina*.'

Both Arran and Carrie laugh and we head back out
into the sunshine.

From every angle you see something new and when it's
viewed for the first time it's a truly inspiring experience. A
rich mixture of light and shade from rocky promontories
way below us and behind, the mountains are almost
breathing down our necks.

'I'm envious but I'm so happy for you both. In fact,
you've made me think about my own life and a few
changes I've decided are overdue.'

We disappear out of view of our guests, between the line of trees and Carrie follows me inside the library, her face in awe.

'This is really something. No wonder Arran fought so hard to retain it and I can see where your motivation came from, now. This is some collection. Of course, you couldn't let him lose it. I'm sorry if, as a friend, I doubted your reasoning, but you know me, always practical. Well, except that all of a sudden, I'm feeling both brave and emotional.'

I indicate for Carrie to take a seat and we both sink down in adjacent arm chairs, cradling our glasses.

'Brave? Don't say you're giving up your job!'

She shakes her head, laughing as she does so.

'No. Can I ask you a question and get an honest answer?'

'Fire away.'

'What did you think of Nicole?'

Ah, now I understand. Nicole was Carrie's plus one the wedding invitation but as soon as we were introduced, I knew she was Carrie's significant other.

'A very strong, likeable personality. Someone my gut instincts told me could be relied upon if you need something doing, or have a problem you want to share. I was surprised we hadn't met before.'

Carrie frowns, taking a sip from her wine glass.

'That's entirely down to me, I'm afraid. We've been together for nearly three years and it's not that we're hiding our relationship, but originally it was a convenience thing. We met at university and kept in touch. When Nic sold her house up north because her department was relocated to the firm's headquarters in Gloucestershire, she came to stay with me. And never left. Everything was fine, until your wedding.'

I grimace. I had no idea there was an upset.

'I hope no one said—'

Carrie holds up her hand to halt my flow of words.

'It wasn't anything anyone said but I've been to a lot of weddings and yours was different. I'll be honest and say most of them are rather boring. A lot of hanging around and not much happening. Everyone is really waiting for the food and the party to begin. But yours and Arran's day was different. The whole thing felt like a party and maybe that was because you kept it small and everyone felt a part of it. When we arrived home Nic thanked me for taking her along. She said she didn't feel like a stranger in the midst of a tight group of family and friends, but someone made welcome because she was special to me.'

I can see that Carrie is moved by the memory and I give her a moment before responding.

'What a lovely thing to say. I know Aunt Grace had a long chat with her and they bonded over their love of greyhounds. Nic and I talked about travelling actually. She has a bucket list and I thought that maybe, well, next summer, the two of you might like to come and stay for a couple of weeks. Perhaps do some touring while you're here.'

Carrie studies my face, intently.

'Now I understand why she felt so welcome.'

'I think it was plain to us all that you meant a lot to each other.'

She grins back at me. 'Well, we've decided we want to formalise our arrangement. Maybe next year, so we will take you up on that offer. What I realised though, was that having someone in your life who you really care about, and who cares about you, is a blessing. It's not something to take for granted and I'd been doing that for a while. Nic doesn't say much, it's not in her nature to moan and groan – that's my job. But she was patiently waiting until I was ready to commit fully. And now I am.'

Carrie stands, and we hug, as best friends do when they have something truly wonderful to celebrate. To love someone and have that emotion returned is a gift and one that many spend their entire lives searching for and never find.

We live in a world where the bad news hits the headlines faster than the good news, if it makes it at all. Good deeds go unrecognised all the time, but I suspect that it's not often they go totally unnoticed, or unappreciated. What many suffer from is a hesitancy to put themselves in a position where they reach out to offer help, love, or simply a listening ear, because they fear rejection. It's humbling to think that our special day sparked such a wonderful and positive reaction. It's true what they say – love begets love.

'I'm so tired I'm talking to you with my eyes closed. That was quite some party, wasn't it?'

Our naked bodies are entwined, but exhaustion has taken over and it's nice to lie here together, listlessly. Tonight, was the final piece in the puzzle that is our wedding tableaux. Every single person we know and care about has now been a part of our celebration in one way or another. That had to span two countries, two very diverse sets of friends, a bit of a language barrier in a few cases and not be blighted by the missing family members who chose not to turn up. What mattered is that everyone who attended came with love and our best interests at heart; and that's what made it so special.

'I thought that was lovely what Nic said to Carrie about our wedding in the UK. It's a pity she couldn't take time off to fly over for the party tonight, but they're both going to come and stay with us next summer. That's okay with you, isn't it?'

Arran's arm squeezes me, gently pulling me even closer.

'Of course. This is our home now, you ask whomsoever you like to stay. Did we run out of your favourite wine? I noticed you were drinking the white stuff this evening and not the pink variety.'

I haul myself up on an elbow to look down at Arran; I love watching his face when he's about to fall asleep. Sometimes he'll say something and the very next second his breathing has dropped and he's sound asleep. It's a quality I envy as often I find it difficult to switch off my mind and achieve that state of pure relaxation. His eyelids flutter but he doesn't succeed in opening his eyes.

'No. I was drinking water, but I wanted it to look like I was drinking wine. It seems that those little sticks in my arm were past their sell by date.'

I count. One, two…

Arran sits bolt upright in bed as if he's on a spring and someone has just released it.

'Okay. I'm awake. Tell me it's not a joke because if it is you are going to have one mightily gutted guy sitting next to you, wide awake. And if I can't sleep—'

I start chuckling. 'Oh, it's no joke and who knows, tonight might be the first time I fall asleep before you do.'

I'm already settling down, nestling the pillow snugly around my face. As my eyes involuntarily close, etched on my mind is the look on Arran's face. Even in the darkness his grin is wide enough for me to know how happy he is and that's all I need to know.

Love sometimes begets babies, too, even when you least expect it, but that doesn't make it any the less of a miracle, does it?

As I sink through the foggy layers of sleep, Arran's voice drifts in and out, as if he's following me.

'A baby… Granddad, I hope you caught that… the Villa is going to have new life breathed into it and I can't wait to be a dad.'

Acknowledgements

IT'S ALL ABOUT TEAM WORK!

When a new book makes its way into the world it's always a mega team effort and that includes *you*, dear reader!

But first, a HUGE thank you to my awesome editor, Lucy Gilmour, whose energy and enthusiasm makes her a joy to work with.

Special thanks, too, go to Dushi Horti, for tightening everything up and Rose Fox for giving the words a polish. Did I mention that I love commas... but now there are a lot less of them!

And a shout out to Vicky Joss, Queen of social media and the much wider team for the behind the scenes work involved in the actual publication and marketing processes.

My lovely agent, Sara Keane, and Aria's Sarah Ritherdon get a special mention as they were instrumental in turning me into an Aria author – for which I'm very, very grateful!

I'm also sending a virtual hug to everyone who has read, reviewed, Tweeted and generally helped spread the word about my Aria titles. The enormous support for *The French Adventure* and *Snowflakes Over Holly Cove* took my breath away and your continued support is a true blessing.

To the growing band of online buddies – wonderful people I may never meet in person, but who have become virtual friends – thank you for brightening my day and being there for me.

It's an honour, as an author, whenever a reader chooses one of your books to escape with for a few hours. I do hope that Brie and Arran's story left you with a smile on your face and a longing to head off on a trip to Italy.

With much love and sincere thanks,

Lucy x

Hello from Aria

We hope you enjoyed this book! Let us know, we'd love to hear from you.

We are Aria, a dynamic digital-first fiction imprint from award-winning independent publishers Head of Zeus. At heart, we're avid readers committed to publishing exactly the kind of books we love to read — from romance and sagas to crime, thrillers and historical adventures. Visit us online and discover a community of like-minded fiction fans!

We're also on the look out for tomorrow's superstar authors. So, if you're a budding writer looking for a publisher, we'd love to hear from you. You can submit your book online at ariafiction.com/we-want-read-your-book

You can find us at:
Email: aria@headofzeus.com
Website: www.ariafiction.com
Submissions: www.ariafiction.com/
we-want-read-your-book
Facebook: @ariafiction
Twitter: @Aria_Fiction
Instagram: @ariafiction